The Journals of the Lewis and Clark Expedition, Volume 10

The Journal of Patrick Gass, May 14, 1804–September 23, 1806

Sponsored by the Center for

Great Plains Studies,

University of Nebraska–Lincoln

and the American

Philosophical Society, Philadelphia

A Project of the Center for
Great Plains Studies,
University of Nebraska–Lincoln
Gary E. Moulton, Editor

The Journals of the Lewis & Clark Expedition

The Journal of Patrick Gass,
May 14, 1804–
September 23, 1806

University of Nebraska Press

Lincoln and London

Publication of this book has been assisted by a grant
from the National Endowment for the Humanities,
an independent federal agency.

⊗ The paper in this book meets the minimum require-
ments of American National Standard for Information Sciences—Permanence of Paper for Printed
Library Materials, ANSI Z39.48-1984.

Library of Congress Cataloging-in-Publication Data
(Revised for volume 8)
The Journals of the Lewis and Clark Expedition.
Vol. 2- Gary E. Moulton, editor; Thomas W. Dunlay,
Assistant editor.
Vol. 2- has title: The Journals of the Lewis & Clark
Expedition.
"Sponsored by the Center for Great Plains Studies,
University of Nebraska – Lincoln, and the American
Philosophical Society, Philadelphia" – vol.1, t. p.
Includes bibliographies and indexes.
Contents: v.1. Atlas of the Lewis & Clark Expedi-
tion – v.2. August 30, 1803-August 24, 1804 – [etc.] –
v.8. June 10-September 26, 1806.
1. Lewis and Clark Expedition – (1804-1806).
2. West (U.S.) – Description and travel – To 1848.
3. United States – Exploring expeditions.   4. Lewis,
Meriwether, 1774-1809 – Diaries.   5. Clark,
William, 1770-1838 – Diaries.   6. Explorers – West
(U.S.) – Diaries.   I. Lewis, Meriwether, 1774-
1809.   II. Clark, William, 1770-1838.   III. Moulton,
Gary E.   IV. Dunlay, Thomas W., 1944-.   V. Univer-
sity of Nebraska – Lincoln. Center for Great Plains
Studies.   VI. American Philosophical Society.
VII. Journals of the Lewis & Clark Expedition.
F592.4   1983   917.8'042   82-8510
ISBN 0-8032-2861-9 (v.1)   ISBN 0-8032-2898-8 (v.7)
ISBN 0-8032-2903-8 (v.8)   ISBN 0-8032-2914-3 (v.9)
ISBN 0-8032-2916-x (v.10)

Contents

Preface

This volume, the previous one, and the one to follow rely largely on the editorial work of previous books in this edition. Therefore, the editorial notes and supporting material in these three books owe a debt to former consultants and friends of the project. Once again we extend our great appreciation to the unselfish work of these generous people.

Nevertheless, we have several persons to thank specifically for help with this volume. The journal of Sergeant Patrick Gass is to be found only in printed form; the original has been lost since its first publication in 1807. We used a copy from the University Archives and Special Collections, University of Nebraska Libraries, which was generously microfilmed for us by Joseph G. Svoboda. We were also aided there by Michele L. Fagan and Lynn R. Beideck-Porn. At our host institution, the University of Nebraska–Lincoln, help came from John R. Wunder, Linda J. Ratcliffe, and Gretchen Walker of the Center for Great Plains Studies, and Thomas W. Dunlay and Doris VanSchooten of the project.

Scholars again provided advice in their respective disciplines. BOTANY: Steven J. Brunsfeld, University of Idaho; A. T. Harrison, Westminster College, Salt Lake City; ENTOMOLOGY: Kenneth P. Pruess, University of Nebraska–Lincoln.

The project received financial support from Samuel H. Douglas III (Whittier, California), Nelson S. Weller (Piedmont, California), the Lewis and Clark Trail Heritage Foundation, and the National Endowment for the Humanities, an independent federal agency.

We extend our sincerest appreciation to all these individuals. Any deficiencies in the present work, however, are entirely the fault of the editor.

Editorial Procedures

For volumes 9, 10, and 11, the final journal-volumes in this edition of the journals of the Lewis and Clark expedition, the principal editorial goal remains that stated in volume 2; that is, to present users with a reliable text largely uncluttered with editorial interference. Readers can find a fuller statement of editing principles in the Editorial Procedures in volume 2. The following paragraphs explain the purpose and extent of editorial annotation included in the present volumes, since the approach to annotation here differs from the method followed with the journals of Lewis and Clark.

Believing that the annotation to Lewis's and Clark's journals in the previous volumes furnished the essential information to understand the events, persons, and inquiries of the expedition, we deemed it unnecessary to reproduce those notes in their entirety in these enlisted men's volumes. We assume that most users turn to Lewis's and Clark's journals as their primary source of information on the expedition and use the enlisted men's journals as supplements. Where the enlisted men provide new or substantially different material in their journals, however, we have commented on that fact and explained the matter as extensively as we did in the captains' journals.

The annotation for the present three volumes falls under four large categories: people, places, animals, and plants. These have been the fields of greatest interest to users of the journals and were the areas most often noticed by the enlisted men. These were also the points on which these men were most likely to provide information not found in the captains' journals. Our aim was to establish a method that was not unnecessarily redundant to previous volumes but that provided readers with essential information so they did not need to refer constantly to other books.

In these volumes the notes have been abbreviated considerably. For example, authoritative sources are not listed in most notes since that information was provided in previous volumes. We do not provide geographic locations for every point mentioned in the enlisted men's journals, nor do we necessarily locate each day's campsite: these locales were discussed in detailed notes to the captains' journals. In the present volumes we try to give a sense of place from day to day by locating the major physical features passed each day. In this way readers should have no trouble determining the party's location at any given time. For natural history matters we provide both the popular and scientific names for flora and fauna. Occasionally we direct readers to notes for the captains' journals for extended discussions of difficult identifications. For the most part the enlisted men were observing and commenting on the same plants and animals as the captains. In fact, there appears to be only one instance in which a biological specimen was mentioned by an enlisted journalist but was not also identified in the captains' journals.

Wherever possible we recognize every Indian tribe noted by the journalists, no matter how indirectly, and name all Indian individuals who we are able to identify. We also transliterate and translate native terms that have not previously been addressed or direct readers to fuller explication in earlier volumes. Sergeant John Ordway seems to have been the only enlisted man to mention Indian terms not noted by Lewis or Clark. It is in fact likely that the enlisted men copied the scant scientific information they have in their diaries from the journals of Lewis and Clark. Because of this we try not to add repetition in the notes to necessary redundancies in the text. Our hope is to give readers sufficient annotation to understand the text without reporting the obvious.

We made some minor changes in Gass's published journal for the present volume. We corrected obvious typographical errors, changed words and phrases set in all capital letters to lower case, and dropped double words. Gass's editor, David McKeehan, or perhaps someone else, added explanatory notes to the text. We have incorporated those notes into our own and designated them "McKeehan's note" (see notes for Gass's entry of May 14, 1804). Aside from these changes, the text is that of the 1807 version.

Introduction to Volume 10

The essential, definitive record of the Lewis and Clark expedition is contained in the journals and observations of the two captains, "the writingest explorers of their time," in the words of Donald Jackson.[1] If no one else associated with the enterprise had written a word we would still have a marvelous narrative replete with geographic, zoological, botanical, and ethnographic information. In fact, however, at least four other members of the party did set down their own daily accounts. This edition brings them together with those of their commanders for the first time.

President Thomas Jefferson did not order the actual keeping of separate journals by anyone other than the captains. In his final instructions to Lewis, however, he did suggest that "several copies of these as well as of your other notes should be made at leisure times, & put into the care of the most trust-worthy of your attendants, to guard, by multiplying them, against the accidental losses to which they will be exposed."[2] All this would seem to require is that some of the "attendants" copy the captains' journals verbatim. Apparently Lewis and Clark, at an early stage, decided to do something else. On May 26, 1804, less than two weeks out from River Dubois, the captains noted that "The sergts . . . are directed each to keep a separate journal from day to day of all passing accurences, and such other observations on the country &c. as shall appear to them worthy of notice.—"[3]

In his last communication to Jefferson from Fort Mandan in April 1805, Lewis wrote: "We have encouraged our men to keep journals, and seven of them do so, to whom in this respect we give every assistance in our power."[4] Lewis had a sense of history; in departing westward from the Mandan villages he compared his little fleet of pirogues and canoes to the vessels of Captain Cook.[5] The significance of his enterprise warranted as complete a record as possible. It might be too much to ask any enlisted men to copy their officers' voluminous journals, but those so inclined could be encouraged to add their bit to the record.

At least some of the men who went with Lewis and Clark seem to have shared that sense of history. They were volunteers, after all, and although some of them no doubt simply hoped to escape from irksome military discipline or to find good beaver streams, others evidently knew very well that this was the chance of a lifetime, that they were involved in something that would survive them, something greater than their individual contribution. The combination of that sense of history with a degree of literacy and considerable diligence made a few of them journal keepers.

To appreciate the work of these men, let us remember the conditions under which they wrote. Most days of the voyage involved hard physical labor, working canoes upstream, loading and unloading bulky equipment, hunting and butchering, tanning leather, making moccasins, cooking, chopping and shaping wood, caring for horses and searching for strays, mounting guard, portaging around falls and rapids, all while exposed to every kind of weather and to the attacks of insects and grizzly bears, with the constant danger of physical injury from accidents. At the end of such a day, perhaps while others were dancing to Pierre Cruzatte's fiddle, a journal keeper would have to write by the light of a campfire in notebooks somehow kept safe from the elements. According to Lewis, seven of the thirty-odd men had the perseverance and the sense of destiny to try.

They wrote under the same conditions as the captains, and like them wrote not only for themselves. It seems probable that they examined each other's journals, and perhaps Lewis and Clark read them, too. We know that on July 14, 1804, having lost his notes for the previous day, Clark had "to refur to the . . . Journals of Serjeants." The enlisted men's journals were intended as part of the record; they were public documents and we cannot expect any deep psychological revelations. No one recorded explicitly, for example, his opinion of Lewis or Clark or Sacagawea.

Literacy was the first requirement. It is probable that some of the men could not even write their own names. Historians have expressed considerable humor over Clark's awkward grammar and his versatility as a speller, but he was little worse than many contemporaries who like him were men of affairs, government officials, and army officers. Comparison of Clark's journal with those of the enlisted men should keep us from laughing too much at Clark. Nor should we be overly amused at the enlisted men, for none of their journals suggests stupidity or dullness. They tried to the best of their ability to record an extraordinary experience.

Sergeants in the army had to be literate, since they kept records for their companies, and it is not too surprising that three of the four enlisted men's journals that we now have are those of sergeants. John Ordway and Charles Floyd held that rank from the start of the trip, and Patrick Gass was promoted some three months out to fill the place of the deceased Floyd. Joseph Whitehouse is the only private whose journal we now have. Ordway's spelling and grammar are, if anything, better than Clark's. We cannot judge Gass's performance, for we do not have his original writing. Floyd and Whitehouse apparently struggled with writing, but there is rarely doubt about what they meant.

We have four enlisted men's journals, in one form or another. Lewis indicated that seven men were keeping journals, and the discrepancy requires some notice, although few hard conclusions can be made. Since the other sergeants were expected to keep journals, one would assume that Sergeant Nathaniel Pryor would also do so, but no document demonstrating this has come to light. Pryor served later on as an army officer and an Indian agent, but other men filled those posts on the frontier who could barely sign their names. On August 12, 1806, Clark noted that Pryor had left behind saddlebags containing his "papers," but Pryor had just returned from being separated from the main party, and the papers could have consisted only of letters he was supposed to deliver to a Canadian trader, and perhaps a journal of his separate trip, which began barely three weeks before. In any case, Pryor went back and recovered the saddlebags, so the papers, whatever they were, were not then lost. There is simply no clear evidence to show that Pryor was one of the seven journal keepers mentioned by Lewis.

It is fairly certain that one private besides Whitehouse kept some sort of journal, because Robert Frazer announced his intention to publish by issuing a prospectus soliciting subscribers barely a month after the party returned to St. Louis, promising "An accurate description of the Missouri and its several branches; of the mountains separating the Eastern from the Western waters; of the Columbia river and the Bay it forms on the Pacific Ocean; of the face of the Country in general; of the several Tribes of Indians on the Missouri and Columbia rivers . . . ," and with all this "a variety of Curious and interesting occurrences during a voyage of two years four months and nine days." The account, Frazer made clear, was "Published by Permission of Captn. Meriwether Lewis."[6] If the journal was anything like what Frazer promised, that it was never published is a great pity. Given the importance of the expedition this is surprising, especially since Patrick Gass was able to secure publication of his work the next year and since there were six further editions of his book in six years. Clearly it was not lack of public interest in Lewis and Clark's discoveries that held Frazer's work back. Whatever the problem was, Frazer passed from view and so did his journal; we have no clue as to its fate.

In April 1805, when Lewis wrote that seven men were keeping journals, Floyd was already dead. If we accept Pryor and Frazer as journal keepers, along with Gass, Ordway, and Whitehouse, we still have two others to account for. It is possible that Lewis counted Floyd, whose journal was sent back from Fort Mandan, even though his record had ceased the previous August. There is a possibility that Private Alexander Willard kept a journal, and with Willard and Floyd we would have Lewis's seven journal keepers.[7] One way or another a considerable part of the record appears to be lost, perhaps forever.

The journals that remain belong with those of Lewis and Clark, supporting them to the best of their ability as they did during the voyage. After the return Lewis evaluated his men, each according to his individual merits, and then wrote of them all: "the Ample support which they gave me under every difficulty; the manly firmness which they evinced on every necessary occasion; and the patience and fortitude with which they submitted to, and bore, the fatigues and painful sufferings incident to my late tour to the Pacific Ocean, entitles them to my warmest approbation and thanks."[8]

PATRICK GASS

Sergeant Patrick Gass, it seems clear, was a tough, lively, enterprising man who did things his own way. He was of Irish ancestry, but the comic brogue those writers of fiction give him is probably the product of their imaginations. Gass was born in 1771 in Pennsylvania. Like John Ordway he was serving in Captain Russell Bissell's company of the First Infantry, stationed at Kaskaskia, Illinois, having joined the army in 1799. Before then he had served on the frontier as a volunteer Ranger, a type of service requiring hardy and self-reliant men, and had become a competent carpenter, one of the most useful of frontier skills. Apparently he was one of those restless young Americans who moved about from one place to another and from one job to another, consciously looking for the right place and the right opportunity, unconsciously savoring the experiences life brought him. The Secretary of War instructed Captain Bissell to furnish Lewis and Clark with "one Sergeant & Eight good men," but Bissell evidently did not wish to lose a good carpenter, for he refused Gass's request to be one of them. Gass was determined and sought out Lewis and presented his case himself. Lewis says nothing of this in his Eastern Journal, but he must have been pleased with the Irishman's initiative. On a later occasion that initiative would please him less.[9]

Gass does not appear in the captains' journals until January 3, 1804, when he is listed in Clark's field journal. It can be assumed that his carpentry skills were useful in building the winter quarters at River Dubois. Although he was in his thirties when he joined the Corps of Discovery and had served four years in the regular army, he was not among the original three sergeants. After Charles Floyd's death in August 1804 Lewis and Clark held an election among the men to choose his successor, and Gass received the most votes. On August 26 Clark noted, "apt. Pat Gass a Sergt. Vice Floyd Deceased." In a Detachment Order the captains told the men:

> The Commanding officers have every reason to hope from the previous faithfull services of Sergt. Gass, that this expression of their approbation will be still further confirmed, by his vigilent attention in future to his duties as a Sergeant. The Commanding officers are still further confirmed in the high opin-

ion they had previously formed of the capacity, deligence and integrety of Sergt. Gass, from the wish expressed by a large majority of his comrades for his appointment as Sergeant.

Nothing in the captains' journals suggests that their confidence was misplaced.

Since Gass furnishes us with the dimensions of Fort Mandan (the only journal keeper who does so), we can assume that his carpentry was important in its construction, and no doubt the same was true of Fort Clatsop and of the many dugout canoes the party constructed at various places along the route. Like Sergeant Ordway he appears in the record chiefly in executing some duty, and the captains make no complaint of him. Like Ordway and Pryor he had a job with a little more authority than the privates and many more demands on his time, energy, and judgment. When Lewis, in July 1806, made a side expedition up the Marias River, the job of supervising the men left at the Great Falls of the Missouri automatically fell to Gass, the only sergeant with Lewis.

Gass accompanied Lewis to Washington after the party's return, then went to Wellsburg, in present West Virginia on the Ohio River, southwest of Pittsburgh. He returned to the army to serve in the War of 1812 and lost an eye, in battle by his own account, in an accident while chopping wood according to army records. He returned to Wellsburg and settled down, and at the age of sixty married a woman of twenty and made up for lost time by fathering six children. Clark, who tried to keep track of the expedition members, thought him dead by about 1825, but in fact he lived until 1870, when he was in his ninety-ninth year. The previous year the Pacific railroad had been completed and Patrick Gass, one of the first Americans to cross the continent and the last survivor of the Corps of Discovery, had lived to see it.[10]

The record gives us reason to believe that Gass was a man of some independence, capable of following orders, but sometimes making his own rules. The history of his journal confirms this impression. The original, unfortunately, is lost to us. Gass acknowledged that he "never learned to read, write, and cipher till he had come of age,"[11] but he still thought his record was worthy of presenting to the world, and he asked no one's permission to do so. In March 1807 the Pittsburgh *Gazette* published a prospectus for "a Journal of the Voyages & Travels of a Corps of Discovery, under the command of Captain Lewis and Captain Clarke of the Army of the United States, from the mouth of the river Missouri through the interior parts of North America to the Pacific Ocean." It promised "An authentic relation of the most interesting transactions during the expedition;—a description of the country, and an account of its inhabitants, soil, climate, curiosities, & vegetable and animal productions."[12]

Lewis had apparently learned of Gass's intention a little earlier, and he was not pleased. He issued a letter to the public more than a week before the publication of Gass's prospectus, "to put them on their guard with respect to such publications, lest from the practice of such impositions they may be taught to depreciate the worth of the work which I am myself preparing for publication before it can possibly appear." The faithful sergeant had now appeared as a rival author. Lewis made sure the public knew that only Robert Frazer had permission to publish and that Lewis had warned Frazer's publishers "not to promise the world anything with which they had not the means of complying." Now there were "several unauthorised and probably some spurious publications now preparing for the press, on the subject of my late tour to the Pacific Ocean by individuals entirely unknown to me." [13]

Whether or not Lewis's fire was directly aimed at Gass, it quickly prompted a return from David McKeehan, Gass's intended publisher. McKeehan's part in the story requires that he receive some attention. His name indicates that he and Gass may have been fellow Irishmen, and like Gass he had resided for a time in Wellsburg. These factors may account for their partnership, and it could even be that McKeehan, who opened a book and stationery store in Pittsburgh in 1807, persuaded Gass to publish. Many publishers of those days were bookstore owners who raised the money for printing and binding by taking subscriptions for prospective volumes. Lewis's denunciation was a threat to McKeehan's venture, and he fired back. [14]

McKeehan obviously had a better than average education for the times, and a facility with the pen. He also had a certain talent for scurrility, which he put to use against "His Excellency Meriwether Lewis, Esquire, Governor of Upper Louisiana," whom he accused of using the dictatorial language of "him who commands and dispenses favours." He charged Lewis with making "amputations and mutilations" in Frazer's journal and denigrating his abilities in order "to deprive poor Frazer, or those who may have purchased from him, of all benefit arising from his publication." McKeehan informed Lewis, in the Pittsburgh *Gazette,* that he intended to publish Gass's narrative without asking Lewis's permission. The rest of a lengthy public letter consisted of gratuitous abuse of Lewis, claiming that he sought to keep all profit or benefit from the expedition for himself, in spite of the rewards he had already received from the government, suppressing any other publication. McKeehan suggested that the public might be interested in Gass's story, even if his scientific qualifications were nil, and implied that the useful geographic information from the captain's journals would be found also in Gass's. Lewis himself, noted McKeehan, was not a trained scientist. The bookseller closed with some sarcasm concerning the wound accidentally inflicted on Lewis by Pierre Cruzatte, "if not *honorable,* near the *place of honor,*" implying it was not an accident. Lewis had the good sense not to reply to this blast. [15]

McKeehan's talents as a writer are relevant because the version of Gass's journal we have is his to a considerable extent. McKeehan himself acknowledged that "I have arranged and transcribed it for the press, supplying such geographical notes and other observations as I supposed would render it more useful and satisfactory to the reader." [16] Estimates of his effort have varied considerably, but most readers have agreed that McKeehan's elegant style was probably very different from that of a rough-and-ready frontier sergeant. There are some gaps in the entries, undoubtedly those of Gass himself, but there is no reason to think that the bookseller substantially altered the facts as Gass presented them. The work agrees well with the captains' journals, and sometimes adds to them. Gass is the only one, as noted, to give any of the dimensions of Fort Mandan and the only expedition journal keeper to describe how the Mandans and Hidatsas built their earth lodges. [17]

Whatever happened to Gass's original, there was little danger of the McKeehan version being lost to the world. By 1814 six additional editions had appeared, in London, Paris, Weimar, and Philadelphia. The Philadelphia editions, published by Mathew Carey, included some quaint and highly imaginative engravings of scenes from the expedition which have often been reproduced in subsequent works. It was the first published work of any length dealing with the expedition, other than some spurious "instant books" based on their generally anonymous authors' imaginations and material lifted from earlier explorers' accounts. One reason for the repeated republication of Gass's work was undoubtedly the delay in the appearance of the official account by Nicholas Biddle. [18]

In his fusillade against Lewis, McKeehan quoted from a certificate he said the captain had given Gass. In it he acknowledges "the ample support, which he gave me under every difficulty; the manly firmness, which he evinced on every necessary occasion; and the fortitude with which he bore . . . the fatigues and painful sufferings incident to that long voyage." [19] These are in fact Lewis's words to the Secretary of War, recommending favorable treatment for all his men, but they apply to Patrick Gass as much as to any man of the party. His account has stood by itself for many years; now it appears with those of his comrades.

NOTES

1. Donald Jackson, ed., *Letters of the Lewis and Clark Expedition with Related Documents, 1783–1854* (2d ed., 2 vols. Urbana: University of Illinois Press, 1978), 1:vii.

2. Jefferson's Instructions to Lewis [June 20, 1803], ibid., 1:62.

3. See the Orderly Book entry for May 26, 1804.

4. Lewis to Jefferson, April 7, 1805, Jackson, ed., *Letters,* 1:232.

5. See Lewis's journal entry for April 7, 1805.

6. The Robert Frazer Prospectus [October 1806], Jackson, ed., *Letters,* 1:345–46.

7. On Willard's journal, see Olin D. Wheeler, *The Trail of Lewis and Clark, 1804–1806* (2 vols. New York: G. P. Putnam's Sons, 1904), 1:124; and Robert B. Betts, "'The writingest

explorers of their time': New Estimates of the Number of Words in the Published Journals of the Lewis and Clark Expedition," *We Proceeded On* 7 (August 1981): 7–8, 8 n. 34.

8. Lewis to Henry Dearborn, January 15, 1807, Jackson, ed., *Letters*, 1:369.

9. Henry Dearborn to Russell Bissell and Amos Stoddard, July 2, 1803, ibid., 1:103; Elliott Coues, ed., *History of the Expedition under the Command of Lewis and Clark.* . . . (1893, Reprint. 3 vols. New York: Dover Publications, 1965), 1:cii.

10. Clark's List of Expedition Members [ca. 1825–28], Jackson, ed., *Letters*, 2:638; Gass to John H. Eaton, March 12, 1829, ibid., 2:646–48; Pension Petition of Patrick Gass, December 23, 1851, ibid., 2:644–50; Affadavit of Patrick Gass [February 17, 1854], ibid., 2:651–53; Charles G. Clarke, *The Men of the Lewis and Clark Expedition: A Biographical Roster of the Fifty-one Members and a Composite Diary of Their Activities from All Known Sources* (Glendale, Calif.: Arthur H. Clark, 1970), 39–40; John G. Jacob, *The Life and Times of Patrick Gass* (Wellsburg, Va.: Jacob and Smith, 1859); Earle R. Forrest, *Patrick Gass: Lewis and Clark's Last Man* (Independence, Pa.: privately published, 1950); James S. and Kathryn Smith, "Sedulous Sergeant, Patrick Gass," *Montana, the Magazine of Western History* 5 (Summer 1955): 20–27; Newman F. McGirr, "Patrick Gass and His Journal of the Lewis and Clark Expedition," *West Virginia History* 3 (April 1942): 205–12.

11. Coues, ed., *History of the Expedition*, 1:xcix.

12. The Patrick Gass Prospectus [March 23, 1807], Jackson, ed., *Letters*, 2:390.

13. Lewis to the Public, March 14, 1807, ibid., 2:385.

14. Paul Russell Cutright, *A History of the Lewis and Clark Journals* (Norman: University of Oklahoma Press, 1976), 21–22.

15. [David McKeehan] to Lewis [April 7, 1807], Jackson, ed., *Letters*, 2:399–408.

16. Ibid., 2:401.

17. Cutright, *History of the Lewis and Clark Journals*, 28–29.

18. Ibid., 29–32.

19. [David McKeehan] to Lewis [April 7, 1807], Jackson, ed., *Letters*, 2:406; compare with Lewis to Henry Dearborn, January 15, 1807, ibid., 1:369.

The Journals of the Lewis and Clark Expedition, Volume 10

The Journal of Patrick Gass, May 14, 1804 – September 23, 1806

Chapter Forty-Nine

Up the Missouri

May 14–September 24, 1804

On Monday the 14th of May 1804, we left our establishment at the mouth of the river du Bois or Wood river, a small river which falls into the Mississippi, on the east-side, a mile below the Missouri, and having crossed the Mississippi proceeded up the Missouri on our intended voyage of discovery, under the command of Captain Clarke. Captain Lewis was to join us in two or three days on our passage.[1]

The corps consisted of forty-three men (including Captain Lewis and Captain Clarke, who were to command the expedition) part of the regular troops of the United States, and part engaged for this particular enterprize. The expedition was embarked on board a batteau and two periogues. The day was showery and in the evening we encamped[2] on the north bank six miles up the river. Here we had leisure to reflect on our situation, and the nature of our engagements: and, as we had all entered this service as volunteers, to consider how far we stood pledged for the success of an expedition, which the government had projected; and which had been undertaken for the benefit and at the expence of the Union: of course of much interest and high expectation.

The best authenticated accounts informed us, that we were to pass through a country possessed by numerous, powerful and warlike nations of savages, of gigantic stature, fierce, treacherous and cruel; and particularly hostile to white men. And fame had united with tradition in opposing mountains to our course, which human enterprize and exertion would attempt in vain to pass.[3] The determined and resolute character, however, of the corps,

**Map of Expedition's
Route, May 14, 1804–
September 23, 1806**

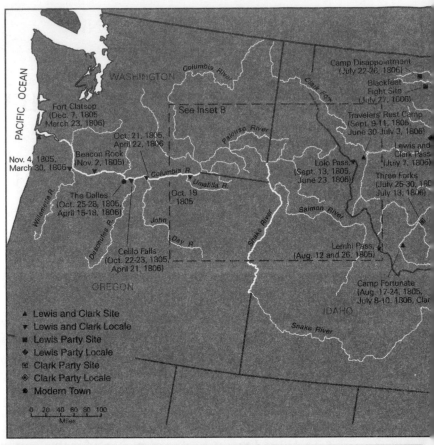

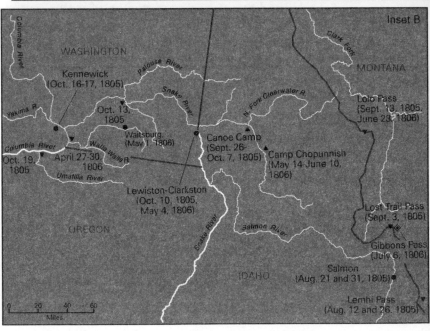

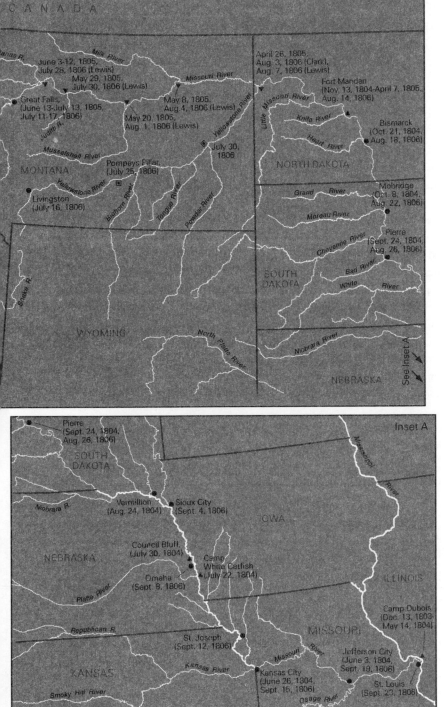

CANADA

Marias R.

Milk River

June 3-12, 1805,
July 28, 1806 (Lewis)
May 29, 1805,
July 30, 1806 (Lewis)

Missouri River

April 26, 1805,
Aug. 3, 1806 (Clark),
Aug. 7, 1806 (Lewis)

Fort Mandan
(Nov. 13, 1804-April 7, 1805,
Aug. 14, 1806)

Great Falls,
(June 13-July 13, 1805,
July 11-17, 1806)

May 8, 1805,
Aug. 4, 1806 (Lewis)

Little Missouri River

Knife River

Heart River

Bismarck
(Oct. 21, 1804,
Aug. 18, 1806)

Judith R.

May 20, 1805,
Aug. 1, 1806 (Lewis)

Yellowstone River

July 30,
1806

Musselshell River

NORTH DAKOTA

MONTANA

Pompeys Pillar,
(July 25, 1806)

Yellowstone River

Bighorn River

Tongue River

Powder River

Grand River

Mobridge
(Oct. 8, 1804,
Aug. 22, 1806)

Livingston
(July 16, 1806)

Moreau River

Cheyenne River

Pierre
(Sept. 24, 1804,
Aug. 26, 1806)

Snake R.

SOUTH
DAKOTA

Bad River

White River

WYOMING

North Platte River

Niobrara River

See Inset A

NEBRASKA

Pierre
(Sept. 24, 1804,
Aug. 26, 1806)

Inset A

Mississippi River

SOUTH
DAKOTA

Niobrara R.

Vermillion
(Aug. 24, 1804)

Sioux City
(Sept. 4, 1806)

IOWA

NEBRASKA

Council Bluff,
(July 30, 1804)

Camp
White Catfish
(July 22, 1804)

ILLINOIS

Omaha
(Sept. 8, 1806)

Platte River

Camp Dubois
(Dec. 13, 1803-
May 14, 1804)

Republican R.

MISSOURI

St. Joseph
(Sept. 12, 1806)

Jefferson City
(June 3, 1804,
Sept. 19, 1806)

KANSAS

Kansas River

Kansas City
(June 26, 1804,
Sept. 15, 1806)

Missouri River

St. Louis
(Sept. 23, 1806)

Smoky Hill River

Osage River

and the confidence which pervaded all ranks dispelled every emotion of fear, and anxiety for the present; while a sense of duty, and of the honour, which would attend the completion of the object of the expedition; a wish to gratify the expectations of the government, and of our fellow citizens, with the feelings which novelty and discovery invariably inspire, seemed to insure to us ample support in our future toils, suffering and dangers.

1. At this point David McKeehan or some person inserted a note for this entry. Such notes were inserted occasionally throughout the book and are reprinted as textual notes in this edition and identified as "McKeehan's note." The first note reads as follows: "The confluence of the Missouri and Mississippi rivers is in latitude about 38 degrees and forty minutes north, and in longitude 92 degrees and an half west of London, or 17 and a third west of Philadelphia. The town of St. Louis is 14 miles below the mouth of the Missouri on the west side of the Mississippi; and Cahokia about 4 or 5 miles lower down on the east side. The longitude of these places is nearly the same with that of the mouth of the river St. Louis at the west end of lake Superior in 46 degrees 45 minutes north latitude; about 2 degrees west of New Orleans in latitude 30 degrees north, and the same number of degrees east of the most western point of Hudson's Bay, in latitude about 59 degrees north: So that a line drawn from New Orleans to Fort Churchhill, at the mouth of Churchhill river on the west side of Hudson's Bay, would pass very near the mouth of the Missouri and the west end of lake Superior." For his notes McKeehan relied mainly on Alexander Mackenzie's *Voyages from Montreal* (London, 1801).

2. Near the mouth of Coldwater Creek, St. Charles County, Missouri, a little above Fort Bellefontaine.

3. Here McKeehan inserted what was probably the way most Americans then pictured the regions beyond the Mississippi and its inhabitants.

Preceding Gass's first entry are several pages of preliminary book material that read as follows:

FRONT MATTER

District of Pennsylvania, to wit:

(L. S.) Be it remembered, That on the eleventh day of April in the thirty-first year of the Independence of the United States of America, A. D. 1807, *David McKeehan,* of the said District hath deposited in this Office, the Title of a Book the Right whereof he claims as Proprietor in the words following, to wit:

"A Journal of the Voyages and Travels of a Corps of Discovery, under the command of Capt. Lewis and Capt. Clarke of the Army of the United States, from the mouth of the river Missouri through the interior parts of North America to the Pacific Ocean, during the years 1804, 1805 and 1806. Containing an authentic relation of the most interesting transactions during the expedition,—A description of the country,—And an account of its inhabitants, soil, climate, curiosities, and vegetable and animal productions.— By *Patrick Gass,* one of the persons employed in the Expedition. With Geographical and Explanatory Notes by the *Publisher."*

In Conformity to the Act of the Congress of the United States, intituled, "An Act for the Encouragement of Learning, by securing the Copies of Maps, Charts, and Books, to the Authors and Proprietors of such Copies during the Times therein mentioned" And also to the Act, entitled "An Act supplementary to Act, entitled, "An Act for the Encouragement of Learning, by securing the Copies of Maps, Charts, and Books, to the Authors and Proprietors of such Copies during the Times therein mentioned," and extending the Benefits thereof to the Arts of designing, engraving, and etching historical and other Prints."

D. Caldwell, Clerk of the District of Pennsylvania

PREFACE

Of the various publications which unite amusement and information, few can be justly held in higher estimation than the Journals and Narratives of Travellers and Voyagers: and in our own highly favoured country, the diffusion of general knowledge, the enterprizing spirit of the people, their commercial pursuits and habits of emigration, render such works particularly valuable and interesting; while the vigorous and unrestrained mind of the free American, by amplifying and embellishing the scenes presented to its view, enjoys the choicest luxuries of the entertainment they are calculated to afford. If it is conceded that discoveries made in North America are more important to the people of the United States than those made elsewhere, it will not be difficult to shew that none could have been made of so much importance to them in any part of the world as in the large tracts of country through which the late expedition, under the command of Captain Lewis and Captain Clarke, passed. For if we take a view of the different discoveries and settlements previously made, we will find that those tracts through which the Missouri and Columbia rivers, and their branches flow, commonly called *unknown regions,* were the only parts remaining unexplored, which could be considered valuable.

The first discovery of the Western World by Europeans of which we have any authentick accounts, being near the southern extremity of North America, drew, as might be expected, their attention to that quarter: and the rage which this grand discovery excited for other enterprizes of the same nature; the avidity, with which avarice was stimulated to seize the precious metals, known to exist in those parts; the means held out for gratifying ambition; and the prospects of a lucrative commerce, with many other objects and considerations tended largely to extend them; while the diminution of the Northern Continent to a narrow isthmus, and its large gulfphs, bays and rivers, furnished and facilitated the means of exploring it. The spirit of enterprize, however, was not confined to the southern extremity; but extending itself to the climates congenial with those which it had left, and connecting with its researches the planting of colonies, important discoveries were made along the Atlantic coast. In the mean time the project of discovering a northwest passage to the East Indies led the boldest naval commanders of Europe through the inland seas, bays and straights of the north; and at length produced surveys of the shores of the Pacific. To these discoveries, and those occasionally made during the settlement of the country within the limits of the United States, and in Canada, the Hudson's Bay company, though not famed for enterprize added something to the stock of general information, and by their establishments aided others in their enterprizes. Mr. Hearne under the direction of this company, in an expedition which lasted from the 7th of December 1770 to the 30th of June 1772, proceeded from Prince of Wales' Fort, on the Churchhill river in latitude 58d. 47½m. north, and longitude 94d 7½m. west of Greenwich, or 19d. west of Philadelphia, to the mouth of the Coppermine river, which according to some accounts is in latitude 72d. north and longitude 119d. west from Greenwich, or 44d. west of Philadelphia; but is laid down by others to be in latitude about 69d. north, and longitude 112d. west from Greenwich or 37d. west from Philadelphia. Whatever the confined views and contracted policy of the Hudson's Bay Company may, however, have omitted in the way of discovery, the enterprize and perseverance of the Canadian traders, sometime since united under the name of the North West Company, have amply supplied. Prior to the year 1789 they had extended their discoveries and establishments along the numerous lakes and rivers situated north of that high tract of country which divides the Mississippi and Missouri waters from those which run towards the north and east, to within a short distance of the Rocky Mountains. In the summer of this year Mr. McKenzie made a voyage from Fort Chepewyan on the lake of the Hills in latitude 58d. 40m. north, and longitude 110d. 30m. west from Greenwich or 35d. 22m. west from Philadelphia, by the way of the Slave river, Slave lake, and a river by which this lake discharges its waters (since called McKenzie's river) to the mouth of that river, where it falls into the North sea, in latitude 69d. 14m. north and longitude 135d. west from Greenwich, or 59d. 52m. west from Philadelphia. He again in the year 1793 penetrated from an establishment on the Peace river in latitude 56d. 9m. north, and longitude 117d. 35m. west from Greenwich, or 41d. 27m. west from Philadelphia, to the Pacific ocean in latitude 52d. 24m. north, and longitude 128d. 2m. west from Greenwich, or 52d. 54m. west from Philadelphia.

By the discoveries alluded to, and those occasionally made during the rapid settlement of the country and the progress of enterprize, the principal divisions of this Northern Continent has been explored and become known. The line separating these from the parts which remained unexplored and unknown, may be considered as commencing at the Pacific ocean in latitude about 38d. north, and running along the high lands and mountains between the waters which fall into the gulphs of California and Mexico and those which fall into the Missouri river, and continuing in that direction to the Mississippi; thence up that river to the source of its highest north western branch; thence along the high tract of country which divides the waters of the Missouri from those which fall into Hudson's Bay and the North sea; from whence it will continue across the Rocky Mountains to the Pacific ocean in latitude about 52d. north. To the south of this general division line, the known countries will be Old and New Mexico and a part of Louisiana; to the southeast, West and East Florida; to the east, the United States; to the northeast, Canada, the Labrador country, part of New South Wales and of other countries round Hudson's Bay; and to the north, part of New South Wales, New

North Wales, the Athabasca and other countries containing the establishments of the Hudson's Bay and North West Companies, and those explored by Hearne and Mc-Kenzie: leaving unknown and unexplored (except so far as the surveys made by navigators of the coast of the Pacific, and the imperfect accounts of traders who have ascended the Missouri have furnished information) all that large intermediate tract, containing in breadth about 1000 miles; and in length in a direct line, about 1800 miles, and by the way of the Missouri and Columbia rivers nearly twice that distance. This tract from its situation may be supposed to contain the chief part of those lands in the great western division of the continent of North America fit for tillage: and this circumstance will therefore in a special manner claim the attention of an agricultural people, render more interesting a description of them, and attach additional value to the history of the country. It will not be forgotten that an immense sum of treasure has been expended in the purchase of this country, and that it is now considered as belonging to the United States. Here at no distant period settlements may be formed; and in a much shorter term than has elapsed since the first were made in America, from which hath arisen a great, powerful and independent nation, the posterity of the present inhabitants of the Union may unfurl the standard of independence on the plains of the Missouri and Columbia.

With respect to the accuracy of the relations given in the following pages, it may be necessary to inform those readers not acquainted with the fact, that the principal object in sending out the expedition was to gain some correct account of the country: and that this might be done more effectually, and the information collected, preserved with more certainty, it was enjoined upon the several persons belonging to the corps, who were considered capable, to keep journals, and every necessary information and assistance given them for that purpose: these journals were also from time to time compared, corrected and any blanks, which had been left, filled up, and unavoidable omissions supplied. By thus multiplying the journals, revising and correcting them, the chances of securing to the country a true account of the progress of the expedition and of the discoveries which should be made, especially should the party be attacked and defeated by the savages or meet with any other disasters in their hazardous enterprize, were also multiplied.

The following is an extract of a certificate delivered by Captain Lewis to Mr. Gass, dated St. Louis 10th Oct. 1806.

"As a tribute justly due to the merits of the said Patrick Gass, I with chearfulness declare, that the ample support, which he gave me, under every difficulty; the manly firmness, which he evinced on every necessary occasion; and the fortitude with which he bore the fatigues and painful sufferings incident to that long voyage, intitles him to my highest confidence and sincere thanks, while it eminently recommends him to the consideration and respect of his fellow citizens."

In determining the form in which the work should appear, the publisher had some difficulty. Two plans presented themselves. The one was to preserve the form of a daily journal (in which the original had been kept) and give a plain description of the country and a simple relation of occurrences equally intelligible to all readers; leaving to every person an opportunity of embellishing the scenes presented to him in his own way. The other plan was to more fully digest the subject, make the narrative more general, and assuming less of the journal form and style, describe and clothe the principal parts of it as his fancy might suggest. However far the latter might have been proper had a foreign country been the subject, and the principal object of the publication, mere amusement, many objections occurred to it in the present case; and rendered the former the most eligible, especially as by it the climate and face of the country will be more satisfactorily described. And Mr. Gass having declared that the beauties and deformities of its grandest scenes were equally beyond the power of description, no attempts have been either by him or the publisher to give adequate representations of them.

The publisher hopes that the curiosity of the reader will be in some degree gratified; that the information furnished will not be uninteresting; and that some aid will be furnished those who wish to acquire a Geographical knowledge of their country. *26th March, 1807*

On the 15th we continued our voyage. It rained in the morning; but in the afternoon we had clear weather, and encamped[1] at night on the north side of the river.

  1. About five miles downstream from St. Charles, St. Charles County, Missouri.

Wednesday 16th. We had a fine pleasant morning; embarked early, and at 2 o'clock in the afternoon arrived at St. Charles,[1] and fired a gun. A number of the inhabitants came to see us. This is an old French village; in the country around which, a number of Americans have settled.

We remained at St. Charles until the 21st, where Captain Lewis arrived from St. Louis and joined us. At 4 o'clock in the afternoon we left this place under a salute of three cheers from the inhabitants, which we returned with three more and a discharge of three guns. This evening was showery, and we again encamped[2] on the north side of the river.

  1. St. Charles, St. Charles County, Missouri.
  2. The camp of May 21, 1804, was about three miles southwest of St. Charles, Missouri.

Tuesday 22nd. We continued our voyage; passed Bonum creek[1] on the south side, and having made fifteen miles, encamped at the Cliffs on the north side of the river. Here we were visited by some Indians.

  1. Bonhomme Creek, St. Louis County, Missouri.

Wednesday 23rd. At 6 o'clock in the morning we proceeded on our voyage with pleasant weather. Passed the mouth of the Osage[1] river on the south side, about a mile and an half below the Tavern Cave, a noted place among the French traders. One mile above this is the Tavern Creek.[2] We encamped this evening on the south side of the river, and had our arms and ammunition inspected.

1. McKeehan's note: "Perhaps Little Osage." McKeehan's information, here as in many other instances, is based on pre–Lewis and Clark knowledge of the trans-Mississippi region. It is Femme Osage River, St. Charles County, Missouri.
2. Tavern Creek, Franklin County, Missouri.

Thursday 24th. We continued our voyage, and encamped[1] at night on the south side. This day our boat turned in a ripple, and nearly upset.

1. About four or five miles below Washington, Franklin County, Missouri.

Friday 25th. We proceeded three miles and passed a creek on the south side, called Wood river;[1] the banks of the river are here high and the land rich: arrived at St. John's,[2] a small French village situated on the north side, and encamped a quarter of a mile above it. This is the last settlement of white people on the river.

1. Dubois Creek, Franklin County, Missouri.
2. La Charette, Warren County, Missouri; called St. John from the one-time Spanish fort located there.

Saturday 26th. This morning two of our people[1] set out by land with a couple of horses. At seven we embarked and had loud thunder and heavy rain; passed Otter creek[2] on the north side, and encamped near its mouth.

1. George Drouillard and John Shields.
2. Loutre River, Montgomery County, Missouri, across from Hermann, which Clark says they passed the next day. All the enlisted men's journals disagree with Clark on this point.

Sunday 27th. We passed Ash creek[1] where there are high cliffs on the south side, and at five in the afternoon arrived at the mouth of Gaskenade river.[2] On the south side one of our party killed a deer.[3] We encamped for the night on an island opposite the mouth of Gaskenade river. This is a very handsome place,—a rich soil and pleasant country:

1. Probably Frame, or Frene, Creek, at Hermann, Gasconade County, Missouri.
2. Gasconade River at Gasconade, Gasconade County.
3. White-tailed deer, *Odocoileus virginianus.*

Monday 28th.   Our provisions and stores were put out to air and dry, and several of our men sent out to hunt. One[1] of them killed a deer. The mouth of the Gaskenade river is 157 yards wide.

1. Reubin Field.

Tuesday 29th.   Seven men were sent out to hunt; six of whom returned. We waited here until 5 o'clock P. M. for the man,[1] who had not come in, and then proceeded three miles, passed Deer creek[2] on the south side, and encamped a short distance above it on the same side. A periogue[3] and eight men had been left for the hunter who had not returned.

1. Joseph Whitehouse.
2. Probably Bailey Creek, Gasconade County, Missouri.
3. The red pirogue, also called the French pirogue.

Wednesday 30th.   After experiencing a very disagreeable night, on account of the rain, we continued our voyage at seven o'clock A. M. and passed a cove where there were high cliffs on the north side opposite an island, called Mombran's Tavern. At twelve we had a heavy shower of rain, accompanied with hail; passed a creek called Rush creek,[1] on the north side; and four miles further Mud creek[2] on the same side. Here the soil is good, with cotton wood, sycamore, oak, hickory, and white walnut; with some grape vines, and an abundance of rushes.[3] We halted and encamped at Grindstone creek[4] on the south side of the river.

1. Perhaps Greasy Creek at Chamois, Osage County, Missouri.
2. Evidently Muddy Creek, Callaway County, Missouri.

3. John Ordway also mentions some of the vegetation this day. The trees are cottonwood, *Populus deltoides* Marsh., sycamore, *Platanus occidentalis* L., an unknown oak, *Quercus* sp., an unknown hickory, *Carya* sp., and white walnut, butternut, *Juglans cinerea* L. The grape is probably river-bank grape, *Vitis riparia* Michx., and the rush is unknown, *Equisetum* sp.

4. "Panther River" to Whitehouse; Ordway gives both names. Now probably Deer Creek, Osage County.

Thursday 31st. We were obliged to remain at this encampment all day, on account of a strong wind from the west. An Indian man and a squaw came down the river with two canoes, loaded with fur and peltry, and remained with us all night. Some of our hunters went out and killed a deer.

Friday 1st June, 1804. Before daylight we embarked and proceeded on our voyage; passed Big Muddy creek[1] on the north side; and on the opposite side saw high banks. Two and an half miles higher up, we passed Bear creek;[2] and at 4 o'clock P. M. arrived at the Osage river;[3] where we remained during the evening and the next day. The Osage river is 197[4] yards wide at its confluence with the Missouri, which, at this place, is 875 yards broad. The country on the south side is broken, but rich: and the land on the other of a most excellent quality. The two men who went by land with the horses, came to us here: they represented the land they had passed through as the best they had ever seen, and the timber good, consisting chiefly of oak, ash, hickory, and black walnut.[5] They had killed in their way five deer. The periogue left at the mouth of Gaskenade river, came up with the man who had been lost. Here our hunters went out and killed three deer. The Osage nation of Indians live about two hundred miles up this river. They are of a large size and well proportioned, and a very warlike people. Our arms and ammunition were all inspected here and found in good order.

1. Probably Auxvasse River, Callaway County, Missouri.
2. Perhaps Loose Creek, Osage County, Missouri.
3. Osage River, at the Osage-Cole county line, Missouri.
4. Clark said it was 397 yards wide.
5. The ash may be white ash, *Fraxinus americana* L. var. *americana,* or green ash, *F. pennsylvanica* March. var. *subintegerrima* (Vahl) Fern.; black walnut is *Juglans nigra* L.

Sunday 3rd. Captain Lewis, with one of the men[1] went out and killed a deer. At five in the afternoon we embarked, and having proceeded six miles, encamped at the mouth of Marrow creek[2] on the south side.

1. Drouillard.
2. Moreau River, Cole County, Missouri, east of Jefferson City.

Monday 4th. Three hunters went out this morning. We continued our voyage, and during the day broke our mast by steering too close to the shore. In the evening we encamped[1] on the south side, near lead mines; when our hunters came in with seven deer.

1. Near "Mine Hill," present Sugar Loaf Rock, northwestern Cole County, Missouri.

Tuesday 5th. We passed Mine creek[1] on the south side, and Little Good-woman creek[2] on the north: also the creek of the Big Rock.[3] We met two Frenchmen in two canoes laden with peltry; passed a high cliff of rocks on the south side, and encamped[4] on the north side. The land about this place is good and well timbered.

1. "Lead Creek" to Charles Floyd, Whitehouse, and Ordway; present Rock Creek or Mud Creek, Cole County, Missouri.
2. Bonne Femme Creek, Boone County, Missouri.
3. Rock Creek or Mud Creek, again.
4. In Boone County, opposite the later town of Sandy Hook, Moniteau County, Missouri.

On the 6th, we passed Saline creek[1] on the south side; and on the 7th the river of the Big Devil[2] on the north; and Big Goodwoman's creek[3] on the same side, where we encamped.

1. Petite Saline Creek, Moniteau County, Missouri.
2. Moniteau Creek on the Howard-Boone county line, Missouri. "Big Devil" must refer to the antlered or horned figures on a nearby rock noted by Clark this day (June 7, 1804).
3. Bonne Femme Creek, Howard County, Missouri.

Friday 8th. We embarked and proceeded five miles, when we met four canoes loaded with fur and peltry: and passed the Mine river[1] on the south side, which is 150 yards wide. The land here is also good and well timbered.

1. Lamine River, near Booneville, Cooper County, Missouri.

Saturday 9th. We passed the Prairie of Arrows, and Arrow creek on the south side.[1] This is a beautiful country, and the land excellent. The Missouri here is only 300 yards wide, and the current very strong. Three miles farther, we passed Blackbird creek[2] on the north side, and encamped. This day going round some drift wood, the stern of the boat became fast, when she immediately swung round, and was in great danger; but we got her off without much injury.

1. The prairie is in the vicinity of the town of Arrow Rock, Saline County, Missouri. "Arrow Creek" is probably Pierre Fresne Creek, Saline County. McKeehan's note: "Prairies are natural meadows, or pastures, without trees and covered with grass."
2. Evidently Richland Creek, Howard County, Missouri.

Sunday 10th. We proceeded five miles and passed a creek, called Deerlick creek[1] on the north side; and three miles further the Two Charlottes[2] on the same side. The mouths of these two rivers are very near each other; the first 70 and the other 100 yards wide. We encamped on the south side of the river at a prairie, and remained there the whole of the next day, the wind blowing too violent for us to proceed.

1. Probably Hurricane Creek, Howard County, Missouri; mentioned by Floyd and Ordway but not by Clark.
2. Little Chariton and Chariton rivers, Chariton County, Missouri.

Tuesday 12th.[1] We set out early, and proceeded until five o'clock in the afternoon, when we met five periogues loaded with fur and peltry from the Sioux nation of Indians. We remained with the people to whom these periogues belonged all night;[2] and got from them an old Frenchman,[3] who could speak the language of the different nations of Indians up the Missouri, and who agreed to go with us as an interpreter.

1. Gass has no entry for June 11; the party remained in their camp of June 10.
2. In south-central Chariton County, Missouri.
3. Pierre Dorion, Sr.

Wednesday 13th. We proceeded early on our voyage; passed a small creek[1] on the north side in a long bend of the river; and encamped at the mouth of Grand river[2] on the North side. This is as handsome a place as I ever saw in an uncultivated state.

1. Perhaps Palmer Creek, Chariton County, Missouri.
2. Grand River is the boundary between Carroll and Chariton counties, Missouri.

Thursday 14th. At five o'clock in the morning we continued our voyage. The river having risen during the night was difficult to ascend. At noon we passed some Frenchmen from the Poenese or Ponis[1] nation of Indians, where they spent the last winter. The evening we passed Snake creek[2] on the north side and encamped on the same.

1. Pawnee Indians.
2. Probably Wakenda Creek, Carroll County, Missouri.

Friday 15th. We renewed our voyage at five in the morning, and had very rapid water. There is a beautiful Prairie on the south side and the land high. Mulberries[1] are in great abundance almost all along the river. We encamped on the north side, opposite an old Indian village.[2]

1. Red mulberry, *Morus rubra* L.
2. A Missouri Indian village, the Gumbo Point site, Saline County, Missouri; see Clark's entry for this date and for June 13.

Saturday 16th. Three men went out this morning to look for timber to make oars, but could find none suitable. On their return we continued our voyage; had cloudy weather and rapid water all day and encamped[1] on the north side.

1. In Carroll County, Missouri, nearly opposite Waverly.

Sunday 17th. This morning was clear and at five we renewed our voyage. Having proceeded about a mile we halted to get timber for oars;[1] and while we remained here to make them, our hunters came in and brought with them a handsome horse, which they had found astray. They also brought a bear,[2] which they had killed.

1. In Carroll County, Missouri, about a mile above the previous camp.
2. Black bear, *Ursus americanus.*

Monday 18th. We remained here all day; and our hunters killed five deer and a bear. On the south side there is high land and a long prairie; on the north the land is level and well timbered, with ash, sugar tree, black walnut, buck-eye, cotton wood and some other timber.[1]

1. Only Gass goes into detail about the timber here. The "sugar tree" is probably sugar, rock, or hard maple, *Acer saccharum* Marsh., or possibly silver, white, or soft maple, *A. saccharinum* L.; the buckeye is either yellow buckeye, *Aesculus octandra* Marsh., or Ohio buckeye, horse chestnut, *A. glabra* Willd.

Tuesday 19th. We passed Tabo creek[1] on the south side, and a small creek on the north;[2] and encamped on the south side opposite a small lake about two miles distant.

1. Tabo Creek, Lafayette County, Missouri.
2. Not mentioned by any other journal keeper; perhaps a very minor nameless watercourse in Carroll County, Missouri, nearly opposite Tabo Creek. The lake was a few miles east of Lexington, Lafayette County.

Wednesday 20th. At five in the morning we continued our voyage, passed Tiger creek,[1] a large creek that flows in from the north, and encamped on an island.[2] The land along here is good on both sides of the river.

1. Apparently Crooked River, Ray County, Missouri; see Clark's entry of this day for the problems surrounding identification of the stream.
2. Perhaps Wolf Island, below Wellington, Lafayette County, Missouri.

On the 21st we had rapid water, and for about a mile had to warp up our boat by a rope. A creek called Du Beau or Du Bois,[1] falls in on the south side behind an island. We encamped in the evening on the south side.

1. Clark and Floyd mention two creeks, Ordway and Gass only one; Clark gives the name as "Eue-beux" and "Eue-bert." Presently there are several, called Little Sni a Bar Creek, Sni Creek, and Big Sni a Bar Creek, in western Lafayette County, Missouri.

Friday 22nd. It rained hard from four to seven in the morning, when we continued our voyage. About 12, one of our men went out and killed a large bear. We encamped at a handsome prairie on the south side opposite a large creek, called the Fire-prairie,[1] and which is 60 yards wide.

1. See Clark's entry for this day for a discussion of the difficulties of locating this stream and the day's camp.

Saturday 23rd. We set out at five in the morning; at 12, the wind blew so strong down the river that we were unable to proceed, and we encamped[1] on an island and inspected the arms and ammunition.— Captain Clarke went out with one of the men[2] and did not return this evening.

1. Near Sibley, Jackson County, Missouri.
2. Apparently Drouillard; see Clark's entry for the day.

Sunday 24th. We had a fine morning, embarked at five and pursued our voyage: at nine Captain Clarke came to us and brought with him two deer and a bear. We passed a creek on the south side called Depie.[1] At 12 we stopped to jirk our meat,[2] and again proceeded at two; passed a creek[3] on the north side and encamped on the south bank of the river.

1. Only Gass uses this name, perhaps from the French *de paille,* "of straw"; it is the Hay, or Hay Cabin, Creek of Clark and other journal keepers, now Little Blue River, Jackson County, Missouri.
2. McKeehan's note: "Jirk is meat cut into small pieces and dried in the sun or by a fire. The Indians cure and preserve their meat in this way without salt."
3. Either Rush Creek or Big Shoal Creek, Clay County, Missouri.

Monday 25th. The morning was foggy and at seven o'clock we pursued our voyage. The river here is narrow with high land on the south side. We passed a creek on the south side called Labenile,[1] and encamped on an island.

1. One of expedition members' several variations of the creek perhaps named for François M. Benoit; present Sugar Creek, Jackson County, Missouri.

Tuesday 26th. We embarked and set out at five o'clock in the morning; passed a creek on the south side, called Blue-Water.[1] This afternoon we had some difficulty in passing a sandbar, the tow-rope having broke; but by the exertions of those on board, the boat was brought to shore without injury. We encamped on the south side on a point at the confluence of the Canzan, or Kanzas river[2] with the Missouri. It was agreed to remain here during the 27th and 28th where we pitched our tents and built bowers in front of them. Canzan or Kanzas, is 230 yards and a quarter wide, and navigable to a great distance. Our hunters killed 4 deer, and a young wolf,[3] and caught another alive. In the afternoon of the 29th we again proceeded on our voyage, and encamped[4] on the north side of the river.

1. Big Blue, or Blue, River, Jackson County, Missouri.
2. Kansas River, at Kansas City, Missouri.
3. Presumably a gray wolf, *Canis lupus,* killed on June 28, according to Ordway and Whitehouse.
4. The camp of June 29 was in the vicinity of Riverside, Platte County, Missouri.

Saturday 30th. The day was clear and we continued our voyage; found high land on both sides of the river; and passed a large creek on the north side, called Platt,[1] fifty yards wide. We broke our mast and encamped[2] on the south side, where there were the most signs of game I ever saw.

1. Platte, or Little Platte, River, Platte County, Missouri, not to be confused with the Platte River in Nebraska.
2. Opposite Diamond Island, no longer in existence, in southeastern Wyandotte County, Kansas.

Sunday 1st July, 1804.   We set out at five in the morning, and having advanced 12 miles, encamped[1] on an island opposite a prairie on the south side of the river.

1. On later Leavenworth Island, opposite Leavenworth, Leavenworth County, Kansas.

Monday 2nd.   At sunrise we continued our voyage, and met a quantity of drift wood which was carried down the stream; this morning we passed a creek[1] on the south side and encamped on the north opposite an old French village and fort,[2] but all vacant.

1. Probably Bee Creek, Platte County, Missouri.
2. Fort de Cavagnial, or Cavagnolle, active from 1744 to 1764, about three miles north of Fort Leavenworth.

Tuesday 3rd.   We proceeded again at five, and continued our voyage until 12, when we stopt at an old trading place on the south side of the river.[1] There we found a grey horse; but saw no appearance of any persons having lately encamped at that place.

1. In Atchison County, Kansas, somewhat above Oak Mills.

Wednesday 4th.   We fired a swivel at sunrise in honour of the day, and continued our voyage; passed a creek on the north side, called Pond creek,[1] and at one o'clock stopt to dine. One of our people[2] got snake bitten but not dangerously. After dinner we renewed our voyage, and passed a creek on the north side, which we called Independence,[3] encamped on the north side at an old Indian village situated in a handsome prairie, and saluted the departing day with another gun.

1. This name is given by no other journal keeper, but it must be the outlet of what Clark calls a "bayou," an oxbow lake in northwestern Platte County, Missouri, perhaps later Bean Lake.
2. Joseph Field.
3. Probably Independence Creek, on the Atchison-Doniphan county line, Kansas. See Clark's entry on this date for the confusion between this and Fourth of July Creek.

Thur. 5th.   We proceeded on our voyage at five in the morning; and found the land high on the south side. We went through a large bend full of sand-bars where we had some difficulty in passing; and encamped[1] on the south side at high prairie land.

1. In Doniphan County, Kansas, some miles northeast of Doniphan.

Friday 6th. We set out early this morning; had a fine day, and made a good day's voyage: and encamped on the south side at Whipperwell creek.[1]

1. Perhaps Peter's Creek, Doniphan County, Kansas, near St. Joseph, Buchanan County, Missouri, on the opposite side.

Saturday 7th. At an early hour we proceeded on our voyage; passed a high handsome prairie on the north side, and killed a wolf and a large wood-rat[1] on the bank. The principal difference between it and the common rat is, its having hair on its tail.

1. No other enlisted man takes note of the animal, probably the eastern woodrat, *Neotoma floridana.*

Sunday 8th. We were under way this morning before day light. The river here is crooked and narrow. At one we came to a large island, with only a small stream on the north side which we went up. A large creek called Na-dowa[1] flows in from the north; and on this side we encamped.

1. Nodaway River, the boundary between Holt and Andrew counties, Missouri.

Monday 9th. Early this morning we continued our voyage. It rained hard till 12 o'clock. We passed a creek on the south side, called Wolf creek.[1] The man that was snake bitten is become well. We encamped on the south side.

1. Wolf Creek, Doniphan County, Kansas.

Tuesday 10th. We set out early this morning and had a fair day and fair wind. There is a handsome prairie on the south side opposite an island. We encamped[1] on the north side.

1. Probably in Holt County, Missouri, nearly opposite the Nebraska-Kansas boundary.

Wed. 11th.   We also embarked early this morning; passed a creek on the north side, called Tarico,[1] and halted at an island, opposite a creek called Moha[2] on the south side of the river. Seven hunters went out to day and two[3] of them brought in five deer. Here we found another horse on the bank of the river, supposed to have been left by a hunting party last winter. Two of our men, who had gone to hunt on the south side of the river, did not return at night.

1. Little Tarkio Creek, Holt County, Missouri.
2. Big Nemaha River, Richardson County, Nebraska.
3. Drouillard and Joseph Field.

Thursday 12th.   We remained here this day, that the men, who were much fatigued, might take some rest. The hunters, who had remained on the south side of the river all night, came in, but had killed nothing. Two more went to hunt on the north side and killed two deer.

Friday 13th.   We were early under way this morning with a fair wind. The day was fine. We passed a creek on the north side, and having made 20 miles and an half, encamped[1] on a large sand bar.

1. Probably in eastern Richardson County, Nebraska.

Saturday 14th.   At day break it began to rain and continued until seven when it abated, and we set forward: but in a short time a gust of wind and rain came on so violent, that all hands had to leap into the water to save the boat. Fortunately this storm did not last long, and we went on to a convenient place and landed. Here we continued two hours and then proceeded. We saw some elk,[1] but could not kill any of them; passed a river on the north side, called Wash-ba-to-nan,[2] and encamped on the south side.

1. *Cervus elaphus.*
2. Nishnabotna River, Atchison County, Missouri; it now mouths farther upstream.

Sunday 15th.   We got under way at six o'clock; passed a creek[1] on the south side; and gathered some ripe grapes. There is high land and prairies on this side. Captain Clarke and two men went by land. At the head of an island, called Elk island, we found some pummice stone among the drift wood. We passed a creek on the south side, called Na-ma-ha,[2] and encamped on the same.

1. Perhaps either Beadow or Deroin creeks, southeastern Nemaha County, Nebraska, noticed but not named by Clark.
2. Little Nemaha River, Nemaha County.

Monday 16th. Early in the morning we proceeded on our voyage opposite a prairie; had a fine day and fair wind, and passed a long island,[1] above which is a place where the bank has slipped into the river. There are high rocky cliffs on the south side, and hills and prairies on the north:[2] on which side we encamped. The river here is two miles wide with rapid water. Two of our hunters met us here with two deer.

1. Clark's Chauvin island, Bald Island later in the century, then later split into McKissock and Hogthief islands.
2. Clark's "Bald-Pated Prairie," on the Missouri-Iowa boundary, much of it now within Waubonsie State Park, Fremont County, Iowa.

Tuesday 17th. We remained here all day; and one of our hunters[1] killed three deer.

1. Drouillard.

Wednesday 18th. Early this morning we prosecuted our voyage with a fair wind and pleasant weather. This is the most open country I ever beheld, almost one continued prairie. Two of our hunters went by land with the horses as usual. On the south side we passed high handsome banks or bluffs of red and blue strata;[1] found some iron ore here, and encamped on the south side, where one of the hunters[2] brought us two deer.

1. McKeehan's note: "By Bluffs in the Western Country is understood high steep banks, which come close to and are washed at their base by the rivers."
2. Drouillard again.

Thursday 19th. At sunrise we renewed our voyage, and passed a number of sand bars, and high land on the south side. Where we halted for dinner we found a great quantity of cherries, called by some choak-cherries.[1] We encamped[2] for the night on an island of Willows.

1. Choke cherry, *Prunus virginiana* L.
2. Probably in Fremont County, Iowa, two or three miles above Nebraska City.

Friday 20th. We embarked early; passed high yellow banks on the south side and a creek, called the Water-which-cries, or the Weeping stream,[1] opposite a willow island, and encamped on a prairie on the south side.

1. Weeping Water Creek, Otoe County, Nebraska.

Saturday 21st. We set out early. It rained this morning but we had a fine breeze of wind. There are a great many willow islands and sand-bars in this part of the river. At nine the wind fell, and at one we came to the great river Platte, or shallow river,[1] which comes in on the south side, and at the mouth is three quarters of a mile broad. The land is flat about the confluence. Up this river live three nations of Indians, the Otos, Panis, and Loos, or Wolf Indians.[2] On the south side there is also a creek, called Butterfly creek.[3]

1. No one else used this name for the Platte River, but it is a free translation—and an accurate description—of the Indian and French names. The river reaches the Missouri between Cass and Sarpy counties, Nebraska.
2. Gass refers to the Oto, the Pawnee, and the Skiri or Loup (Wolf) Pawnee Indians.
3. Papillion, or Big Papillion, Creek, Sarpy County.

Sunday 22nd. We left the river Platte and proceeded early on our voyage, with fair weather. There is high prairie land on the south side, with some timber on the northern parts of the hills. We came nine miles from the mouth of Platte river, and landed on a willow bank.[1] The hunters killed five deer and caught two beaver.[2]

1. The party's Camp White Catfish, on the Mills-Pottawattamie county line, Council Bluffs, Iowa.
2. American beaver, *Castor canadensis*.

Monday 23rd. Six men were sent out to make oars; and two[1] to a nation of Indians up the Platte river,[2] to inform them of the change of government in this country, and that we were here ready to treat with them. We hoisted a flag, and sent them another.

Our people were all busily engaged in hunting, making oars, dressing skins, and airing our stores, provisions, and baggage. We killed two deer and caught two beaver. Beaver appear plenty in this part of the country.

We continued here to the 27th. On the 24th there were some showers; but during the remainder of the time there was clear weather. Our people were generally employed as before. The hunters killed five more deer; and the two men returned from the Indian village, without finding any of the natives.

1. Drouillard and Pierre Cruzatte.
2. To the Oto village east of Yutan, Saunders County, Nebraska.

Friday 27th. This forenoon we were engaged in loading the boats and preparing to start. At 12 we proceeded with a fair wind, and pleasant weather; went twelve miles, and encamped[1] on a handsome prairie on the south side.

1. Within the limits of Omaha, Douglas County, Nebraska, in the vicinity of the Douglas Street Bridge (Interstate 480).

Saturday, 28th. We set out early; had a cloudy morning: passed some beautiful hills and prairies, and a creek called Round-Knob creek,[1] on the north side; and high bluffs on the south. We encamped[2] on the north side. Here two of our hunters came to us, accompanied by one of the Oto Indians.[3]

1. Ordway and Whitehouse use this name, Clark has it as Indian Knob Creek, and Floyd calls it Beaver Creek; now probably Pigeon Creek, Pottawattamie County, Iowa.
2. In Pottawattamie County, a little north of Council Bluffs.
3. A Missouri Indian, according to Clark. Drouillard was one of the hunters.

Sunday, 29th. We embarked early, and continued our voyage. One of our Frenchmen[1] went with the Indian to bring more of them to meet us at some convenient landing place. At 12 one of our hunters came in with a deer and some elk meat. We renewed our voyage at 3, passed a bank, where there was a quantity of fallen timber, and encamped[2] on the north side.

1. La Liberté, who took the opportunity to abandon the expedition; see Appendix A, vol. 2, and Clark's entry for this day.

2. Apparently in Pottawattamie County, Iowa, somewhat above the Washington-Douglas county line in Nebraska, opposite.

Monday 30th.   Our grey horse died last night.[1] We set out early, and the hunters[2] met us with a deer. At 9 we came to some timber land at the foot of a high bluff and encamped[3] there in order to wait for the Indians. At the top of the bluff is a large handsome prairie, and a large pond, or small lake about two miles from camp on the south side of the river. Two of our hunters went out and killed an animal,[4] called a prarow, about the size of a ground hog and nearly of the same colour. It has a head similar to that of a dog, short legs and large claws on its fore feet; some of the claws are an inch and an half long. Our hunters[5] again went out, but did not return this day.

1. The horse found running loose on July 3.
2. Reubin and Joseph Field.
3. At the party's Council Bluff, near the town of Fort Calhoun, Washington County, Nebraska.
4. Badger, *Taxidea taxus;* see Clark's entry for this day. Gass's "prarow" is his attempt at the French term for the animal, *blaireau.*   Joseph Field was one of the hunters.
5. The Field brothers.

Tuesday 31st.   One of our men went to visit some traps he had set, and in one found a young beaver, but little hurt and brought it in alive. In a short time he went out again and killed a large buck.[1] Two other hunters[2] came in about 12, who had killed two deer; but lost the horses. One of them with two other persons were sent out to hunt for them, who returned at dark without finding them; and supposed they had been stolen by the Indians.

1. Ordway and Whitehouse agree with Gass, naming Drouillard in both cases; Clark says that Reubin and Joseph Field brought in the beaver kit, and Drouillard killed the buck.
2. The Field brothers.

Wednesday 1st Aug. 1804.   Three of our men again went out to hunt the horses, but returned without them. They brought a deer, and two of our other hunters[1] killed two more.

1. According to Ordway's journal, Shields, Joseph Field, and George Gibson brought in deer, but only Drouillard was out looking for the horses. Whitehouse has Drouillard and John Colter looking for horses and Gibson looking for the Otos and La Liberté. Clark does not name any of the men.

Thursday 2nd. Some hunters went out this morning; and two[1] of them returned with the horses and an elk they had killed. The others brought in two large bucks and a fawn. The Indians we expected came at dark; but our Frenchman[2] was not with them. We supposed he had been lost. This place we named Council-Bluff, and by observation we found to be in latitude 41d 17m north.

1. Drouillard and Colter.
2. La Liberté, who had no intention of returning.

Friday 3rd. Captain Lewis and Captain Clarke held a council with the Indians, who appeared well pleased with the change of government, and what had been done for them. Six of them were made chiefs,[1] three Otos and three Missouris.

We renewed our voyage at 3 o'clock; went six miles and encamped[2] on the south side; where we had a storm of wind and rain, which lasted two hours.

1. See Clark's entry for this date for their names.
2. Some miles south of Blair, Washington County, Nebraska, but perhaps on the Iowa side, in Harrison County.

Saturday 4th. We were early under way this morning, and had a fair day. We passed a creek[1] on the south side, which came out of ponds. One of our men[2] went out this morning and did not return: another came to us and brought a deer. We encamped[3] on the south side.

1. Apparently Fish Creek, near Blair, Washington County, Nebraska.
2. Moses B. Reed, who deserted.
3. In either Washington County, Nebraska, or Harrison County, Iowa.

Sunday 5th. We set out early, but a storm of rain and wind obliged us to stop two hours. It then cleared and we continued our voyage; passed prairies on both sides, and encamped[1] on the north side. The river here is very crooked and winding. To arrive at a point only 370 yards from this place, the passage by water is twelve miles.

1. In Harrison County, Iowa, near the Burt-Washington county line in Nebraska, on the opposite shore.

Monday 6th.   We proceeded at an early hour this morning, after a stormy night of wind and rain; passed a creek on the north side, at the back of an island, called Soldiers creek;[1] and encamped on the south side.

1. Soldier River, Harrison County, Iowa. The camp was apparently in Harrison County, roughly halfway between Soldier and Little Sioux rivers.

Tuesday 7th.   We set out early this morning and continued our voyage till 12, when four[1] of our people were dispatched to the Oto nation of Indians after the man who had not returned on the 4th, with orders to take him, dead or alive, if they could see him. There is no timber in this country, except some cotton wood and willows in the bends of the river. All the high land is a continued prairie. We encamped[2] on the north side. The musquetoes here are very numerous and troublesome.

1. Drouillard, Reubin Field, William Bratton, and François Labiche were sent to apprehend Reed.
2. Probably in northwest Harrison County, Iowa, a few miles below the Little Sioux River.

Wednesday 8th.   We embarked early, passed a small river on the north side, called Little Sioux.[1] Captain Clarke and one of the men[2] went out to hunt and killed an elk. One of the hunters[3] killed a pelican[4] on a sand bar, and Captain Lewis killed another, very large. We encamped[5] on the north bank. In a bag under the bill and neck of the pelican, which Captain Lewis killed, we put five gallons of water.

1. Little Sioux River in Harrison County, Iowa.
2. John Collins.
3. John Dame.
4. American white pelican, *Pelecanus erythrorhynchos.*

5. Probably in southwest Monona County, Iowa, a little above the Harrison County line. A river shift may have placed the site in Burt County, Nebraska.

Thursday 9th.   The fog was so thick this morning, that we could not proceed before 7, when we went on under a gentle breeze, and having advanced eleven miles, came to a place where the river by cutting through a narrow neck of land, reduced the distance fifteen miles. Captain Clarke and one of the men went out to hunt and killed a small turkey.[1] We encamped[2] on the south side, where we found the musquetoes very troublesome.

1. Wild turkey, *Meleagris gallopavo.*
2. A site now in Harrison County, Iowa, on the west side of Guard Lake, a little south of Onawa.

Friday 10th.   We embarked early, passed high yellow banks on the south side, and encamped[1] on the north.

1. In Monona County, Iowa, a few miles above the Thurston-Burt county line on the opposite side in Nebraska.

Saturday 11th.   A storm came on at three o'clock this morning and continued till nine, notwithstanding which, we kept under way till ten, when we came to a high bluff,[1] where an Indian chief had been buried, and placed a flag upon a pole, which had been set up at his grave. His name was Blackbird, king of the Mahas; an absolute monarch while living, and the Indians suppose can exercise the power of one though dead. We encamped[2] in latitude 42d 1m 3s 3, as ascertained by observation.

1. Blackbird Hill, Thurston County, Nebraska, near Macy. Gass says more about the Omaha Indian Chief Blackbird himself than Clark, showing that the Blackbird legend was already well developed a few years after the chief's death.
2. A few miles east of the present river course, Monona County, Iowa, near present Badger Lake, the 1804 course of the Missouri.

Sunday 12th.   We embarked and got under way before day light. The musketoes last night were worse than I ever experienced. We went round a bend, of eighteen miles, the neck of which was only 974 yards across; passed high bluffs of yellow clay on the south side of the river and low land on the north; and encamped[1] on a sand island.

1. In either Monona or Woodbury County, Iowa, near the county line.

Monday 13th. We proceeded this morning with a fair wind; and at 2 landed on a sandy beach, near the Maha village,[1] on the south side of the river. A sergeant and one man[2] were sent to the village, who did not return this day.

1. The Omaha village known as Tonwontonga, or Big Village, Dakota County, Nebraska, about one mile north of Homer. The camp was in Dakota County, or in Woodbury County, Iowa, a few miles south of Dakota City, Nebraska.

2. According to Clark the detachment consisted of Ordway, Cruzatte, George Shannon, William Werner, and the mysterious "Carrn," for whom see Clark's entry for this date and vol. 2, Appendix A.

Tuesday 14th. The sergeant and man returned from the village; but they had found no Indians there. Some of our hunters went out but killed nothing. Game appears scarce here. While at this place we provided ourselves with a new mast.

Wednesday 15th. Captain Clarke and ten of the party[1] went to the Maha creek[2] to fish, and caught 387 fish of different kinds. We discovered smoke on the opposite side of the river, and four men crossed to see if any of the Mahas or Sioux Indians were there; but could not discover any. There had been fire there some days, and the wind lately blowing hard had caused the fire to spread and smoke to rise. We continued at this place until the 20th. Captain Lewis went with a party of twelve men to fish and took 709 fish, 167 of which were large pike.[3] The fish here are generally pike, cat,[4] sun perch[5] and other common fish. What we caught were taken with trails or brush nets. On the 18th the party who had been sent in pursuit of the man who had been absent since the 4th returned with him, and eight Indians and a Frenchman;[6] but left our Frenchman[7] behind who had gone out to hunt the horses. On the 19th a council was held with these Indians, who appeared to wish to make peace with all nations. This day Sergeant Floyd became very sick and remained so all night. He was seized with a complaint somewhat like a violent colick.[8]

1. Including Sergeant Floyd.
2. Perhaps Omaha Creek, Dakota County, Nebraska.
3. Perhaps northern pike, *Esox lucius,* or some fish resembling it.
4. Possibly channel catfish, *Ictalurus punctatus,* or stonecat, *Noturus flavus.*
5. Perhaps the "perch" that Clark on this date calls a silverfish, otherwise white perch and now freshwater drum, *Aplodinotus grunniens.*
6. Drouillard, Reubin Field, Bratton, and Labiche, with the deserter Reed and the Oto and Missouri chiefs. Ordway also mentions the Frenchman, but Clark says nothing about him on this date. He was evidently not one of the party, but a trader or trapper living among the Indians. He may have been François (or Pierre, Jr.) Dorion, son of Pierre Dorion (see Clark's entry of August 19); or he may have been the mysterious "Far fonge" (see Clark for August 2).
7. La Liberté, who escaped from the party sent to catch the deserters.
8. "A violent colic" would probably describe the symptoms observable to the party if Floyd was suffering from appendicitis.

Monday 20th.   Sergeant Floyd continued very ill. We embarked early, and proceeded, having a fair wind and fine weather, till 2 o'clock, when we landed for dinner. Here Sergeant Floyd died, notwithstanding every possible effort was made by the commanding officers, and other persons, to save his life. We went on about a mile to high prairie hills on the north side of the river,[1] and there interred his remains in the most decent manner our circumstances would admit; we then proceeded a mile further to a small river on the same side and encamped.[2] Our commanding officers gave it the name of Floyd's river; to perpetuate the memory of the first man who had fallen in this important expedition.

1. Within Sioux City, Woodbury County, Iowa, on a bluff overlooking the river.
2. Floyd River, Sioux City, Woodbury County.

Tuesday 21st.   We set out early; passed handsome pale coloured bluffs, willow creek[1] and the Sioux river[2] on the north side: and having come upwards of 20 miles, encamped on the south side.

1. Perry Creek, at Sioux City, Woodbury County, Iowa.
2. Big Sioux River is now the South Dakota–Iowa boundary.

Wednesday 22nd.   We proceeded early upon our voyage; passed bluffs on the south side, where there is copperas, allum and ore of some kind; also passed a creek.[1] The high land on the south side for nine or ten miles runs close to the river, where there are cedar bluffs of various colours. We encamped on the north side.

1. Probably Aowa, or Ayowa, Creek, Dixon County, Nebraska, near Ponca.

Thursday 23rd.   We proceeded early this morning with a fair wind. The river here becomes more straight than we had found it for a great distance below. Captain Clarke and one of the men killed a deer and a buffaloe, and some of the men were sent to dress and bring the buffaloe to the boat.[1] We stopped at a prairie on the north side, the largest and handsomest, which I had seen. Captain Clarke called it Buffaloe prairie. The men having returned, we again went on; but the wind changed and we were obliged to halt for the present. While we were detained here we salted two barrels of buffaloe meat. At five in the evening we proceeded some distance and encamped[2] on the south side.

1. Lewis led the party and Ordway was one of them. The first buffalo, *Bison bison,* taken by the expedition; see Clark's entry for the confusion about which one of the Field brothers killed it.
2. In Dixon County, Nebraska, or Clay County, South Dakota.

Friday 24th.   This morning was cloudy with some rain. Captain Clarke went by land. We passed cedar[1] bluffs on the north side, a part of which were burning; and there are here to be found mineral substances of various kinds. There is also a quantity of small red berries,[2] the Indian name for which in English means rabbit berries. They are handsome small berries and grow upon bushes about 10 feet high. Captain Clarke came to us and had killed two elk and a fawn, we passed a creek called White-stone creek;[3] landed and remained here all night to jirk our meat.

1. Probably eastern red cedar, *Juniperus virginiana* L.
2. Buffaloberry, *Shepherdia argentea* (Pursh) Nutt., whose colloquial name is given also by the other enlisted men but not by Clark.
3. Vermillion River, Clay County, South Dakota.

Saturday 25th. Two of our men last night caught nine catfish, that would together weigh three hundred pounds.[1] The large catfish are caught in the Missouri with hook and line. Captain Lewis and Captain Clarke went to see a hill[2] on the north side of the river where the natives will not or pretend that they will not venture to go, and say that a small people live there, whom they are afraid of. At 11 o'clock, the gentlemen not having returned, we set sail with a gentle breeze from the S. E. passed black bluffs on the south side, and continued on nine miles and encamped.[3] Two of our hunters came in who had killed a large elk.[4] Captains Lewis and Clarke did not return this evening.

1. Perhaps channel catfish.
2. Spirit Mound, Clay County, South Dakota, eight miles north of Vermillion.
3. The main party, with Sergeant Nathaniel H. Pryor in charge, continued on and camped on the Nebraska side, near the Cedar-Dixon county line.
4. Reubin Field and Shannon.

Sunday 26th.[1] Some of the men went out to dress and bring in the elk. About 10 o'clock Captain Lewis and Captain Clarke with the party accompanying them came to camp; but had not been able to discover any of those small people. The hill is in a handsome prairie: and the party saw a great many buffaloe near it. About 11 we renewed our voyage and passed some timberland on the south side; and black and white bluffs on the same side, we encamped on the north side opposite a creek called Pettit-Ark, or Little-bow.[2]

1. This day Clark notes, "apt. Pat Gass a Sergt. Vice Floyd Deceased." Gass (or his editor) did not think his promotion worth mentioning.
2. Bow Creek, Cedar County, Nebraska.

Monday 27th. Got under way at sunrise, and passed white bluffs on the south side. At 2 we stopped for dinner, and an Indian of the Mahas nation, who lives with the Sioux came to us here, at the mouth of the Sacque river;[1] and while we remained here two more came in. A sergeant with our old Frenchman and another man[2] went with two of the Indians to their camps, and the other went with us in the boat. We encamped on a sand beach on the north side.[3]

31

1. Gass's version of the Rivière aux Jacques, now James River, Yankton County, South Dakota.
2. Pryor, Pierre Dorion, Sr., and "a Frenchman."
3. In Yankton County, between the James River and Yankton.

Tuesday 28th. We set forward early. The day was pleasant, and a fair wind from S. E. At 8 we halted for breakfast, when our young Indian left us to go to his camp at a handsome prairie, gently rising from the river on the north side; a small distance above which are beautiful groves of Cotton wood on both sides of the river. About 12 one of the periogues run against a snag which broke a hole in it. We then crossed to the south side to mend the periogue, and to wait to receive the Indians we expected; and landed a little below some high bluffs. Our camp[1] was in a wide bottom, in which are large elm[2] and oak trees.

1. Below Gavins Point Dam, Cedar County, Nebraska.
2. Probably the American elm, *Ulmus americana* L.

Wednesday 29th. At 8 o'clock last night a storm of wind and rain came on from the N. west, and the rain continued the greater part of the night. The morning was cloudy with some thunder. We are generally well supplied with Catfish, the best I have ever seen. Some large ones were taken last night. In the afternoon the men who had gone to the Indian camp returned and brought with them sixty Indians of the Sioux nation. They encamped for the evening upon the opposite shore, and some corn and tobacco were sent over to them. The sergeant who had gone to their camp informed me that their lodges, forty in number, are about nine miles from the Missouri on the Sacque river. They are made of dressed buffaloe and elk skins, painted red and white, and are very handsome. He said the women are homely and mostly old; but the young men likely and active. They killed a dog as a token of friendship. One of our men[1] killed a deer.

1. Drouillard.

Thursday 30th. A foggy morning, and heavy dew. At nine o'clock the Indians came over the river. Four of them, who were musicians, went backwards and forwards, through and round our camp, singing and making a noise. After that ceremony was over they all sat in council. Captain Lewis and Captain Clarke made five of them chiefs, and gave them some small presents. At dark Captain Lewis gave them a grained deer skin to stretch over a half keg for a drum. When that was ready they all assembled round some fires made for the purpose: two of them beat on the drum, and some of the rest had little bags of undressed skins dried, with beads or small pebbles in them, with which they made a noise. These are their instruments of musick. Ten or twelve acted as musicians, while twenty or thirty young men and boys engaged in the dance, which was continued during the night. No Squaws made their appearance among this party.

Friday 31st. A clear morning. The Indians remained with us all day, and got our old Frenchman[1] to stay and go with their chief to the city of Washington. Some of them had round their necks strings of the white bear's[2] claws, some of the claws three inches long.

1. Dorion, Sr.
2. The grizzly bear, *Ursus horribilis,* not encountered by the party until October 20.

Saturday 1st Sept. 1804. We renewed our voyage early; passed high bluffs on the south side, and high prairie land on the north; on this side, the hills come close to the river; and are so near on both sides, as not to be more than two miles from each other. During last night we had hard wind and some rain, which continues to fall occasionally during the day.— About 1 o'clock we passed a rich prairie on the south side, and encamped on the north side, at the lower end of an island.[1]

1. Bon Homme Island, Bon Homme County, South Dakota, now inundated by Lewis and Clark Lake.

Sunday 2nd. At 1 o'clock last night we had hard thunder, lightning and rain, which continued about two hours. We set out early in the morning, along the north side of the island: there is handsome prairie land on the south. Three of our men[1] went on the island to hunt. When we landed for breakfast, we heard several guns fired on the island, and saw six elk swimming across the river about a mile above where we had halted. Two of our men went up and killed one of them; those on the island killed three.[2] About twelve, the wind blew so hard down the river, that we could not proceed, and we landed on the north side, where there is an extensive prairie.[3] It was cloudy and rained till 4 when it cleared up. We remained here for the night and dried our meat. On the bank opposite our camp is an ancient fortification or breastwork,[4] similar to those which have been occasionally discovered on the western waters. The two ends run at right angles to the river, and the outside, which is 2500 yards in length, parallel to it: there is no breastwork thrown up next to the river, the bank as is supposed, serving as a sufficient defence on that side.[5]

1. Drouillard, Reubin Field, and John Collins.

2. The successful hunters were Drouillard, Reubin Field, Thomas P. Howard, and John Newman.

3. In Bon Homme County, South Dakota.

4. Gass, like the rest of the party, believed these natural sand ridges opposite Bon Homme Island in Knox County, Nebraska, to be a man-made fortification; see Clark's detailed survey of this date and McKeehan's note for the day.

5. McKeehan's note: "The description of this Breastwork corresponds exactly with the accounts given of numerous ancient fortifications discovered in the Western Country, which are known and represented to be generally of an oblong form, situated on strong and well chosen ground, and contiguous to water. These works from the examinations which have been made, are supposed to have been erected more than 1000 years ago; or 700 before the discovery of America by Columbus. They appear to have existed about the same period, throughout all, or the greater part of that vast tract of Country bounded by the Alleghany Mountains on the east and the Rocky Mountains on the west, and including the most favourable latitudes of North America. Perhaps some have been found east of the Allegheny Mountains. Have numerous ancient nations, more civilized and disposed to labour than any of the modern Indian tribes, inhabited this Country? And have these fortifications been their humble substitutes for the walled and fortified Cities of the old world in remote ages? Or, has this been the Roman Empire of the New World? and has it been destroyed by other hordes of barbarians, as fierce and cruel as those who destroyed that of the old[?]"

Monday 3rd.   We set out early, and had a clear day; passed yellow bluffs on the north side, and a small creek, called Plumb creek.[1] Here the river turns at right angles to the left, till it reaches the hills on the south side, then winds gradually to the right. There is no timber in this part of the country; but continued prairie on both sides of the river. A person by going on one of the hills may have a view as far as the eye can reach without any obstruction, or intervening object; and enjoy the most delightful prospects. During this day's voyage we found the hills on the opposite sides of the river generally not more than two miles apart, and the river meandering through them in various directions. We encamped[2] on the south side.

1. Probably Emmanuel Creek, Bon Homme County, South Dakota.

2. In Knox County, Nebraska, probably near the western boundary of the Santee Sioux Indian Reservation.

Tuesday 4th.   We proceeded early on our voyage, passed a creek on the south side about 30 yards wide, called Paint creek;[1] and high yellow bluffs on the same side. About a mile and an half further, we passed another creek on the same side 50 yards wide, called White-paint creek;[2] and yellow bluffs on the north side. About four miles higher up, we passed a river, on the south side, 152 yards wide, called Rapid-water river:[3] up this river the Poncas nation of Indians lived not long since. We encamped on the south side among some cedar trees.

1. Lost Creek, Knox County, Nebraska; see Clark's entry for this day.

2. Bazile Creek, Knox County.

3. Niobrara River, Knox County, with a Ponca village nearby.

Wednesday 5th.   We set sail early this morning with a fair wind, and had a clear day. We passed a long island covered with timber, and three men[1] went to hunt on it. On the north side are yellow bluffs, out of which issue several beautiful springs. Opposite the head of the island, on the south side, flows in a river, called Pania river;[2] and about three miles higher up, on the north side, a creek, called Goat creek.[3] On the hills above this creek we saw some goats or antelopes, which the French call cabres.[4] About 4 we encamped[5] on an island, where we made and put in a new mast. The three men, who went to hunt on the long island killed a deer and an elk; and two more went out from camp and killed another deer and an elk, both young.

1. The Field brothers and Drouillard.
2. Like Clark, Gass uses "Pania" (Pawnee) for "Ponca." This is Ponca Creek, Knox County, Nebraska.
3. Chouteau Creek, between Bon Homme and Charles Mix counties, South Dakota.
4. Pronghorn, *Antilocapra americana*.
5. On an island between Charles Mix County, South Dakota, and Knox County, Nebraska.

Thursday 6th. We set out early and had cloudy morning: passed a handsome bottom prairie on the north side; at the upper end of which is a grove of cotton wood, and a long range of dark coloured bluffs on the south side. About 9 o'clock it began to rain and we had strong wind ahead. There are a great number of sand bars, and we had much difficulty in getting along. We encamped[1] on the north side and one of our men[2] killed two deer.

1. In Charles Mix County, South Dakota, a little below the Knox-Boyd county line in Nebraska, opposite.
2. Reubin Field.

Friday 7th. We set sail early, and had a clear day: passed high prairie land on both sides; but there is some cotton wood on the low points in the bottoms. On the south side we found a scaffold of meat neatly dried. This had been left by one of our men,[1] who had gone out on the 26th of the last month to hunt the horses, and supposing we had got a distance ahead, proceeded up the river several days journey, before he discovered his error. Captain Lewis and Captain Clarke with some of the men went to view a round knob[2] of a hill in a prairie, and on their return killed a prairie dog,[3] in size about that of the smallest species domestic dogs.

Having understood that the village of those small dogs was at a short distance from our camp, Captain Lewis and Captain Clarke with all the party, except the guard, went to it; and took with them all the kettles and other vessels for holding water; in order to drive the animals out of their holes by pouring in water; but though they worked at the business till night they only caught one of them.

1. Shannon.
2. Old Baldy, or the Tower, Boyd County, Nebraska.
3. Gass takes the French traders' designation *chien*, or dog, literally. The prairie dog, *Cynomys ludovicianus*, is a rodent.

Saturday 8th. We proceeded early on our voyage, and had a clear day and fair wind from the S. E. Passed the bed of a creek[1] without water. At 9 I went out with one of our men, who had killed a buffaloe and left his hat to keep off the vermin and beasts of prey; but when we came to the place, we found the wolves had devoured the carcase and carried off the hat. Here we found a white wolf dead, supposed to have been killed in a contest for the buffaloe. We passed high bluffs on the south side and burnt prairie on the north. We encamped on an island[2] covered with timber; and having a number of buf-faloe on it. Captain Lewis who had been out with some of the men hunting informed us he had passed a trading house, built in 1796.[3] This day we killed two buffaloe, a large and a small elk, a deer and two beaver.

1. Clark crossed out his only apparent reference to this stream; if they are the same, it is some three miles above the last camp, in Boyd County, Nebraska, just below the South Dakota state line, and bears no name on any map.
2. Chicot, or Strehlow, Island, on the Charles Mix–Gregory county line, South Dakota.
3. Jean Baptiste Truteau wintered here in 1794–95, some thirty miles above the mouth of the Niobrara River, in Charles Mix County.

Sunday 9th. We set out early, and passed two small creeks[1] on the north side, high bluffs on the south, and at one o'clock landed for dinner at a small creek[2] on the south side. One of our hunters[3] brought in a deer and two fawns. This day we saw several gangs or herds, of buffaloe on the sides of the hills: One of our hunters[4] killed one, and Captain Clarke's black servant[5] killed two. We encamped[6] at sunset on the south side.

1. Either Spring and Pease creeks, or Pease and Campbell creeks, Charles Mix County, South Dakota.
2. Perhaps Scalp Creek, Gregory County, South Dakota.
3. Drouillard.
4. Reubin Field.
5. York.
6. In Gregory County, South Dakota, opposite Stony Point.

Monday 10th. We had a foggy morning, but moved on early; passed high bluffs on the north side, and saw some timber in the bottom on the south side. At 12 we came to black sulphur bluffs on the south side.[1] On the top of these bluffs we found the skeleton or back bones of a fish, 45 feet long, and petrified: part of these bones were sent to the City of Washington. One of our sergeants[2] discovered a large salt spring about a mile and an half from the river. A hunter went up the bank and killed an elk. We left a periogue for the men who were dressing the elk, and proceeded up the north side of the river two miles, when we were obliged to return on account of sand bars, and to take the south side. Here we saw eight elk swimming the river, and had seen a great many buffaloe during the day. We encamped[3] on an island and killed one buffaloe.

1. At Mulehead Point, Gregory County, South Dakota, where they found the fossil remains of a plesiosaur.
2. Sergeant Pryor, along with Drouillard.
3. On Pocahontas, or Toehead, Island, between Gregory and Charles Mix counties, South Dakota.

Tuesday 11th.   We set sail before day light with a fair wind; passed an island covered with timber, and high hills and prairie on both sides of the river. At 1 o'clock it began to rain. We saw some person[1] coming down the river on horseback, when we came to land and found it was the man who had preceded us with the horses. He had left one of the horses that had failed. We now had only one horse left. This man had been absent 16 days, and his bullets being expended, he subsisted 12 days almost wholly on grapes. The hills here come close to the river on both sides. One of the men went by land with the horse, and we continued our voyage, until night, though it rained very hard; and encamped[2] on the south side. Captain Clarke with two or three of the men[3] who had gone out to hunt, killed two elk, four deer and one porcupine.[4]

1. Shannon.
2. A little south of the Lyman-Gregory county line, South Dakota.
3. Sergeants Ordway and Pryor, and perhaps Gibson.
4. Porcupine, *Erethizon dorsatum.*

Wednesday 12th.   We set out as usual and had a cloudy day; passed a long range of black bluffs on the south side, and an island covered with timber, which is all the timber that can be seen from this place. The country round is all hills and prairie. Captain Clarke, myself and another[1] went out to hunt, and did not return till after dark. The boat had much difficulty in passing on account of the sand bars and strong current, and did not make to day more than four miles.[2]

1. Newman.
2. They camped in Brule County, South Dakota.

Thursday 13th. Four beaver were taken last night. We set sail early; the morning was cloudy with some rain and wind ahead; passed a creek and a long range of bluffs on the south side. Some of our men[1] went out to hunt; but did not return this evening. We encamped[2] on the north side.

1. Sergeants Ordway and Pryor, and Shannon.
2. The main party camped in Brule County, South Dakota.

Friday 14th. We proceeded as yesterday, and with the same kind of weather. Had considerable difficulty in getting along, on account of the shallowness of the river; all hands in the water dragging the boat. At 8 we halted for breakfast, and the men who went to hunt yesterday came in, and had only killed a porcupine. Three beaver were caught last night. The musketoes are as troublesome as they have been any time in summer. We passed black bluffs on the south side, and an island with timber on it. Passed a creek on the same side and encamped[1] on it. The man who had gone by land with the horse came to us here; had killed a hare.[2] Captain Clarke killed a goat or antelope.

1. Near the mouth of Bull Creek, Lyman County, South Dakota.
2. Shields got the "hare," a white-tailed jackrabbit, *Lepus townsendii.*

Saturday 15th. A cloudy morning. We continued our voyage early, and passed a creek[1] on the south side and black bluffs on the north. Passed White river[2] on the south side; one of the men[3] and myself went up it to examine the country, and encamped about twelve miles from the mouth, where it is 150 yards broad. We found good bottoms on this creek; but timber scarce, and none upon the hills. The current and colour of the water are much like those of the Missouri.

1. Bull Creek (see previous entry).
2. White River, reaching the Missouri in Lyman County, South Dakota.
3. Reubin Field.

Sunday 16th. We set out for the boat across the hills, on the tops of which are level plains with a great number of goats and buffaloe on them. Came to the head waters of a creek[1] and kept down it a S. E. course, and on our way killed three deer. We proceeded on to its mouth, which I computed to be 14 miles from that of the White river. Having found the boat had passed we proceeded up the river, and came to a handsome bottom, where our people had encamped[2] to dry the provisions and stores. In our absence the men had killed some deer and two buffaloe.

1. The party's Corvus Creek, now American Creek, Lyman County, South Dakota.
2. Near Oacoma, Lyman County.

Monday 17th. As the weather was fair we remained here during the day. Captain Lewis and some men went out to hunt, and killed thirteen common, and two black-tailed deer;[1] three buffaloe and a goat. The wild goat in this country differ from the common tame goat, and is supposed to be the real antelope. The black-tailed, or mule deer have much larger ears than the common deer and tails almost without hair, except at the end, where there is a bunch of black hair. There is another species of deer in this country with small horns and long tails.[2] The tail of one which we killed was 18 inches long. One of our men caught a beaver, and killed a prairie wolf.—[3] These are a small species of wolves, something larger than a fox, with long tails and short ears.

1. Lewis and Clark gave the mule deer, *Odocoileus hemionus*, its popular name.
2. Western white-tailed deer, *Odocoileus virginianus dacotensis*.
3. The coyote, *Canis latrans*.

Tuesday 18th. We continued our voyage; the day was clear and pleasant: passed some timber land on the south side, and hills and prairies on the north; also an island and a great number of sand bars. Yesterday captain Lewis while hunting killed a bird[1] not common in the states: it is like a magpie and is a bird of prey. This day we killed eleven deer and a wolf, and halted and encamped[2] on the south side of the river in order to jirk our meat.

1. Black-billed magpie, *Pica pica.*
2. In Lyman County, South Dakota, a few miles northeast of Oacoma.

Wednesday 19th. We set out early and had a clear day passed large bottoms on both sides of the river covered with timber. We saw some buffaloe swimming the river and killed two of them. There is an island here, opposite which a river flows in on the north side.[1] This river is formed of three, which unite their waters just above its mouth; and immediately above the confluence is a crossing place, called the Sioux-crossing-place of the three rivers. At the upper end, a creek called, Elm creek,[2] comes in on the south side, and two miles above another creek called Wash creek,[3] falls in on the same side. About two miles further we passed another creek called Night creek where we encamped on the south side. Three black tailed deer were killed this day.

1. The "Sioux Pass of the Three Rivers"; the streams are Crow, Elm (or Wolf), and Campbell creeks, behind Des Lauriens Island, all in Buffalo County, South Dakota.
2. See note to Clark's entry of this day for the problems about creek names. Elm Creek is perhaps Good Soldier Creek or Counselor (Camel) Creek, Lyman County, South Dakota.
3. Not named by Clark; it may be Counselor (Camel) Creek, in which case Night Creek, where they camped, would be Fish (Brule) Creek, Lyman County.

Thursday 20th. We renewed our voyage at an early hour, and had a clear day and fair wind. Passed handsome rising prairies on the north side, and bottoms covered with timber on the south side. Two of the men[1] with the horse went across the neck of the Long, or Grand bend,[2] which we were obliged to go round with the boat, a distance of 30 miles. At one o'clock we stopped for dinner, and Captain Lewis and one of the men[3] went to hunt, Captain Clarke had gone out in the morning. At 2 we proceeded again on our voyage, and passed a long chain of bluffs on the north side, of a dark colour. From these and others of the same kind the Missouri gets its muddy colour. The earth of which they are composed dissolves like sugar; every rain washes down great quantities of it, and the rapidity of the stream keeps it mixing and afloat in the water, until it reaches the mouth of the Mississippi. We encamped[4] at 7 o'clock on a sand beach on the north side. Here Captain Lewis, Captain Clarke and the other man joined us. They had killed two goats and two deer. At 1 o'clock at night, the bank where we were stationed began to fall so much, that we were obliged to rouse all hands, and go on a mile and cross the river before we could again encamp.

1. Drouillard and Shields.
2. The Big Bend of the Missouri River, enclosing land in Lyman County, South Dakota.
3. Reubin Field.
4. In Hughes County, South Dakota.

Friday 21st.   We set out early, the day was clear, and we proceeded on four miles along bluffs on the south side, when came to the termination of the Grand bend, about a mile from the place of our encampment on the 19th.— We again went on, having black bluffs on the south and a handsome bottom on the north side; and beyond these a cedar bottom on the south side and bluffs on the north; passed a creek on the south side, called Tyler's creek;[1] and encamped on the north side.

1. Medicine River, Lyman County, South Dakota.

Saturday 22nd.   We embarked early in a foggy morning, saw some timber on the south side and high plains on the north. About 3 o'clock we passed cedar island, one of the Three-Sisters, where Mr. Lucelle had built a fort of cedar.[1] The space picketed in is about 65 or 70 feet square, with centry boxes in two of the angles. The pickets are 13½ feet above ground. In this square he built a house 45½ by 32½ feet, and divided it into four equal parts, one for goods, one to trade in, one to be used as a common hall and the other for a family house. Here the two men[2] came to us with the horse. They had killed a white wolf and some deer. We proceeded on, passed a creek,[3] and islands of the three sisters;[4] and an old Indian camp, where we found some of their dog-poles, which answer for setting poles. The reason they are called dog-poles, is because the Indians fasten their dogs to them, and make them draw them from one camp to another loaded with skins and other articles.[5] We encamped[6] on the north side.

1. Régis Loisel's *Fort aux Cedres,* built in 1800, or perhaps two years later, for the Sioux trade. It was on later Dorion Island No. 2, Lyman County, South Dakota. The site was not precisely determined before the island was inundated by Big Bend Reservoir.

2. Drouillard and Shields.

3. Cedar Creek, Lyman County, Clark's Three Sisters Creek.

4. The "Three Sisters" are presumably the two Dorion Islands and a third later joined to the shore, all in Lyman County, and all now inundated by Big Bend Reservoir.

5. A dog travois, used by many plains tribes before the introduction of the horse. Mc-Keehan's note: "Mr. Mackenzie speaking of the Knisteneaux, a numerous nation of Indians spread over a vast extent of country extending south westerly from the coast of Labrador, north of the St. Laurence and its Lakes and the Lake Winnipic, east of Elk river, south of the Lake of the Hills, and west, south and east of James's Bay and the southern part of Hudson's Bay, says, 'In the winter when the waters are frozen, they make their journies, which are never of any great length, with sledges drawn by dogs.' *General History of the Fur Trade.*"

6. In Hughes County, South Dakota, nearly opposite the mouth of Loiselle Creek (see Clark's entry and note for this date).

Sunday 23rd. We went on early, and had a clear morning; passed some timber on the north side and high land on the south; also a creek on the north side called Smoke creek;[1] passed Elk island, a handsome bottom on the north side covered with timber and barren hills on the south. At six in the evening we saw four Indians on the south side and encamped[2] on the north. Three of the Indians swam over to us: they belonged to the Sioux, and informed us that there were more of their nation not far distant. We sent them over the river again. One of our men[3] killed an antelope.

1. La Chapelle, or Chapelle, Creek, Hughes County, South Dakota.

2. In Hughes County, just below the mouth of Antelope Creek on the opposite side.

3. Reubin Field.

Monday 24th. We set sail early with fair weather, and passed a small creek on the south side.[1] About 3 o'clock the man[2] who had gone by land with the horse came to us, and informed us that he had gone that morning on an island to kill elk, and that while he was there the Indians had stolen the horse. He had killed three elk, and the periogues remained behind to bring on the meat. We saw five Indians on the bank, but we could not understand each other. We cast anchor to wait for the periogues; one of which having come up, we went on to the mouth of the Tinton or Teeton river,[3] where we anchored about 100 yards from the shore on the south side. The guard and cooks only landed, the rest slept in the boat. The five Indians remained with us all night. We had a Frenchman aboard a periogue, who understood and could speak a little of the Sioux language.[4] The Indians gave us to understand the chiefs would come to-morrow, and that if their young men had taken the horse, they would have him given up. These Indians are a band of the Sioux, called the Tinton or Teeton-Band.[5]

1. Antelope Creek, Stanley County, South Dakota.
2. Colter.
3. Bad River, Stanley County, opposite Pierre.
4. Probably Cruzatte or Labiche, speaking Omaha.
5. Teton Sioux; see note at Clark's entry for this date.

Chapter Fifty

Winter at the Knife River

September 25, 1804–April 6, 1805

Tuesday 25th.   We stayed here to wait for the Indians, who were expected to arrive, and at 10 o'clock they came, about 50 in number. The commanding officers made three of them chiefs[1] and gave them some presents. Five[2] of them came on board and remained about three hours. Captain Clarke and some of our men in a periogue went ashore with them; but the Indians did not seem disposed to permit their return. They said they were poor and wished to keep the periogue with them. Captain Clarke insisted on coming to the boat; but they refused to let him, and said they had soldiers as well as he had. He told them his soldiers were good, and that he had more medicine aboard his boat than would kill twenty such nations in one day.[3] After this they did not threaten any more, and said they only wanted us to stop at their lodge, that the women and children might see the boat. Four of them came aboard; when we proceeded on a mile, and cast anchor at the point of an island[4] in the middle of the river. The Indians remained with us all night.

   1. Black Buffalo, Buffalo Medicine, and Partisan.
   2. The chiefs named above and probably Warzingo and Second Bear (see Clark's entry), but perhaps some unnamed "soldiers."
   3. Clark says only that "I felt my Self warm & Spoke in verry positive terms."
   4. The captains called it Bad Humored Island, for obvious reasons; probably later Marion Island, Stanley County, South Dakota, opposite Pierre.

Wednesday 26th.   We set out early, and proceeded on four miles. The bank of the river on the south side was covered all the way with Indians; and at 10 o'clock we met the whole band, and anchored about 100 yards from the shore.[1] Captain Lewis, the chiefs, and some men went on shore, the Indians were peaceable and kind. After some time Capt. Lewis returned on board, and Capt. Clarke went on shore. When the Indians saw him coming they met him with a buffaloe robe, spread it out and made him get into it, and then eight of them carried him to the council house. About an hour after some of them came for Captain Lewis, and he landed; and eight of them carried him to the council house in the same manner, they had carried Captain Clarke. They killed several dogs for our people to feast on, and spent the greater part of the day in eating and smoking. At night the women assembled, and danced till 11 o'clock: then the officers came on board with two chiefs, who continued with us until the morning.

1. In Stanley County, South Dakota, about four miles north of Fort Pierre.

Thursday 27th.   We remained here all day. Capt. Lewis, myself and some of the men went over to the Indian camp. Their lodges are about eighty in number, and contain about ten persons each; the greater part women and children. The women were employed in dressing buffaloe skins, for clothing for themselves and for covering their lodges. They are the most friendly people I ever saw; but will pilfer if they have an opportunity. They are also very dirty: the water they make use of, is carried in the paunches of the animals they kill, just as they are emptied, without being cleaned. They gave us dishes of victuals of various kinds; I had never seen any thing like some of these dishes, nor could I tell of what ingredients, or how they were made.[1]

About 15 days ago, they had a battle with the Mahas, of whom they killed 75 men and took 25 women prisoners, whom they have now with them. They promised to Capt. Lewis that they would send the prisoners back and make peace.

About 3 o'clock we went aboard the boat accompanied with the old chief and his little son.[2] In the evening Captain Clarke and some of the men went over, and the Indians made preparations for a dance. At dark it commenced. Captain Lewis, myself and some of our party went up to see them perform. Their band of musick, or orchestra, was composed of about twelve persons beating on a buffaloe hide, and shaking small bags that made a rattling noise. They had a large fire in the centre of their camp; on one side the women, about 80 in number, formed in a solid column round the fire, with sticks in their hands, and the scalps of the Mahas they had killed, tied on them. They kept moving, or jumping round the fire, rising and falling on both feet at once; keeping a continual noise, singing and yelling. In this manner they continued till 1 o'clock at night, when we returned to the boat with two of the chiefs. On coming aboard, the periogue run across the bow of the boat and broke the cable. All hands were roused to tow the boat ashore; the chiefs called aloud, and a number of the warriors came to our assistance, but we did not need it: the circumstance, however, shewed their disposition to be of service.[3] This unfortunate accident lost to us our anchor.

1. Clark's entry of September 26 mentions pemmican, dog, and "ground potatoe" (perhaps Indian potato, ground nut, *Apios americana* Medic.).

2. Not identified, but the captains regarded Black Buffalo as the ranking chief. On September 30, Gass calls Buffalo Medicine "our old chief."

3. The captains thought the incident demonstrated that the Sioux intended to rob them, but apparently they did not relay this suspicion to the enlisted men.

Friday, 28th. This morning we dragged the river all around where the boat lay, but could not find the anchor. At 9 o'clock we made preparations to sail; some of the chiefs were on board, and concluded to go some distance with us. When we went to shove off, some of the Indians took hold of the rope and would not let it go. This conduct had like to be attended with bad consequences, as Captain Lewis was near giving orders to cut the rope and to fire on them. The chiefs, however, went out and talked with them: they said they wanted a carrot of tobacco, and that if we gave that we might go. The tobacco was given them, and we went off under a gentle breeze of wind. We passed high land on the north side and bottom on the south. We proceeded 4 miles, and then saw an Indian[1] following us along the beach, when Captain Lewis went in a periogue and brought him on board. He informed us that 300 more Indians had come to their camp, and desired we should stop and talk with them. We did not then stop, but proceeded on, and he remained on board. We passed a fine bottom covered with timber on the north side, and bare hills on the south. We made two large stones serve the purpose of an anchor, and at sunset anchored for the night,[2] near a small sand-bar in the middle of the river.

While I was at the Indian camp yesterday they yoked a dog to a kind of car, which they have to haul their baggage from one camp to another; the nation having no settled place or village, but are always moving about.[3] The dogs are not large, much resemble a wolf, and will haul about 70 pounds each.

1. Buffalo Medicine.

2. Between Stanley and Hughes counties, South Dakota, some three miles above Oahe Dam.

3. McKeehan's note: "It appears that these people, (in some respects resembling the wandering Arabs) are an unsettled, ferocious, blood-thirsty race, and have been great destroyers of the Algonquin nation, who inhabit the country about lake Superior. Mr. McKenzie states the following circumstance, 'Within three miles of the last portage' (a place near lake Superior) 'is a remarkable rock, with a smooth face, but split and cracked in different parts, which hang over the water. Into one of its horizontal chasms a great number of arrows have been shot, which is said to have been done by a war party of the Nadowasis or Sieux, who had done much mischief in this country, and left these weapons as a warning to the Chebois or natives, that, notwithstanding its lakes, rivers and rocks, it was not inaccessible to their enemies.' *General History of the Fur Trade.*"

Saturday 29th. We set sail early and had fair weather; passed a handsome bottom covered with timber on the north side, and bluffs on the south. We saw several Indians on the south side walking up the shore; spoke to them and found they were some of those we left yesterday. There were one or two of the chiefs with them. They requested us to give them a carrot of tobacco for the chiefs of the other band to smoke. We sent them two carrots to a sand bar, where they could get it; but told them we should not go on shore again, until we came to the nation of the Aricaris, commonly called Rickarees, Rickrees, or Rees. The Missouri is very shallow at this time and full of sand bars. We passed an old village[1] on the south side, where the Rickarees lived five years ago, and raised corn in the bottom, around the village. We encamped[2] on a sand beach on the south side of the river.

1. An Arikara village on Chantier Creek, Stanley County, South Dakota, believed to have been abandoned about 1794.

2. Between Stanley and Sully counties, South Dakota, about three and one-half miles above Chantier Creek.

Sunday 30th. We set out early in a cloudy morning; passed black buffs on the south side, and handsome bottom prairie on the north; saw an Indian on the shore, and the chief we had on board spoke to him. He said he wished to come on board and go with us to the Rees; but we did not take him. The wind was fair and we made 9 miles by 10 o'clock. We saw a great number of Indians coming down to the river on the south side. We stopt for breakfast about 200 yards from the shore; then proceeded about a mile; near to the place where the Indians were encamped on the south side; we halted and spoke to them[1] and then went on under a fine breeze of wind.

A short time before night, the waves ran very high and the boat rocked a great deal, which so alarmed our old chief, that he would not go any further. We encamped[2] on the north side.

1. See Clark's account of this conversation.
2. Either on Cheyenne Island or on the nearby shore of Sully County, South Dakota.

Monday 1st Oct 1804. We early continued our voyage, the morning was cloudy but the wind fair and we sailed rapidly. At 9 we passed the river De Chien, or Dog river;[1] a large river that comes in on the south side. A short distance above this river, the sand bars are so numerous, that we had great difficulty to get along; and encamped[2] on one in the middle of the river. There were some French traders on the other bank of the river, and one[3] of them came over and remained with us all night.

1. Cheyenne River, Stanley County, South Dakota. Gass repeats Clark's confusion of "Cheyenne" and the French *chien,* or dog.
2. In Dewey County, South Dakota, a few miles above Cheyenne River.
3. Apparently the unnamed "boy" who came over in a canoe from Jean Vallé's trading post.

Tuesday 2nd. We set sail before day light. A Frenchman[1] came on board, who could speak English. He mentioned it as his opinion, that we should see no more Indians, until we should arrive at the nation of Rees. We passed a range of black bluffs on the north side and a large bottom on the south, where there was some timber on the bank of the river. About 2 o'clock we discovered some Indians on the hills on the north side, and one of them came down to the bank and fired a gun; the object or intention we did not well understand, but were ready to meet an attack. We passed black bluffs on the south side, an island covered with timber, and a handsome bottom on the north side. We halted and spoke to the Indian, who said he belonged to the Jonkta or Babarole band,[2] and that there were 20 lodges of them. We told him we had seen two of their chiefs, and given them a flag and medal.[3] We passed a creek on the south side, and encamped[4] on a sand bar in the middle of the river.

1. Jean Vallé, a trader of Ste. Genevieve, Missouri.
2. Evidently either the Yankton or Bois Brulé divisions of the Sioux.
3. Presenting medals to Indian dignitaries was a longstanding custom. Lewis and Clark carried medals of various sizes and inscriptions. The most common displayed the profile of President Jefferson on one side, while the reverse showed clasped hands and crossed tomahawk and pipe.
4. Just above Plum Island, between Sully and Dewey counties in South Dakota.

Wednesday 3rd.   The morning was cloudy, and some rain fell. The land is high on both sides of the river. About 12 o'clock the wind began to blow so hard down the stream, that we were unable to proceed, and we halted under some high bluffs, where drift wood was plenty. At 3 we continued our voyage; passed a long range of dark colored bluffs on the south side and bottom, with some timber, on the north. We encamped[1] on the south side.

1. Near the Potter-Dewey county line, South Dakota. See note to Clark's entry for the problems of this day's courses.

Thursday 4th.   We set out early; but were obliged to return to the place where we halted yesterday at 12 and to take the other side of the river; the water was so shallow and sand bars so numerous. At 9 o'clock an Indian swam across the river to see us, when we stopped for breakfast. We informed him that we were not traders, that we had seen his chief and told him all we had to say. We proceeded on, passed a creek on the south side, called Teel creek,[1] and encamped on the upper part of an island.

1. Stove (perhaps actually Stone), or Cherry, Creek, Dewey County, South Dakota.

Friday 5th.   This morning there was a white frost; the day clear and pleasant. About 11 we saw some goats swimming the river, when one of our hunters ran up the shore and killed four of them, and we took them into the boat and periogues as they floated down. We passed a creek on the north side, called Hidden creek,[1] and high black bluffs on the south side.[2] Some of our hunters having gone on an island to hunt scared a prairie wolf into the river, which we killed. We passed a creek on the south side called White Goat creek,[3] and encamped on the north side.

1. Little Cheyenne River, or Cheyenne Creek, Potter County, South Dakota.
2. McKeehan's note: "To prevent mistakes, owing to the very winding course of the river, Starboard side and Larboard side were made use of in the original journal, instead of north side and south side; during the remainder of the voyage up the Missouri; but have been changed to north side and south side, as being better understood, and sufficiently representing the general course of the river."
3. White Brant Creek, according to Clark, retained that name until late in the nineteenth century, but later became Swift Bird Creek, Dewey County, South Dakota.

Saturday 6th.   We continued our voyage early, and had a clear day; passed bluffs on the south side and a bottom covered with timber on the north. About 11 we passed a handsome bottom, where a band of the Rees lived last winter. They had left a number of round huts covered with earth, some of their water craft made of buffaloe hides,[1] and some garden truck, such as squashes. We proceeded on and passed a small creek[2] on the south side; a handsome bottom on the north; and encamped on a sand beach on the north side.

1. Bullboats.
2. Perhaps Four Bears Creek, Dewey County, South Dakota, mentioned by Ordway but not by Clark.

Sunday 7th.   We set forward early and had a clear day: passed a willow bottom on the south side, and a creek on the north.[1] At the beginning of some timber land we passed a small river on the south side, called Cer-wer-cer-na,[2] about 90 yards wide. It is not so sandy as the Missouri, and the water is clear, with a deep channel. At the mouth of this river is a wintering camp of the Rickarees of 60 lodges. We saw two Sioux Indians on the north side, gave them some meat and proceeded on. We passed an island, on which Captain Clarke and one of the men went to hunt and killed a deer and a prarow. We encamped[3] on the north side opposite the head of the island.

1. Probably Clark's Otter Creek, now Swan Creek, Walworth County, South Dakota.
2. Moreau River, Dewey County, South Dakota.
3. Just above Blue Blanket Island, Walworth County, near Mobridge.

Monday 8th.   The morning was pleasant and we set out early: passed high land on the south side and bottom on the north. The river here is very shallow and full of sand bars. We passed a run on the south side called slate run.[1] Two of our hunters went out to some timber land on the north side to look for game. At 12 we came to a river on the south side, 120 yards wide, called the Marapa,[2] where we halted for dinner. The hunters came up, but had killed nothing. We passed a long range of hills on the north side; about two miles from the Marapa we passed a creek 25 yards wide;[3] and about four miles further came to an island,[4] where one band of the Rickarees live; and encamped at the upper end.

1. Deadman Creek, Corson County, South Dakota.
2. Gass is apparently in error here; according to Clark the stream 120 yards wide is the "We tar hoo," the present Grand River, Corson County; the "Maropa" is the next stream on the same side, Rampart, or Oak, Creek, also in Corson County.
3. This is Oak Creek (see previous note).
4. Ashley Island, site of an Arikara village.

Tuesday 9th.   The day was stormy, and we remained here preparing to hold a Council with the nation. Captain Lewis with some of the men went down to their lodges, and were used very kindly and friendly. Two Frenchmen live with them, one to trade and the other to interpret.[1]

1. The trader would be Pierre-Antoine Tabeau; the interpreter was Joseph Gravelines or perhaps Joseph Garreau. See Clark's entries for October 8 and 9.

Wednesday 10th.   This day I went with some of the men to the lodges, about 60 in number. The following is a description of the form of these lodges and the manner of building them.

In a circle of a size suited to the dimensions of the intended lodge, they set up 16 forked posts five or six feet high, and lay poles from one fork to another. Against these poles they lean other poles, slanting from the ground, and extending about four inches above the cross poles: these are to receive the ends of the upper poles, that support the roof. They next set up four large forks, fifteen feet high, and about ten feet apart, in the middle of the area; and poles or beams between these. The roof poles are then laid on extending from the lower poles across the beams which rest on the middle forks, of such a length as to leave a hole at the top for a chimney. The whole is then covered with willow branches, except the chimney and a hole below to pass through. On the willow branches they lay grass and lastly clay. At the hole below they build a pen about four feet wide and projecting ten feet from the hut; and hang a buffaloe skin, at the entrance of the hut for a door. This labour like every other kind is chiefly performed by the squaws. They raise corn, beans, and tobacco. Their tobacco[1] is different from any I had before seen: it answers for smoking, but not for chewing. On our return, I crossed from the island to the boat, with two squaws in a buffaloe skin stretched on a frame made of boughs, wove together like a crate or basket for that purpose.[2] Captain Lewis and Captain Clarke held a Council with the Indians, and gave them some presents.

1. *Nicotiana quadrivalvis* Pursh.
2. A bullboat again.

Thursday 11th.   A clear day. We waited for an answer from the Indians. About 12 o'clock, they came, and brought some corn, beans and squashes, which they presented to us. The chief said he was glad to see us, and wished our commanding officers would speak a good word for them to the Mandans; for they wanted to be at peace with them. These are the best looking Indians I have ever seen. At 1 o'clock P. M. we proceeded on our voyage; passed a creek[1] on the south side 20 yards wide and a handsome bottom covered with timber. Having made about four miles, we came to the second Village of the Rickarees,[2] situated in a prairie on the south side. They had the American flag hoisted which Captain Lewis gave them yesterday. Their lodges are similar to those in the first village, and the same, or perhaps more, in number. They are the most cleanly Indians I have ever seen on the voyage; as well as the most friendly and industrious. We anchored about 50 yards from shore, and sent a periogue over the river for wood. We all slept on board except the cooks, who went on shore to prepare provisions for the next day.

1. Clark's Kakawissassa Creek, later Cathead Creek, now Fisher Creek, Carson County, South Dakota.

2. In Campbell County, South Dakota.

Friday 12th. We had a pleasant morning, and remained here the forenoon to hear the chief of this village speak. Last night the Indians stole an axe from our cook, which of course in some degree diminished our confidence, and lessened the amicable character we had conceived of them. At 9 o'clock Captain Lewis, Captain Clarke and myself went to the 2nd Village, and talked with its chief; then to the third Village, about half a mile beyond a small creek,[1] and talked with the chief of that Village; and got some corn and beans[2] from them. The third village is nearly of the same size of the second, and has in it a great number of handsome and smart women and children: the men are mostly out hunting. About 12 we left the village and proceeded on our voyage. One of the natives agreed to go with us as far as the Mandans. We encamped[3] on the north side. After dark we heard some person hallooing on the opposite shore; and a periogue went over and brought an Indian and two squaws, who remained with us all night.[4]

1. The two villages are Rhtarahe and Waho-erha, Corson County, South Dakota.

2. The beans were the product of the hog peanut, *Amphicarpa bracteata* (L.) Fern.

3. In Campbell County, South Dakota.

4. Gass says nothing of the mutinous conduct of Newman this day, or the confinement of Newman and Reed.

Saturday 13th. We proceeded on early and had a cloudy day; passed Pond river[1] on the north side, about 50 yards wide. One of the squaws went on with us. At 12 it rained some, and we halted to hold a court martial.[2] At 2 continued our voyage, and did not get landing until after dark, the bank was so high and steep on one side and the water so shallow on the other. We encamped[3] on the north side.

54

1. Clark's Stone Idol Creek, now Spring, or Hermaphrodite, Creek, Campbell County, South Dakota. Gass's name reflects its supposed origin in a nearby small lake.

2. Newman was found guilty of "having uttered repeated expressions of a highly criminal and mutinous nature." He was sentenced to receive seventy-five lashes on the bare back and to be dismissed from the party. He would spend the winter at labor and was sent back with the return party in the spring.

3. In Campbell County, South Dakota, about a mile south of the North Dakota state line, their last camp in South Dakota on the westbound journey.

Sunday 14th. We had a cloudy morning and some rain. We proceeded early on our voyage; passed a bottom covered with timber on the south side and low ground covered with willows on the north; passed a creek[1] and black bluffs on the south side and encamped[2] on the north. It rained slowly during the whole of the day.

1. They called this stream Piaheto, or Eagle Feather, Creek, after an Arikara chief, presumably the one who accompanied them. It is now Bald Head Creek in Corson County, South Dakota.

2. They camped in Emmons County, North Dakota, their first camp in that state, roughly opposite Fire Heart Butte.

Monday 15th. It rained all last night, and we set out early in a cloudy morning. At 7 we saw a hunting party of the Rickarees, on their way down to the villages. They had 12 buffaloe-skin canoes or boats laden with meat and skins; besides some horses that were going down the bank by land. They gave us a part of their meat. The party consisted of men, women and children. At 8 we went on again; passed a fine bottom covered with cotton wood on the north side, and naked hills on the south. About 10, we saw another party of hunters, who asked us to eat and gave us some meat. One of these requested to speak with our young squaw,[1] who for some time hid herself, but at last came out and spoke with him. She then went on shore and talked with him, and gave him a pair of ear-rings and drops for leave to come with us; and when the horn blew for all hands to come on board, she left them and came to the boat. We passed a creek[2] on the south side, and encamped at dusk on the north; where there was a party of Indians about 30 in number. Our squaw remained with this party: they gave us some meat and appeared very glad to see us.

1. Clark says nothing about this young woman on this day, although he notes, "their women fond of our men— &c." Ordway is also silent on the matter. She may be one of the "2 Handsom squars" who followed the party and "persisted in their Civilities" on October 12, when Gass notes their spending the night. See Clark's entry and note for October 12.

2. Perhaps Clark's Sharha Creek, either Long Soldier or Porcupine Creek, Sioux County, North Dakota.

Tuesday 16th. We early renewed our voyage; and had a clear morning, passed a creek[1] on the south side. The timber is more plenty than it has been for a considerable distance down the river. The sand bars, gave us a great deal of trouble, and much retarded our progress. In the evening a short time before we encamped, we met with another hunting party of the Rickarees. They had a flock of goats, or antelopes, in the river, and killed upwards of forty of them. Captain Lewis, and one of our hunters went out and killed three of the same flock. We encamped[2] on the south side. This day we saw more than an hundred goats.

1. Probably Clark's Girl Creek, either Porcupine or Battle Creek, Sioux County, North Dakota.

2. In Sioux County, some two miles above the mouth of Beaver Creek.

Wednesday 17th. We renewed our voyage early, and had a clear morning. Last night eight of the Indians came over to see us, brought us some meat and remained all night. Captain Lewis, gave them some presents this morning. At half past ten the wind blew so hard down the river that we were obliged to halt. At four we proceeded on with the assistance of the tow line, though the wind still continued against us, and having made about two miles, encamped[1] on the south side. Several hunters went out this day and killed six deer: one of them did not join us at night.

1. A mile or two south of the entrance of Cannonball River, Sioux County, North Dakota.

Thursday 18th. We had a clear pleasant morning with some frost. We set sail early, and a hunter went up each shore. Having proceeded two miles we met a couple of Frenchmen in a canoe,[1] who had been up at the Mandan nation hunting, and met with a party of that nation, who robbed them of their arms, ammunition, and some fur which they had; and therefore they had to return down the river; but, meeting us, went back in hopes of recovering their property. We passed a small river, on the south side called Cannon-ball river.[2] Several hunters went out here. We passed a creek on the north side, called Fish Creek,[3] on which I killed a deer. At night we encamped on the south side, and all the hunters came in having killed six deer, four goats and a pelican.

1. On the question of their identity, see Clark's entry for this date. One of them was probably Grenier, an employee of Gravelines.

2. Cannonball River, on the boundary between Sioux and Morton counties, North Dakota.

3. Badger Creek, Emmons County, North Dakota.

Friday 19th. Early this morning we renewed our voyage, having a clear day and a fair wind: passed a creek on the south side. While out hunting yesterday I saw about three hundred goats, and some buffaloe. Deer are not so plenty here as lower down the river; but elk, buffaloe and goats, are very numerous. Four hunters went out to day and in the evening returned with 7 deer and three elk. We encamped[1] on the north side.

1. This campsite is somewhat uncertain, but it was evidently a few miles north of Huff, Morton County, North Dakota.

Saturday 20th. We were early under way this morning, which was very pleasant. Two hunters went out and at breakfast time brought a deer to the boat; when four more went out. We passed a creek on the north side,[1] about 20 yards wide; bottom covered with timber on both sides, and a small river[2] on the south side opposite the lower point of an island. At the upper end we passed bluffs on the south side and bottom on the north. We, this day, saw a number of buffaloe, and goats on the sides of the hills. We encamped on the south side, and our hunters came in having killed 14 deer, a goat and a wolf; and one of them wounded a large white bear.[3]

1. Probably Clark's Shepherd's Creek, modern Apple Creek, Burleigh County, North Dakota.

2. Little Heart River, Morton County, North Dakota.

3. Pierre Cruzatte had the party's first encounter with the grizzly bear.

Sunday 21st. We had a disagreeable night of sleet and hail. It snowed during the forenoon, but we proceeded early on our voyage, passed bottom on the south side and hills on the north. We also passed a small river on the south side, called Chischeet river;[1] and encamped on the south side. Two of the hunters, who had gone out in the morning came in, and had killed a buffaloe and an otter.[2]

1. Heart River, Morton County, North Dakota.
2. River otter, *Lutra canadensis.*

Monday 22nd. Some snow fell last night, and the morning was cloudy and cold. We embarked early and went on. At 9 we saw 11 Indians of the Sioux nation coming down from the Mandans, who, notwithstanding the coldness of the weather, had not an article of clothing except their breech-clouts. At 1 o'clock the day became clear and pleasant and we encamped[1] at night on the south side.

1. Probably in southeast Oliver County, North Dakota, just above the Morton County line.

Tuesday 23rd. Some snow again fell last night, and the morning was cloudy. At 8 it began to snow, and continued snowing to 11, when it ceased. We passed the place where the Frenchmen had been robbed but no Indians could be seen. The hills here are futher from the river than they are for some distance down it; and there are fine large bottoms on both sides covered with cotton wood. We encamped[1] on the south side where we found a great quanity of rabbit berries.[2] Three hunters were out to day, but killed nothing.

1. Near Sanger, Oliver County, North Dakota.
2. Buffaloberry again.

Wednesday 24th. We set out early in a cloudy morning. At 9 it began to rain and continued to rain for an hour. At 12 we came to a hunting party of the Mandan nation of Indians, and remained with them untill 2 and then continued our voyage. There were three lodges of these Indians on an island,[1] which has been cut off the Grand Bend, a short distance below the Mandan village. We encamped[2] on the north side. Five of the Indians came to us, and our Indian[3] went over with them and returned in the morning.

1. The old river bend formed an oxbow lake, Painted Woods Lake, McLean County, North Dakota.

2. About two miles below Washburn, McLean County.

3. The Arikara chief, Toone or Arketarnashar, who had accompanied them in hopes of making peace with the Mandans. See note to Clark's entry of October 9, 1804.

Thursday 25th. The morning was pleasant, and we set sail early with a fair wind. Passed a beautiful bottom on the south side, and hills on the north. A great many of the natives, some on horseback and some on foot appeared on the hills on the north side, hallooing and singing. At 2, we stopped for dinner, and as we could not get our boat to shore on the north side, the water being shallow, our Indian was sent over to them. In the afternoon we passed a bottom covered with timber on the north side and hills on the south, and encamped[1] on the north side. Here our Indian returned, accompanied by one of the Mandans.

1. In the vicinity of later Fort Clark, in either Oliver or McLean counties, North Dakota, depending on river shifts.

Friday 26th. We set out early and had a clear morning; passed a large Willow bottom on the south and high land on the north side. The Mandan Indian left us early in the morning. At 10, we came to a hunting party of the Mandans, consisting of men, women and children. There was an Irishman[1] with them, who had come from the North West Company of traders. We remained here an hour, and then proceeded. A number of the Indians kept along the shore opposite the boat all day, on the south side, on which side we encamped.[2] Some of them remained with us till 12 at night and then returned to their village.

1. Hugh McCracken, who may have been an independent trader rather than a North West Company man.

2. About half a mile below the Mandan village of Mitutanka (known to archaeologists as the Deapolis site, Clark's Matootonha), perhaps in McLean County, North Dakota, rather than Mercer County, due to later river shifts.

Saturday 27th. The morning was clear and pleasant and we set out early. At half past seven we arrived at the first village of the Mandans,[1] and halted about two hours. This village contains 40 or 50 lodges built in the manner of those of the Rickarees. These Indians have better complexions than most other Indians, and some of the children have fair hair.[2] We passed a bluff on the south side with a stratum of black resembling coal. There is a bottom on the north side, where the second Mandan village[3] is situated. We went about a mile above it, and encamped[4] in the same bottom, for the purpose of holding a council with the natives. This place is 1610 miles from the mouth of the river du Bois, where we first embarked to proceed on the expedition. There are about the same number of lodges, and people, in this village as in the first. These people do not bury their dead, but place the body on a scaffold, wrapped in a buffaloe robe, where it lies exposed.[5]

1. Mitutanka village, Mercer County, North Dakota.

2. This trait led to speculation that the Mandans were the fabled Welsh Indians.

3. Rooptahee to Clark, otherwise Ruptáre village, McLean County, North Dakota. Archaeologists call it the Black Cat site after the village chief.

4. North of Ruptáre, McLean County, opposite Stanton, Mercer County.

5. McKeehan's note: "See Mackenzie's account of the funeral rites of the Knisteneaux, in his General History of the Fur Trade."

Sunday 28th. The day was clear, and we remained here; but could not sit in council, the wind blew so violent.

Monday 29th. We had again a clear day, and some of the principal men came from each village of the Mandans, from the Watasoons,[1] Sioux,[2] and one from the Grossventers;[3] and all sat in council together. At 11 o'clock, when the Council met, a shot was fired from our bow piece, and the commanding officers took the chiefs by the hand. Captain Lewis, through an interpreter, delivered a speech; gave a suit of clothes to each of the chiefs and some articles for their villages. He also sent a suit to the chief of the Grossventers. At three o'clock another gun was fired at the breaking up of the council, and they all appeared satisfied. Captain Lewis gave an iron mill to the Mandan nation to grind their corn, with which they were highly pleased.

1. The Awaxawi Hidatsas; see Clark's October 27, 1804, entry and note for the involved nomenclature of this group.

2. Clark does not mention the presence of any Sioux on this occasion. It may be McKeehan's misreading of Gass. Whitehouse's copyist writes it "Water Sioux."

3. *Gros Ventres,* French for "big bellies," was a common designation for the Hidatsas. Clark mentions two chiefs of the Hidatsas proper at this council, Black Moccasin and Little Fox. For the names of all the chiefs, see his entry for this day.

Tuesday 30th.   We remained here to know the answer of the Indians. The day was clear and pleasant. At 10, Captain Lewis[1] with a party of our people, and an Indian or two, went about 6 miles up the river to view an island, in order to ascertain whether or not it would suit for winter quarters. At 5 P. M. they returned and were of opinion, that it was not an eligible place.

1. Actually Clark—not Lewis—went on this excursion.

Wednesday 31st.   A pleasant morning. We remained here also to day, the Indians having given no answer. At 12, Captain Clarke and some of the men went down to the village, and the chief gave 9 or 10 bushels of corn, and some buffaloe robes.

Thursday 1st Nov. 1804.   At 3 o'clock P. M. we returned down the river, to look for a place where we could fix our winter quarters. At dark we had descended 9 miles, and came to a bottom covered with cotton wood, where we encamped.[1]

1. In McLean County, North Dakota, a little north of Mitutanka village.

Friday 2nd.   Captain Lewis, myself and some of the men, went up to the first village of the Mandans, who gave us some corn. Captain Clarke and the rest of our party, having dropt half a mile lower down the river, began to clear a place for a camp and fort.[1] We pitched our tents and laid the foundation of one line of huts.

1. The site of Fort Mandan, McLean County, North Dakota, some fourteen miles west of Washburn, where they would remain until April 7, 1805. The actual site has been washed away by the Missouri.

Saturday 3rd.[1] A clear day; we continued building, and six men went down the river in a periogue to hunt. They will perhaps have to go 30 or 40 miles before they come to good hunting ground.— The following is the manner in which our huts and fort were built;[2] the huts were in two rows, containing four rooms each, and joined at one end forming an angle. When rasied about 7 feet high a floor of puncheons or split plank were laid, and covered with grass and clay; which made a warm loft. The upper part projected a foot over and the roofs were made shed-fashion, rising from the inner side, and making the outer wall about 18 feet high. The part not inclosed by the huts we intended to picket. In the angle formed by the two rows of huts we built two rooms, for holding our provisions and stores.

1. After this date Gass begins to skip several days' entries at a time through the Fort Mandan winter. Discrepancies of dating from Clark, Ordway, or Whitehouse, the other journalists for the period, will be noted.

2. Gass gives the most detailed information available about the construction of Fort Mandan. The fort was roughly triangular in outline. Ordway indicates that each row of huts consisted of four rooms each fourteen feet square, making each row approximately 56 feet in length.

About the 16th, the weather became very cold, and the ice began to run in the river. We sent a Frenchman[1] down to enquire about the hunters and the periogue. He and one of the hunters returned to the fort, having left the periogue and the rest about 30 miles below. The Frenchman was sent down again with a rope, and returned by land. On the 19th the hunters came up with the periogue loaded with the meat of about thirty deer, eleven elk and some buffaloe. In the cold weather we moved into the huts, though not finished. From the 20th to the 27th we had fine pleasant weather, and on the evening of the latter finished the roofs of our huts. These were made of puncheons split out of cotton wood and then hewed. The cotton wood resembles the lombardy poplar, and is a light soft wood.[2] The largest trees are in thickness about eighteen inches diameter. On the night of the 27th the snow fell seven inches deep, and the 28th was stormy.

1. The unnamed Frenchman, either one of the expedition *engagés* or one of the trappers or interpreters who joined them for the winter, set out on November 14 and returned on the fifteenth, according to Clark.

2. The cottonwood is plains cottonwood again, while the Lombardy poplar is an introduced European species, *Populus nigra* L. var. *italica* DuRoi.

Thursday 29th. This day was clear, but cold. We went to unrig the boat, and by an accident one of the sergeants had his shoulder dislocated.[1] The 30th the weather continued the same. Early in the morning of this day we saw an Indian on the opposite side of the river, and brought him over. He informed us that, a few days ago, eight of his nation were out hunting, and were attacked by a party of the Sioux tribe, who killed one and wounded two more; and also carried off their horses. Captain Clarke and twenty-three men immediately set out with an intention of pursuing the murderers. They went up to the first village of the Mandans, but their warriors did not seem disposed to turn out. They suggested the coldness of the weather; that the Sioux were too far gone to be overtaken; and put off the expedition to the spring of the year. Captain Clarke and his party returned the same evening to the fort. We have been daily visited by the Indians since we came here. Our fort is called Fort Mandan, and by observation is in latitude 47. 21. 32. 8.[2]

1. Pryor; see Clark's entry for this date.

2. This latitude must be from the captains' observation of November 11, 1804. McKeehan's note: "The course of the Missouri, and distances of places on it appear to be very erroneously laid down upon the maps of Louisiana generally. On these the villages of the Mandans are placed in about 43½ degrees north latitude and 112½ of west longitude from Greenwich. This would place them about 500 miles nearer the mouth of the Columbia on the Pacific ocean, than the mouth of the Missouri: supposing the mouth of the Columbia to be about 124 degrees west of London. But the nearest practicable route from the Mandan villages to the mouth of the Columbia, according to Captain Clarke's estimate, places them 335 miles nearer the mouth of the Missouri than that of the Columbia; and by the route actually taken by the expedition to the mouth of the Columbia, they are 900 miles nearer the mouth of the Missouri.

"By Captain Lewis's observations these villages are in latitude 47. 21. 32. 8. and according to Mr. Mackenzie, Mr. Thompson astronomer to the North West company, in the year 1798, determined the northern bend of the Missouri to be in latitude 47. 32. north, and longitude 101. 25. west. Now this is probably near the longitude of the Mandan villages; for as it appears by the above statement, and by other observations of Captain Lewis nearer the mouth of the Missouri, that the course up the river is, for a considerable distance, nearly due west, and afterwards nearly due north, the difference of longitude and latitude, between the mouth of the Missouri and the point where Mr. Thompson took his observations, may be added together, in estimating the distance: and this will give about 8½ degrees of latitude [a]nd 9 degrees of longitude making in the whole 17½ degrees, which from the very meandring course of the Missouri, may be sufficient to include 1610 miles of it, the distance from the mouth to the villages. In the map of North America included in the Atlas accompanying Pinkerton's Geography, published in 1804, this part of the Missouri appears pretty accurately laid down; but in the map of Louisiana in the same set it is equally erroneous with any other."

Saturday 1st December, 1804.   The day was pleasant, and we began to cut and carry pickets to complete our fort. One of the traders from the North West Company[1] came to the fort, and related that the Indians had been troublesome in his way through. An Indian came down from the first Mandan village, and told us that a great number of the Chien or Dog nation[2] had arrived near the village.

  1. George Henderson, actually of the Hudson's Bay Company, and thus a competitor of the North West Company traders.
  2. Cheyennes; Gass is still confusing the name with *chien,* or dog.

Sunday 2nd.   The day was pleasant, and the Snow melted fast. A party of the Chien Indians with some of the Mandans came to the fort: they appeared civil and good natured.

The 3rd 4th and 5th were moderate and we carried on the work; but the 6th was so cold and stormy, we could do nothing. In the night the river froze over, and in the morning was covered with solid ice an inch and an half thick.

Friday 7th.   A clear cold morning. At 9 o'clock, the Big-white[1] head chief, of the first village of the Mandans, came to our garrison and told us that the buffaloe were in the prairie coming into the bottom. Captain Lewis and eleven more of us went out immediately, and saw the prairie covered with buffaloe and the Indians on horseback killing them. They killed 30 or 40 and we killed eleven of them. They shoot them with bows and arrows, and have their horses so trained that they will advance very near and suddenly wheel and fly off in case the wounded buffaloe attempt an attack.[2]

  1. For Big White (Sheheke), see Clark's entry of October 29, 1804.
  2. Gass is the first of the expedition to note the Indians' training of buffalo horses.

Saturday 8th. In our hunt of yesterday, two men had their feet frost-bitten. Captain Clarke and another party went out though the cold was extreme, to hunt the buffaloe; and killed nine and a deer. One man got his hand frozen; another his foot;[1] and some more got a little touched. Two men encamped out to take care of the meat.

1. York suffered frostbite on his feet and apparently some slight frostbite on his penis, according to Clark.

Sunday 9th. Captain Lewis and twelve more of us, went down to the bottom where the two men were taking care of the meat. We found some buffaloe had come into the woods, and we killed ten of them and a deer. Having dressed them we loaded four horses with meat and sent them with some of the party to the fort: Captain Lewis and the rest of us encamped out, and had tolerable lodging with the assistance of the hides of the buffaloe we had killed.

Monday 10th. After breakfasting on marrow bones, Captain Lewis and four of us set out for the fort. Four hunters and another man to keep camp remained out. On our return we met one of our men, who said that a party had gone down with the horses for more meat. This day was very cold: an experiment was made with proof spirits, which in fifteen minutes froze into hard ice. In the evening two of our hunters came in with the horses, but had killed nothing.[1] Five encamped out.

1. Ordway says that Drouillard killed two buffalo and a deer, and brought in the deer. Clark says one of the buffalo was "too pore to Skin."

Tuesday 11th. Captain Lewis and Captain Clarke thinking the weather too cold to hunt, sent men down to the camp to bring up the remainder of the meat, and orders for the hunters to return. The hunters came in at dark. They had killed four buffaloe, and had dressed two of them. The cold was so severe they could do nothing with the other two.

Wednesday 12th. We all remained at the garrison, the weather being intensely cold. We made three small sleds to haul in the meat with.

Thursday 13th. The weather this day, began to be more moderate. Two hunters[1] went out and killed two buffaloe. One came in, and he and some of the men went out and brought in the meat.

1. One was Joseph Field.

Friday 14th. This day was more moderate, and light snow showers fell. Captain Clarke and fourteen men went out to hunt; and took the three sleds with them. In the evening five of them returned. Captain Clarke and the other 9 encamped out, and killed two deer. The snow fell about three inches deep.

Saturday 15th. A cloudy day. Some of the natives paid us a visit, and brought presents of meat to the commanding officers. About one o'clock Captain Clarke and his party returned, but had killed nothing more. The buffaloe were gone from the river. Some slight showers of snow fell during the day.

Sunday 16th. A clear cold day; I went up with some of the men to the 1st and 2nd village of the Mandans, and we were treated with much kindness. Three of the traders from the N. W. Company came to our fort,[1] and brought a letter to our commanding officers. They remained with us all night. The object of the visits we received from the N. W. Company, was to ascertain our motives for visiting that country, and to gain information with respect to the change of government.[2]

1. Hugh Heney and François-Antoine Larocque of the North West Company and George Bunch, or Budge, of the Hudson's Bay Company. Heney and Larocque delivered a letter from Charles Chaboillez, North West Company factor on the Assiniboine River. See Clark's entries for October 26, November 26, and this date.

2. McKeehan's note: "The North West Company was first formed in the winter of 1783–4, by the merchants of Canada engaged in the fur trade, uniting their interest. The concern was divided into sixteen shares, without any capital being deposited; each party furnishing his proportion of the articles necessary for carrying on the trade. After a severe struggle and rival competition with others engaged in the trade, in the year 1787 more partners were admitted, the shares extended to twenty and the establishment, which was no more than an association of commercial men agreeing among themselves to carry on the fur trade, founded on a more solid basis.

"This and Hudson's Bay Company, have engrossed and carry on almost the whole of the fur trade in that extensive country, situated between Hudson's Bay, the Rocky mountains, and that high tract of country, west of lake Superior, which seperates the southern from the northern waters: and have factories, forts and trading establishments on the Winnipic, Assiniboin, Sturgeon, Saskatchiwine, Elk, and most of the other great lakes and rivers, which communicate with or discharge themselves into Hudson's Bay, and the North sea. It is said some change has since taken place in the establishment of the North West Company."

Monday 17th.   This was a cold clear day, and we all remained in the garrison. A sled was fitted up for one of the N. W. traders to return in. In the evening one of the natives came down and told us the buffaloe were again come to the river.

Tuesday 18th.   A very cold day. Six of us went out to look for the buffaloe; but could see nothing but some goats. At 9 we returned and found the men from the N. W. Company had set out on their return, notwithstanding the severity of the weather.

Wednesday 19th.   This was a more pleasant day and we began to set up the pickets.

The 20th and 21st were quite warm and pleasant, and we advanced with our work.

Saturday 22nd.   The weather continued clear, pleasant and warm. A great number of the natives came with corn, beans and mockasins to trade, for which they would take any thing— old shirts, buttons, awls, knives and the like articles.

Sunday 23rd.   The weather continued pleasant, and we proceeded in our operations in setting up the pickets.

Monday 24th.   Some snow fell this morning; about 10 it cleared up, and the weather became pleasant. This evening we finished our fortification. Flour, dried apples, pepper and other articles were distributed in the different messes to enable them to celebrate Christmas in a proper and social manner.

Tuesday 25th. The morning was ushered in by two discharges of a swivel, and a round of small arms by the whole corps. Captain Clarke then presented to each man a glass of brandy, and we hoisted the American flag in the garrison, and its first waving in fort Mandan was celebrated with another glass.— The men then cleared out one of the rooms and commenced dancing. At 10 o'clock we had another glass of brandy, and at 1 a gun was fired as a signal for dinner. At half past 2, another gun was fired, as a notice to assemble at the dance, which was continued in a jovial manner till 8 at night; and without the presence of any females, except three squaws, wives to our interpreter,[1] who took no other part than the amusement of looking on. None of the natives came to the garrison this day; the commanding officers having requested they should not, which was strictly attended to. During the remainder of the month we lived in peace and tranquility in the garrison, and were daily visited by the natives.

1. The wife of René Jusseaume and Toussaint Charbonneau's two wives, including Sacagawea; see Clark's entries of October 27 and November 4, 1804.

Tuesday 1st Jan. 1805. Two shot were fired from this swivel, followed by a round of small arms, to welcome the New year. Captain Lewis then gave each a glass of good old whiskey; and a short time after another was given by Captain Clarke.

About 11 o'clock one of the interpreters and half of our people, went up, at the request of the natives, to the village, to begin the dance; and were followed some time after by Captain Clarke, and three more men.[1] The day was warm and pleasant. Captain Lewis in the afternoon issued another glass of whiskey; and at night Capt Clarke and part of the men returned from the village, the rest remained all night.

1. Ordway says that he was there, and so probably was François Rivet. York was also there, probably accompanying Clark, and probably both interpreters, Jusseaume and Charbonneau. See Clark's and Ordway's entries for the day.

Wednesday 2nd. Some snow fell this morning. The men, who remained at the village last night, returned. Captain Lewis, myself and some others, went up to the second village and amused ourselves with dancing &c. the greater part of the day. In the evening we in general returned and a great number of the natives, men, women and children, came to see us, and appeared highly pleased.

This day I discovered how the Indians keep their horses during the winter. In the day time they are permitted to run out and gather what they can; and at night are brought into the lodges, with the natives themselves, and fed upon cotton wood branches: and in this way are kept in tolerable case.[1]

1. Clark notes this practice on November 9, 1804, and Lewis on February 12, 1805. One reason for bringing the horses inside at night was to prevent their being stolen.

Thursday 3rd. From this to the 13th the weather was generally very cold; but our hunters were frequently out. One of them killed a beautiful white hare.[1] These animals are said to be plenty. We killed a small buffaloe, 3 elk, 4 deer and two or three wolves. Three of the hunters going to a distance down the river, killed nothing for two days, but a wolf, which they were obliged to eat; and said they relished it pretty well, but found it rather tough. A number of the natives being out hunting in a very cold day, one of them gave out on his return in the evening; and was left in the plain or prairie covered with a buffaloe robe. After some time he began to recover and removed to the woods, where he broke a number of branches to lie on, and to keep his body off the snow. In the morning he came to the fort, with his feet badly frozen, and the officers undertook his cure.[2]

1. Probably a white-tailed jackrabbit.
2. This was the thirteen-year-old boy whose toes Lewis had to amputate on January 27 and 31.

Sunday 13th. A clear cold day. A number of the natives went down the river to hunt with our men. In the evening one of our interpreters[1] and another Frenchman who had gone with him to the Assiniboins for fur returned. They had their faces so badly frost bitten that the skin came off, and their guide was so badly froze that they were obliged to leave him with the Assiniboins. This nation live near the Rocky Mountains, and about 90 miles from fort Mandan.[2]

1. Charbonneau.

2. McKeehan's note: "It is presumed, no part of the great chain of Rocky Mountains comes as near as 90 miles to fort Mandan; but it is not improbable that there may be a mountain, connected with them, which runs a considerable distance eastward along the great dividing ridge; and on some maps a mountain is laid down running east and west, south of the Assiniboin river and lake, which would appear to be not more than 90 or 100 miles from the Mandan villages." McKeehan may have misread Gass's original journal. Whitehouse gives the distance as about 190 miles.

Monday 14th.   Some snow fell this morning. Six more hunters went out to join those with the natives. In the evening one of the hunters[1] that first went out, returned. They had killed a buffaloe, a wolf and two porcupine and one of the men[2] had got his feet so badly frozen that he was unable to come to the fort.

1. Shannon.
2. Whitehouse.

During the 15th and 16th the weather was warm, and the snow melted fast. Horses were sent for the lame man, and he was brought to the fort his feet were not so bad as we had expected.

On the 17th it became cold; the wind blew hard from the north, and it began to freeze.

Friday 18th.   Clear cold weather. Two of our hunters returned, and had killed four deer, four wolves and a prarow. Two men belonging to the N. W. company,[1] who stay at the Grossventers village, came to the fort. They say this animal which the French call a prarow, or brarow, is a species of the badger.

1. Larocque and Charles McKenzie; for a discussion of the latter see Clark's entry of November 27, 1804.

Saturday 19th.   Two men were sent with horses for meat, to the hunters' Camp, which is thirty miles down the river.

Sunday 20th.   I went up with one of the men to the villages. They treated us friendly and gave us victuals. After we were done eating they presented a bowlful to a buffaloe head, saying, "*eat that.*" Their superstitious credulity is so great, that they believe by using the head well the living buffaloe will come and that they will get a supply of meat.[1]

1. Gass and Whitehouse note this particular custom, which was indeed intended to placate the spirit of the buffalo, so that the animals would come near and offer themselves as food.

Monday 21st. A clear cold day. Our hunters returned to the fort, and brought with them three horse load of vension and elk meat.

The weather on the 22nd and the 23rd was warm, and we commenced cutting the ice from about our craft, in order to get them out of the river. The snow fell about three inches deep.

Thursday 24th. A cold day. Some of our hunters went out, but killed nothing.

Friday 25th. All hands were employed in cutting away the ice, which we find a tedious business.

Saturday 26th. A pleasant day and all hands employed in cutting wood, to make charcoal. We have a blacksmith[1] with us, and a small set of black-smith tools. The blacksmith makes war-axes, and other axes to cut wood; which are exchanged with the natives for corn, which is of great service to us as we could not bring much with us.

1. Shields.

On the 27th and 28th the weather became much more settled, warm and pleasant than it had been for some time.

Tuesday 29th. We attemped another plan for getting our water craft disengaged from the ice: which was to heat water in the boats, with hot stones; but in this project we failed, as the stones we found would not stand the fire, but broke to pieces.

71

Wednesday 30th.   I went up the river and found another kind of stones, which broke in the same manner: so our batteaux and periogues remained fast in the ice.

Thursday 31st.   Some snow fell last night. Five hunters went out with two horses. In the morning the wind blew and was cold, toward the middle of the day the weather became moderate, and the afternoon was pleasant.

Friday 1st Feb. 1805.   A cold day. About 11 our hunters came home, but had killed nothing. One of the men at the fort went out a short distance, and killed a small deer. On the next day he went out and killed another deer. This and the third were cold.

Monday 4th.   A fine day. Captain Clarke and 18 more went down the river to hunt. We proceeded on 20 miles and could see no game.[1]

1. Gass summarizes in his next entry the events of this hunting trip of February 4–12. The camp of this night was in the vicinity of Mandan Island, four or five miles below Washburn and a little above Sanger; it may have been on the island, in McLean County on the east side of the river, or in Oliver County on the west, all in North Dakota.

Tuesday 5th.   We proceeded on to some Indian camps[1] and there we killed three deer. The next day we went on to more Indian camps[2] and killed some deer. On the 7th we encamped in a bottom on the south side of the Missouri,[3] and the next day turned out to hunt. We killed 10 elk and 18 deer, and remained there all night. On the 9th we built a pen,[4] to secure our meat from the wolves, which are very numerous here; and in the evening went further down and encamped.[5] The next morning we set out on our return towards the fort; and killed some elk and deer in our way. On the 12th we arrived at the fort; and found that one of our interpreter's wives had in our absence made an addition to our number.[6] On the 13th we had three horses shod to bring home our meat.

1. Probably one of the abandoned earthlodge villages below Mandan Island.
2. Near the mouth of Square Butte Creek (Clark's Hunting Creek), Oliver County, North Dakota, a little below the Morton County line.

3. Gass seems to indicate that they moved camp this day, but Clark seems to say that they remained in the camp near Square Butte Creek. Neither gives any details.

4. Clark seems to indicate that they built the pen on February 8. Gass also appears to leave out a day in his reckoning on the return trip to the fort. He may have written a sketchy summary in his journal from memory after returning to Fort Mandan, and McKeehan may have confused matters further in his version.

5. The camp of February 9 was apparently in one of the abandoned villages between Heart River and Fort Mandan.

6. Jean Baptiste Charbonneau was born on February 11, 1805.

Thursday 14th. Four men[1] set out early with the horses and sleds to bring home our meat; and had gone down about 25 miles when a party of Indians (they did not know of what nation) came upon them and robbed them of their horses one of which they gave back, and went off without doing the men any further injury. The same night the men came back and gave information of what had happened. At midnight Captain Lewis called for twenty volunteers who immediately turned out.[2] Having made our arrangements, we set out early accompanied by some Indians; and having marched thirty miles, encamped in some Indian huts.[3]

1. Drouillard, Robert Frazer, Silas Goodrich, and Newman.
2. Including Ordway and Gass.
3. One of the abandoned villages in Oliver County, North Dakota.

Saturday 16th. We renewed our pursuit early, and had a cold morning. Having proceeded twelve miles we discovered fresh smoke arising at some old camps, where we had hid some meat before[1] when Captain Clarke was down; and therefore advanced with caution. Having arrived at the place we found the savages were gone; had destroyed our meat, burnt the huts and fled into the plains. This morning the Indians, who had come down with us and one of our men whose feet had been a little frozen, returned home. We hunted the 17th and 18th and got a good deal of meat which we brought to a place were some more had been secured. The 19th we loaded our sleds very heavy, and fifteen men drew one and the horse the other, which was a small one. On the next day we arrived at the fort much fatigued.

1. Probably the villages where Clark's party camped on February 9. See Clark's entry of February 13, 1805.

Thursday 21st.   Some rain fell to day, the first that has fallen since November. In the evening the weather became clear and pleasant.

Friday 22nd.   Was a fine day and we again began to cut away the ice, and succeeded in getting out one of the periogues.

Saturday 23rd.   We had fine pleasant weather, and all hands were engaged in cutting away the ice from the boat and the other periogue. At 4 o'clock in the afternoon we had the good fortune to get both free from the ice; and in the three following days succeeded in getting them all safe upon the bank. On the 27th we made preparations for making periogues to pursue our voyage in.

Thursday 28th.   Sixteen of us went up the river about six miles, where we found and cut down trees for four canoes. While we were absent an express arrived from the Rickarees village[1] with news that the Sioux had declared war against us, and also against the Mandans and Grossventers. They had boasted of the robbery of the 14th at the Rickarees village in their way home, and that they intended to massacre the whole of us in the spring. By this express we therefore found out that it was the Sioux who had taken the horses from our men.

1. Letters from Tabeau were carried by Gravelines and two Frenchmen, one of them, according to Ordway, a "Mr. Roie," who may be the expedition *engagé* Peter Roi, who may have gone to the Arikara villages after being discharged at Fort Mandan.

Friday 1st March, 1805.   The same party encamped out to make the canoes, and continued until six were made.

On the 20th and 21st we carried them to the river about a mile and an half distant: There I remained with two men to finish them, and to take care of them, until the 26th, when some men came up from the fort, and we put the canoes into the water. As the river had risen there was some water between the ice and the shore. We got three of them safe to the fort; but the ice breaking before the other three were got down, so filled the channel, that we were obliged to carry them the rest of the way by land. On the 27th we put one of the canoes into the water to ascertain what weight they would carry. We found they would not carry as much as was expected, and Captain Lewis agreed to take a large periogue along. The remainder of the month we were employed in preparing our craft for a renewal of our voyage.

Monday 1st April 1805.   As our large boat was to return immediately to St. Louis, the whole of our craft was put into the water. A considerable quantity of rain fell this day; the first of any consequence that had fallen here for six months. The 2nd, was a fair day but windy. On the 3rd the weather was fine and pleasant. Some boxes were made, in which it was intended to have packed skins of different animals, which had been procured in the country, to be sent down in the batteaux.

Thursday 4th.   A fine clear day. We packed the boxes[1] full of skins, buffaloe robes, and horns of the Mountain ram, of a great size for the president; and began to load the boat.

1. Clark lists the boxes and their contents on April 13, 1805.

Friday 5th.   This was a clear day and the wind blew hard and cold from the N. W. We took all our goods, stores and baggage out, divided and put them aboard our craft, that we might be ready to continue our voyage.

If this brief Journal should happen to be preserved, and be ever thought worthy of appearing in print: some readers will perhaps expect, that, after our long friendly intercourse with these Indians, among whom we have spent the winter; our acquaintance with those nations lower down the river and the information we received relative to several other nations, we ought to be prepared now, when we are about to renew our voyage, to give some account of the *fair sex* of the Missouri; and entertain them with narratives of feats of love as well as of arms.[1] Though we could furnish a sufficient number of entertaining stories and pleasant anecdotes, we do not think it prudent to swell our Journal with them; as our views are directed to more useful information. Besides, as we are yet ignorant of the dangers, which may await us, and the difficulty of escape, should certain probable incidents occur, it may not be inconsistent with good policy to keep the Journal of as small and portable a size as circumstances will make practicable. It may be observed generally that chastity is not very highly esteemed by these people, and that the severe and loathsome effects *of certain French principles* are not uncommon among them.[2] The fact is, that the women are generally considered an article of traffic and *indulgencies* are sold at a very moderate price. As a proof of this I will just mention, that for an old tobacco box, one of our men was granted the honour of passing a night with the daughter of the headchief of the Mandan nation. An old bawd with her punks, may also be found in some of the villages on the Missouri, as well as in the large cities of polished nations.

1. In this passage McKeehan, like many another publisher, seeks to titillate his readers without actually risking the accusation of indecency. Explorers' accounts of the day, such as those describing South Sea expeditions, commonly described the sexual encounters of European explorers and native women in some detail.

2. A statement with a double meaning; it alludes, of course, to popular American notions about French behavior, and probably to French Revolutionary ideas. It also alludes to the fact that syphilis was commonly known as the "French disease" or the "French pox."

Saturday 6th.   The day was clear and pleasant. This morning we heard that some of the Rickarees had come up to the mandan villages. Our interpreter[1] and some of the men were sent over to ascertain the truth of the report; and we were detained all day waiting their return.

1. Probably Gravelines. The captains wanted to know if any Arikara chiefs were ready to go to Washington.

Chapter Fifty-One

Great Falls of the Missouri

April 7–July 14, 1805

Sunday 7th.　The men returned and four of the Rickarees with them. The commanding officers held a conversation with these Indians; and they concluded that some of them would go down in the boat from their village to St. Louis. About 5 o'clock in the afternoon we left fort Mandans in good spirits. Thirty one men and a woman went up the river and thirteen returned down it in the boat.[1] We had two periogues and six canoes, and proceeded about four miles, and encamped[2] opposite the first Mandan village, on the North side.

　　1. Gass counts all the party, including York and the two captains, but not the baby Jean Baptiste Charbonneau, making thirty-three persons in the permanent party who would go to the Pacific and return. Gass also did not add the unnamed Mandan who started with them but dropped out on April 9. See the captains' entries for this day for names of the permanent party and a note on the composition of the return party.
　　2. Opposite Mitutanka, McLean County, North Dakota, about three miles below Stanton.

Monday 8th.　We set out early and had a clear day. The wind blew hard from the N. W. At 12 the word was passed from a canoe in the rear that it was sinking, when we halted in front and Captain Clarke went back to see what was the matter. This forenoon we passed two villages[1] of the Grossventers, or Big-bellys nation of Indians on the South side and a small river on the same side called Cutteau or Knife river. The canoe which had been in distress, came up, and had received little damage except wetting some powder on board. The woman that is with us is a squaw of the Snake nation of Indians,[2] and wife to our interpreter. We expect she will be of service to us, when passing through that nation. In the afternoon we passed very high bluffs on the South side; one of which had lately been a burning vulcano. The pumice stones lay very thick around it, and there was a strong smell of sulphur.[3] We came about fourteen miles and encamped[4] on the North side.

1. There were three Hidatsa villages along the Knife River in McLean County, North Dakota. Gass may be excluding the Awaxawi Hidatsas' village, Mahawha (Amahami site), because these people were somewhat distinct from the other two, and only counting Metaharta (Sakakawea site) and Menetarra (Big Hidatsa site) villages.

2. Meaning the Shoshone Indians.

3. McKeehan's note: " 'Mr. Mackay informed me, that in passing over the mountains, he observed several chasms in the earth that emitted heat and smoke, which diffused a strong sulphureous stench.' *Mackenzie's Voyage*. These appearances were near the eastern side of the Rocky mountains where they were crossed by Mr. Mackenzie's party; and in about lat. 56 North, and long. 120 West."

4. In McLean County, a mile or so below Garrison Dam.

Tuesday 9th. We set out early, and had a fine day; about 1 o'clock we passed a party of Grossventers hunting: made about twenty-two miles and encamped[1] on the North side.

1. In McLean County, North Dakota, above Douglas Creek and a few miles southwest of Garrison.

Wednesday 10th. We proceeded again early, and had rapid water and a great many sand-bars; but a fine pleasant day. Having proceeded about nineteen miles we encamped[1] on the North side.

1. Just above the later site of Fort Berthold, McLean County, North Dakota.

Thursday 11th. We got under way early, had a fine clear pleasant day, and went on very well. We saw some Indians on the South side, but did not speak with them. We came about twenty-one miles and encamped[1] on the North side.

1. In McLean County, North Dakota, a few miles below the mouth of the Little Missouri River.

Friday 12th. Another fine day. We set out early as usual. About 8 we came to the mouth of the Little Missouri,[1] a handsome small river that comes in on the South side where we halted and took breakfast. The river is very properly called the Little Missouri, for it exactly resembles the Missouri in colour, current and taste.[2] It was thought adviseable to remain here the remainder of the day, and air our loading. Some hunters went out and killed a deer, and Captain Clarke killed a hare,[3] which was now changing its colour from white to grey.

1. The mouth of Little Missouri River is now in McLean County, North Dakota; it may have shifted over the years. They camped below the mouth.

2. McKeehan's note: "The maps of Louisiana place the Mandan villages west of the little Missouri, whereas it is ascertained by this expedition to be 92 miles higher up the Missouri than the Mandans."

3. White-tailed jackrabbit.

Saturday 13th. We had a pleasant day and a fair wind; but our small canoes could not bear the sail. Some of the party caught some beaver, and some Frenchmen who were out trapping[1] caught 7 of them. We passed a large creek on the South side, called Onion creek.[2] We came 23 miles and encamped[3] on the North side, where we found a wild goose[4] nest on a tree about 60 feet high. One of the men climbed the tree and found one egg in the nest.

1. They encountered these three French trappers on April 10.

2. Deepwater Creek, McLean County, North Dakota.

3. In Mountrail County, North Dakota, in what was once called Fort Maneury Bend, now under Garrison Reservoir.

4. Canada goose, *Branta canadensis*. See Clark's entry for a discussion of the bird nesting in trees.

Sunday 14th. We started early as usual, and had a fine morning. As we were setting out a black dog came to us, and went along, supposed to have belonged to a band of the Assiniboins, who had been encamped near this place a few days ago. We passed a hill resembling a large haystack, all but about 10 feet of the top which was as white as chalk. The hills in general are much higher here than lower down the river; but the bottoms much the same. In the afternoon we passed a creek, called after our interpreter, Sharbons creek.[1] He had been, before, this far up the Missouri, and no white man any further, that we could discover. We made 16 miles and encamped[2] on a handsome bottom on the North side.

1. Charbonneau Creek to the party, now Bear Den Creek, near the McLean-Dunn county line, North Dakota.
2. In Mountrail County, North Dakota, opposite and a little above the mouth of Bear Den Creek.

Monday 15th. We had a pleasant day and a fair wind; set forward early as usual, and went on very well. Passed a large creek on the North side, called Goat-pen creek.[1] We saw a number of buffaloe and two bears on the bank of the river. After going 23 miles we encamped on the South side.

1. Little Knife River, Mountrail County, North Dakota. Clark named the creek after the Indian pen, or pound, for catching pronghorns which he found there.

Tuesday 16th. We had a clear pleasant day; and in the early part of it, a fair gentle wind. Captain Clarke went out and killed a Cabre or Antelope, the same kind of an animal, which we before called a goat. The wind became flawy,[1] and the sailing bad. After making 18 miles we encamped on the South side in a point of woods called the Grand point.[2]

1. Gusty.
2. In McKenzie County, North Dakota, a little above Beaver Creek on the other side. Expedition maps show a Grand, or Great, Bend some distance above this camp.

Wednesday 17th. We proceeded on early as usual with a fair wind. The day was fine and we made good way. Passed a beautiful plain and two large creeks on the North side, and another creek on the South.[1] We saw a great many buffaloe and elk on the banks. At 1 o'clock we halted for dinner, when two men went out and in a few minutes killed 2 buffaloe. We made 26 miles and encamped[2] on the South side, and found that some rain had fallen during the day, where we encamped, though there was none where we had been.

1. The captains have little to say about any of these streams. The one on the south is apparently later Clark Creek in McKenzie County, North Dakota. The first on the north is

probably their Hall's Strand Creek, later Tobacco Creek in Mountrail County. The last is probably the "run" which Clark notes falling in among burning hills, perhaps later Garden Creek.

  2. In McKenzie County, North Dakota.

Thursday 18th. The men caught some beaver, and killed a wild goose. The morning was fine and we went on very well until 1 o'clock, when the wind blew so hard down the river, we were obliged to lie to for 3 hours, after which we continued our voyage. This day Captain Clarke went by land and met us in the afternoon on the bank with an elk and a deer. We came about 14 miles and encamped[1] in a good harbour on the North side, on account of the wind, which blew very hard all night accompanied with some drops of rain.

  1. In Williams County, North Dakota, where they remained until April 20.

Friday 19th. A cloudy morning, with high wind. We did not set out until the next day. While we lay here, I went out to the hills, which I found very high, much washed by the rain, and without grass. I saw a part of a log quite petrified, and of which good whetstones—or hones could be made.— I also saw where a hill had been on fire, and pumice stone around it. There is a great quanitity of hysop[1] in the vallies. We killed an elk and some wild geese, and caught some beaver.

  1. Some type of sagebrush, *Artemisia* sp.

Saturday 20th. We set out again and had a cold disagreeable morning; rapid water and a strong wind. Some of the canoes took in a good deal of water; and we made but 6 miles, when we were obliged again to lie too,[1] on account of the wind, and to dry our loading. While we lay here we killed three elk and got a number of Geese eggs out of their nests, which are generally built on trees.

  1. In Williams County, North Dakota.

Sunday 21st. We proceeded on early; and had a fine clear morning, but cold: there was a sharp frost. We saw a great number of elk, buffaloe and deer on both sides of the river. About 12 the wind again rose and was disagreeable, but we continued our voyage. Two of our hunters went out this afternoon and caught three young buffaloe calves. We passed a small river called White Clay river[1] on the North side and having gone 15 miles encamped on the South side.

1. The captains' White Earth River, but not the present stream of that name, which they passed on April 16. This is Little Muddy River, Williams County, North Dakota.

Monday 22nd.   Before daylight we continued our voyage; passed a beautiful bottom on the North side, covered with game of different kinds. The wind was unfavourable to day, and the river here is very crooked. We came about 14 miles, then encamped[1] on the South side and caught some beaver.

1. In McKenzie County, North Dakota, a few miles above Williston, on the opposite side.

Tuesday 23rd.   We set our early and had a fine day; but the wind was ahead, and we were obliged to lie to about three hours. We went 15 miles and encamped[1] on the North side. Captain Clarke killed 3 blacktailed deer and a buffaloe calf.

1. In Williams County, North Dakota, where they remained until April 25.

Wednesday 24th.   This was a clear day, but the wind blew so hard down the river we could not proceed. While we lay here some of the men went to see some water at a distance which appeared like a river or small lake. In the afternoon they returned, and had found it only the water of the Missouri, which had run up a bottom. One of the men caught six young wolves[1] and brought them in, and the other men killed some elk and deer.

1. The captains say these were wolves "of the small kind," that is, coyotes.

Thursday 25th.   We set out as usual and had a fine day; but about 11 were obliged to halt again the wind was so strong ahead. Captain Lewis and four men set off by land from this place to go to the river Jaune, or Yellow Stone river, which it is believed is not very distant. I remarked, as a singular circumstance, that there is no dew in this Country, and very little rain. Can it be owing to the want of timber? At 5 o'clock in the afternoon, we renewed our voyage; and having this day advanced about 13 miles, encamped[1] on the South side.

1. In Williams County, North Dakota, in the vicinity of Glass Bluffs on the opposite side.

Friday 26th. A fine day. We set out early, and having proceeded 10 miles came at 12 o'clock to the mouth of the Jaune[1] and halted: Captain Lewis and his party had not arrived. I went up the point about 9 miles, where there are the most beautiful rich plains, I ever beheld. I saw a large pond or lake.—[2] Captain Clarke while I was absent measured both rivers; and found the breadth of the Missouri to be 337 yards of water, and 190 of a sand-beach; total 527 yards. That of the Yellow Stone river 297 yards of water and 561 of sand; total 858 yards.[3] The mouth of this river is 1888 miles from the mouth of the Missouri, 278 from Fort Mandan, and 186 from the mouth of Little Missiouri.

The river Jaune is shallow, and the Missouri deep and rapid. In the evening Captain Lewis with his party joined us; and had brought with them a buffaloe calf, which followed them 7 or 8 miles. We killed a number of calves, and found they made very good veal. There are a great many signs of beaver in this part of the country. We encamped on the point all night.

1. The Yellowstone (*Roche Jaune* in French) River, McKenzie County, North Dakota, just east of the Montana state line.
2. Probably Nohly Lake, Richland County, Montana.
3. Compare with the figures in Clark's entry for this date.

Saturday 27th. About 9 o'clock in the forenoon we renewed our voyage. The day was fine, but on account of a strong wind we were obliged at 1 to halt, till 4, when we again went on; and having this day made 8 miles, encamped[1] on the North side.

1. The party's first camp in Montana, in Roosevelt County, about a mile below and opposite the village of Nohly, Richland County.

Sunday 28th. We set out early, had a fine day and went on very well. About 9 we halted for breakfast under very high bluffs on the North side. About 15 miles above the Yellow Stone river, the banks on the Missouri are not so high as below it, and the sand bars are more in the middle of the river. We came 24 miles and encamped[1] on the North side in a handsome bottom. The bottoms here are not so large, and have less timber on them than those below the Jaune.

1. In Roosevelt County, Montana, near Otis Creek, opposite in Richland County.

Monday 29th. We again set out early, had a clear morning and went on at a good rate. This forenoon we passed some of the highest bluffs I had ever seen; and on the top of the highest we saw some Mountain sheep,[1] which the natives say are common about the Rocky mountains. These were the first we had seen, and we attempted to kill some of them but did not succeed. Captain Lewis, and one of the men, travelled some distance by land and killed a white bear.—[2] The natives call them white, but they are more of a brown grey. They are longer than the common black bear, and have much larger feet and talons. We went 25 miles and encamped[3] on the bank of a small river, which comes in on the North side about 70 yards wide.

1. Bighorn sheep, *Ovis canadensis,* also "ibex" to the party; see Lewis's entry of April 26 and note for a possible subspecies.
2. Their first actual specimen of the grizzly bear, from which Lewis wrote the first scientific description.
3. Just above Big Muddy Creek, Roosevelt County, Montana. To Ordway it was "little yallow River"; Clark named it "Martheys river in honor to the Selebrated M. F.," a woman whose identity remains a mystery.

Tuesday 30th. We embarked at sunrise; had a fine morning and went on very well. We passed through a handsome Country, with a rich soil, and the prairies rising beautifully on both sides of the river. We went 24 miles and encamped[1] on the North side. Captain Lewis killed a large elk here.

1. In the vicinity of Brockton, Richland County, Montana.

Wednesday 1st May, 1805.   We set out early in a cool morning; and went on till 12 o'clock, when the wind rose so high, that our small canoes could not stand the waves. We made only 10 miles this day.[1]

1. They camped in the vicinity of later Elkhorn Point, Roosevelt County, Montana.

Thursday 2nd.   At day break it began to snow; and the wind continued so high, we could not proceed until the afternoon. While we lay here our hunters went out and killed some buffaloe and deer. They found some red cloth at an old Indian camp, which we supposed had been offered and left as a sacrifice; the Indians having some knowledge of a supreme being and this their mode of worship. The snow did not fall more than an inch deep. At four we set out, went six miles, and encamped[1] on the North side in a beautiful bottom.

1. In Richland County, Montana, in the vicinity of the crossing of Montana Highway 251.

Friday 3rd.   We proceeded on our voyage this morning, though very cold and disagreeable, and a severe frost. The snow and green grass on the prairies exhibited an appearance somewhat uncommon. The cotton wood leaves are as large as dollars, notwithstanding the snow and such hard frost. We passed a small river on the north side called the 2000 mile river. About a mile above we passed a large creek on the South side, called Porcupine creek.—[1] We came this day about 20 miles and encamped[2] on the North side.

1. Like Sergeant Ordway, Gass transposes the two streams. The first, the captains' Porcupine River, is on the north side and is now Poplar River, Roosevelt County, Montana. Their 2000 Mile Creek, on the south, is Redwater River, McCone County, Montana.
2. In McCone County, three or four miles above Poplar, Roosevelt County.

Saturday 4th.   This day was more pleasant: in the forenoon we passed a creek[1] on the South side, about 40 yards wide. The river has been more straight for two or three days than it was before; the bottoms larger and more timber on them. We went about eighteen miles and encamped[2] on the North side. One of the men[3] became sick this morning and has remained so all day.

1. Probably Antelope, or later Nickwall, Creek, McCone County, Montana.
2. In Roosevelt County, Montana.
3. Joseph Field; see Lewis's entry of this day for the symptoms and treatment.

Sunday 5th. The morning was fine with some white frost. During this day the country appeared beautiful on both sides of the river. We went sixteen miles and encamped[1] on the North side. The sick man has become better. Here we killed a very large brown bear, which measured three feet five inches round the head; three feet eleven inches around the neck; round the breast five feet 10½ inches; the length eight feet 7½ inches; round the middle of the fore leg 23 inches; and his talons four inches and three eights of an inch.

1. In McCone County, Montana, southeast of Wolf Point. Shifts of the river have placed the site on the opposite side of the river.

Monday 6th. We set sail with a fair wind and pleasant weather. At 12 a few drops of rain fell, but it soon cleared up. We passed a river on the South side about 200 yards wide; but the water of this river sinks in the sand on the side of the Missouri.[1] We went twenty-six miles and encamped[2] on the South side.

1. The party passed three dry steams on the south side this day; the last and largest they called Little Dry River, now Prairie Elk Creek, McCone County, Montana.
2. In McCone County, a few miles southwest of Oswego.

Tuesday 7th. We again set out early and went on very well till 12 when it began to blow hard, and being all under sail one of our canoes turned over. Fortunately the accident happened near the shore; and after halting three hours we were able to go on again. Having this day made sixteen miles we encamped[1] on the South side.

1. In either McCone or Valley County, Montana, depending on shifts in the river, a few miles southwest of Fraser.

Wednesday 8th. We were again very early under way in a cloudy morning; about 12 some rain fell: at 2 we passed a handsome river on the North side about 200 yards wide called Milk river.[1] There is a good deal of water in this river which is clear, and its banks beautiful. Our distance this day was about twenty-seven miles, and we encamped[2] in a beautiful bottom on the South side.

1. Milk River, reaching the Missouri in Valley County, Montana, still bears the name the captains gave it.

2. Probably in Valley County, a mile or two above Fort Peck Dam.

Thursday 9th. We proceeded on early and had a fine day. The country on both sides begins to be more broken, and the river more crooked. At 1, we passed a creek[1] on the South side, and having made about 25 miles we encamped at the mouth of a creek on the North side, called by the name of Warner's creek.[2]

1. The party's Big Dry River, still called Big Dry Fork, or Creek, in McCone and Garfield counties, Montana.

2. This camp was a few miles above the town of Fort Peck, Valley County, Montana. Warner's Creek, present Duck Creek, was named for William Werner of the party.

Friday 10th. We set out early in a fair morning; but having gone five miles were obliged to halt and lye by during the day,[1] on account of hard wind. Some small showers of rain occasionally fell. Here we killed some deer and buffaloe and took some beaver.

1. In either Garfield or Valley County, Montana, on a site now inundated by Fort Peck Reservoir.

Saturday 11th. The morning was fine, we started at the usual hour: at 1 passed a small creek on the South side.[1] This day we saw several great gangs of buffaloe, and other game in plenty. One of the men killed another large brown bear, about the size of the one lately killed. We came seventeen miles and encamped[2] on the South side.

1. Not noticed by the captains and not found on any *Atlas* map. If Gass means the north side, there are at least three small creeks now largely drowned by Fort Peck Reservoir in the day's course, none of which the captains thought worth mentioning.

2. In Garfield County, Montana, on a site now inundated by Fort Peck Reservoir.

Sunday 12th. We early renewed our voyage and had a pleasant morning; passed some hills on the North side, covered with pine and cedar,[1] the first timber of any kind we have seen on the hills for a long time. At 1 we halted for dinner and a violent storm of wind then arose, which continued until night when some rain fell. Our distance this day only 13½ miles.[2]

1. Probably ponderosa pine, *Pinus ponderosa* Laws., and Rocky Mountain red cedar, *Juniperus scopulorum* Sarg.
2. The party camped in Garfield County, Montana, on a site now inundated by Fort Peck Reservoir.

Monday 13th The weather continued stormy, and some few drops of rain fell. At 1 P. M. we embarked; passed three creeks, one on the North side and two on the South; went seven miles and encamped[1] in a large bottom.

1. The captains do not mention a creek on the north side, nor does one appear on expedition maps. The two on the south are Sheep and Crooked Creeks, Garfield County, Montana. The party camped a mile or two above the latter.

Tuesday 14th. There was some white frost in the morning, we proceeded on early; passed black hills close to the river on the South side and some covered with pine timber at a distance. About 12 the day became warm. Banks of snow were seen lying on the hills on the North side. This forenoon we passed a large creek on the North side[1] and a small river on the South.[2] About 4 in the afternoon we passed another small river on the South side[3] near the mouth of which some of the men discovered a large brown bear, and six of them went out to kill it. They fired at it; but having only wounded it, it made battle and was near seizing some of them, but they all fortunately escaped, and at length succeeded in dispataching it. These bears are very bold and ferocious; and very large and powerful. The natives say they have killed a number of their brave men. The periogues having gone ahead, while the people belonging to the canoes were dressing the bear, a sudden gust of wind arose, which overset one of the periogues before the sail could be got down. The men who had been on board, turned it again and got it to shore, full of water. It was immediately unloaded and the cargo opened, when we found a great part of the medicine, and other articles spoiled. Here we encamped, having come to day 18½ miles.

1. Probably the party's Gibson's Creek (after expedition member George Gibson), now Sutherland Creek, Valley County, Montana.
2. Probably their Stick Lodge Creek, now Hell Creek, Garfield County.
3. The party's Brown Bear Defeated Creek, present Snow Creek, Garfield County.

Wednesday 15th.   We remained here all day to dry our baggage that had got wet. It was cloudy and unfavourable for the purpose, and some rain fell.

Thursday 16th.   This was a fine day, and by 4 o'clock in the afternoon we had all our articles dry and on board again. At that time we proceeded on our voyage; passed high barren hills on both sides of the river, with only a few pine trees on them. We advanced seven miles and encamped[1] in a handsome bottom on the South side where there are a number of old Indian huts.

1. In Garfield County, Montana, on a site now under Fort Peck Reservoir; see Lewis's entry and note for further discussion of this campsite.

Friday 17th.   The morning was fine and we embarked early. The hills here come very close to the river on both sides, and have very little timber on them. They are very high and much washed. There are some of them, which at a distance resemble ancient steeples. We passed two rivers one on each side.[1] During the whole of this day's voyage the Missouri was very handsome, and about 300 yards wide. We made 20¼ miles, and encamped on the South side.

1. The first is the captains' Bratton's Creek, after William Bratton of the party, now Timber Creek, Phillips County, Montana. The second, their Burnt Lodge Creek, is now Seven Blackfoot Creek, Garfield County. See Lewis's entry for confusion about the party's names for these creeks.

Saturday 18th.   A cloudy morning. We proceeded as usual. The country much the same as yesterday; until about 12 o'clock, when the bottoms became more extensive on both sides of the river. There is still a small quantity of pine timber on the hills. We had some showers of rain in the forenoon; hail in the afternoon; and a fine clear evening. We went nineteen miles and encamped[1] on the South side opposite an island.

1. In Garfield County, Montana, about two miles upstream from the Devils Creek Recreation Area. The island may be the later Elk Island; the area is now under Fort Peck Reservoir.

Sunday 19th.   The morning was foggy and there was some dew. The river is handsome and the country mountainous. We made 20¼ miles and encamped[1] on the North side in a small bottom.

1. In either Phillips or Garfield County, Montana, at or near later Long Point, now under Fort Peck Reservoir.

Monday 20th.   We set sail early and had a fine morning. Passed a creek on the south side[1] and about 11 came to the mouth of the Muscle-shell river,[2] a handsome river that comes in on the South side. The water of the Missouri is becoming more clear. We here spent the remainder of the day, having come seven miles. Captain Lewis had an observation here, which gave 47° 00 24 North latitude: and Captain Clarke measured the rivers. The Missouri here is 222 yards wide, and the Muscle-shell 110 yards. The water of the latter is of a pale colour, and the current is not rapid; its mouth is 660 miles above Fort Mandans.

1. The party's Blowing Fly Creek, later Squaw Creek, Garfield County, Montana.
2. Musselshell River, here dividing Garfield and Petroleum counties, Montana, still bears the party's name.

Tuesday 21st.   We proceeded on early and had a fine morning; towards the middle of the day the wind blew hard; but we went on very well for 20 miles, and encamped[1] on a sand-beach on the North side.

1. In Phillips County, Montana, now inundated by Fort Peck Reservoir.

Wednesday 22nd.   A cloudy morning. The wind blew so hard this morning, we did not get under way until 9 o'clock. The forenoon was cold and disagreeable, but the afternoon became more pleasant. We killed a brown bear and some other game on our way. Having gone 16⅓ miles we encamped[1] on the North side.

1. In Phillips County, Montana, just below CK, or Kannuck, Creek, the party's Teapot Creek.

Thursday 23rd. The morning was clear with a white frost, and ice as thick as window glass. We passed two creeks, one on each side of the river:[1] and two islands which are not common.[2] There are very few between these and fort Mandans; not more than six or eight. In the evening we killed a large bear in the river; but he sunk and we did not get him.[3] We went 28½ miles and encamped.[4]

1. The one on the north side would be either CK Creek or Sevenmile Creek, both in Phillips County, Montana; the one on the south side would be Carroll Creek, Fergus County.
2. One of these is probably later Ryan Island; the other may be Chippewa, or Rocky, Island.
3. McKeehan's note: "It is said that bears, beavers, otters, and such animals will sink unless shot dead."
4. A little below the mouth of Rock (their North Mountain) Creek, Fergus County.

Friday 24th. There was again some white frost this morning. We embarked early; passed a large creek on the North side[1] and a beautiful island close on the southern shore. At the head of the island, came in another creek on the South side.[2] The bottom of the river, and sand-bars have become much more gravelly than we found them at any place lower down. The water is high, rapid and more clear. At dinner time a party was sent out to bring the meat of some animals that had been killed at a distance. Here we left two canoes to wait for them and proceeded on. We passed a creek on the North side, and having made 24¼ miles encamped[3] on the South side. The hills are near, on both sides of the river, and very high.

1. Lewis and Clark's North Mountain Creek, now Rock Creek, Phillips County, Montana.
2. The captains' Little Dog Creek, after a prairie dog village on the other side of the river, now Sand Creek in Fergus County, Montana.
3. In Fergus or Phillips County, some three miles above where U.S. Highway 191 crosses the Missouri.

Saturday 25th. We waited here in the morning until the canoes came up; and about 7 proceeded on our voyage. The forenoon was pleasant. We passed two creeks opposite to each other on the opposite sides of the river.[1] About 12 we passed a bottom on the North side with one solitary tree on it, upon which there was an eagle's nest. The bottoms here are very small. As we went on this afternoon some of the party killed three of what the French and natives call mountain sheep;[2] but they very little resemble sheep, except in the head, horns and feet. They are of a dun colour except on the belly and round the rump, where they are white. The horns of the male are very large; those of the female small. They have a fine soft hair. Captain Clarke calls them the Ibex,[3] and says they resemble that animal more than any other. They are in size somewhat larger than a deer. The hills here are very high and steep. One of our men[4] in an attempt to climb one had his shoulder dislocated; it was however replaced without much difficulty. These hills are very much washed in general: they appear like great heaps of clay, washing away with every shower; with scarcely any herbs or grass on any of them. This evening we passed an island all prairie except a few trees on the upper end of it. We went 18 miles and encamped[5] on the South side.

1. Two Calf Creek, Fergus County, Montana, and Antelope Creek, Phillips County; the captains did not name either of them.

2. Their first specimens of the bighorn sheep.

3. "Ibex" refers to several species of Old World mountain goats. Clark, not Lewis, uses the term in reference to the bighorn on this day, and Gass's reference suggests that Clark had done some reading in natural history, even though Lewis usually wrote the scientific descriptions of species.

4. Whitehouse indicates that it was Gibson. The captains do not mention this episode.

5. In Fergus County, some five or six miles below Cow Island Landing Recreation Area and near the ferry crossing the Missouri. They called the island Goodrich's Island, after Silas Goodrich of the party.

Sunday 26th. We set out early in a fine morning, and passed through a desert country; in which there is no timber on any part, except a few scattered pines on the hills. We saw few animals of any kind, but the Ibex or mountain sheep. One of our men killed a male, which had horns two feet long and four inches diameter at the root.[1] We passed two creeks this forenoon on the North side;[2] and in the evening one of the men killed a buffaloe. At dark we came to large rapids,[3] where we had to unite the crews of two or three canoes, to force them through. It was some time after night before we could encamp. We at length, after having gone twenty-one miles encamped[4] on the South side in a small grove of timber, the first we had seen during the day.

1. McKeehan's note: "'The Ibex resembles the goat in the shape of it's body; but differs in the horns which are much larger. They are bent backwards, full of knots; and it is generally asserted that there is a knot added every year. There are some of these found if we may believe Bellonius, at least two yards long. The Ibex has a large black beard, is of a brown colour, with a thick woven coat of hair. There is a streak of black runs along the top of the back; and the belly and back of the thighs are of a fawn colour. It is a native of the Alps, the Pyrenees, and mountains of Greece; extremely swift and capable of running with ease along the edges of precipices, where even the Wolf or the Fox, though instigated by hunger, dares not pursue it.' Goldsmith.

"Such is the description given of the Ibex; but which to us does not appear to suit the animal found about the Rocky mountains called the mountain Ram. From what we have before heard of that animal, and from Mr. Gass's verbal description, we are led to believe, that it much more nearly resembles the wild sheep, called the Mufflon or Musmon, to be found in the uncultivated parts of Greece, Sardinia, Corsica and in the desart of Tartary; and which is thought to be the primitive race and the real sheep in its wild and savage state. Perhaps it may be found to be exactly the same; of which we find the following description.

"'The Mufflon, or Musmon, though covered with hair, bears a stronger similitude to the Ram than to any other animal; like the Ram it has the eyes placed near the horns; and its ears are shorter than those of the goat: it also resembles the Ram in its horns, and in all the particular contours of its form. The horns also are alike; they are of a white or yellow colour; they have three sides as in the Ram, and bend backwards in the same manner behind the ears. The muzzle and inside of the ears are of a whitish colour tinctured with yellow; the other parts of the face are of a brownish grey. The general colour of the hair over the body is of a brown, approaching to that of the red deer. The inside of the thighs and belly are of a white tinctured with yellow. The form upon the whole seems more made for agility and strength than that of the common sheep; and the Mufflon is actually found to live in a savage state, and maintain itself either by force or swiftness against all the animals that live by rapine. Such is its extreme speed that many have been inclined rather to rank it among the deer kind, than the sheep. But in this they are deceived, as the Musmon has a mark that entirely distinguishes it from that species, being known never to shed its horns. In some these are seen to grow to a surprizing size; many of them measuring, in their convolutions, above two ells long.' Goldsmith."

2. The first is the captains' Windsor's Creek, after Richard Windsor of the party, now Cow Creek in Blaine County, Montana. The second is their Soft Shell Turtle Creek, now Bullwhacker Creek in Blaine County.

3. The party's Elk Fawn Rapids, now Bird Rapids.

4. In Fergus County, Montana, above the rapids.

Monday 27th.   We have now got into a country which presents little to our view, but scenes of barrenness and desolation; and see no encouraging prospects that it will terminate.[1] Having proceeded (by the course of this river) about two thousand three hundred miles, it may therefore not be improper to make two or three general observations respecting the country we have passed.

From the mouth of the Missouri to that of the river Platte, a distance of more than six hundred miles, the land is generally of a good quality, with a sufficient quantity of timber; in many places very rich, and the country pleasant and beautiful.

From the confluence of the river Platte with the Missouri to the Sterile desert we lately entered a distance of upwards of fifteen hundred miles the soil is less rich, and except in the bottoms, the land of an inferior quality; but may in general be called good second rate land. The country is rather hilly than level, though not mountainous, rocky or stony. The hills in their unsheltered state are much exposed to be washed by heavy rains. This kind of country and soil which has fallen under our observation in our progress up the Missouri, extends it is understood, to a great distance on both sides of the river. Along the Missouri and the waters which flow into it, cotton wood and willows are frequent in the bottoms and islands; but the upland is almost entirely without timber, and consists of large prairies or plains the boundaries of which the eye cannot reach. The grass is generally short on these immense natural pastures, which in the proper seasons are decorated with blossoms and flowers of various colours. The views from the hills are interesting and grand. Wide extended plains with their hills and vales, stretching away in lessening wavy ridges, until by their distance they fade from the sight; large rivers and streams in their rapid course, winding in various meanders; groves of cotton wood and willow along the waters intersecting the landscapes in different directions, dividing them into various forms, at length appearing like dark clouds and sinking in the horizon; these enlivened with the buffaloe, elk, deer, and other animals which in vast numbers feed upon the plains or pursue their prey, are the prominent objects, which compose the extensive prospects presented to the view and strike the attention of the beholder.

The islands in the Missouri are of various sizes; in general not large and during high water mostly overflowed.

There are Indian paths along the Missouri and some in other parts of the country. Those along that river do not generally follow its windings but cut off points of land and pursue a direct course. There are also roads and paths made by the buffaloe and other animals; some of the buffaloe roads are at least ten feet wide. We did not embark this morning until 8 o'clock. The day was fine, but the wind ahead. We had difficult water, and passed through the most dismal country I ever beheld; nothing but barren mountains on both sides of the river, as far as our view could extend. The bed of the river is rocky, and also the banks and hills in some places; but these are chiefly of earth. We went thirteen miles and encamped[2] in a bottom, just large enough for the purpose, and made out to get enough of drift wood to cook with.

1. The party was traveling through the Missouri River Breaks.
2. In Fergus County, Montana, near later McGarry Bar.

Tuesday 28th.   We set sail early, had a fine morning, and proceeded on through this desert country untill about 4 o'clock P. M. when we came to a more pleasant part. We made twenty-one miles and encamped[1] on the North side.

1. In Chouteau County, Montana, near Judith Landing Recreation Area, opposite Dog Creek (the party's Bull Creek), Fergus County.

Wednesday 29th.   We proceeded on early and had a fine morning; passed two rivers, one on each side.[1] At 12 it became cloudy and began to rain. We went about eighteen miles and halted at a handsome grove of timber on the South side. It rained a little all the afternoon. Some of the men went out to hunt and killed an elk. Last night[2] about 12 o'clock a buffaloe swimming the river happened to land at one of the periogues, crossed over it and broke two guns, but not so as to render them useless. He then went straight on through the men where they were sleeping, but hurt none of them. As we came along to day we passed a place where the Indians had driven above an hundred head of buffaloe down a precipice and killed them.

95

1. Judith River, Fergus County, Montana, named by Clark for his future wife, Julia Hancock, and Chip Creek, the party's Valley Creek, Chouteau County. Gass does not mention their Slaughter River, today's Arrow Creek, although he notes the mass of dead buffalo, which they took to be an Indian "buffalo jump," and which inspired the captains' name for the stream. See notes to the captains' entries for problems about stream names.

2. The night of May 28–29.

Thursday 30th. The forenoon was cloudy, with some rain. We did not set out till late in the day. The hills came in close on the river again, but are not so high. Some of them are as black as coal and some white as chalk.[1] We see a great many fresh Indian tracks or signs as we pass along. It rained a little all day; we went on slow and encamped[2] early on the North side, in a small bottom with some cotton wood, having proceeded on eight miles. There are no pines to be seen on the hills.

1. The party is entering the White Cliffs area of the Missouri River Breaks, Chouteau County, Montana.

2. In Chouteau County, nearly opposite the mouth of Sheep Shed Coulee.

Friday 31st. We embarked early in a cloudy morning; passed through a mountainous country, but the game is more plenty, and we killed some buffaloe in our way. About 11 o'clock it began to rain slowly, and continued raining two hours, when it cleared up. We passed some very curious cliffs and rocky peaks, in a long range. Some of them 200 feet high and not more than eight feet thick. They seem as if built by the hand of man, and are so numerous that they appear like the ruins of an ancient city. We went 17½ miles and encamped[1] at the mouth of a handsome creek on the North side.

1. Just above the mouth of Eagle Creek, the party's Stonewall Creek, Chouteau County.

Saturday 1st June, 1805. We embarked early. The morning was cloudy, but without rain. We passed through a more handsome country, than for some days past. It appears more level and there are some good bottoms on both sides of the river, but not large; also a number of beautiful small islands covered with cotton wood. We saw a number of mountain sheep. Yesterday our men killed three of them, that had remarkable large horns; one pair weighed 25 pounds. We passed a small river on the North side about

11 o'clock.[1] The water is not so rapid to day as usual, but continues high. In the afternoon we passed a creek[2] about 30 yards wide, and several small islands. We went 24 miles and encamped[3] on a small island.

1. The streams Gass mentions today the captains did not deem worthy of notice even in their courses and distances, though the streams appear, nameless, on expedition maps. The first may be Little Sandy Creek, Chouteau County, Montana.
2. An apparently nameless watercourse in Chouteau County.
3. Boggs Island, Chouteau County.

Sunday 2nd.   We embarked early in a fine morning. The hills come close on the river, but are not so high nor so broken, as we found them a short distance lower down. This forenoon we passed two creeks,[1] one on each side, and several islands covered with cotton wood; but there is not a stick of timber to be seen any where upon the hills. Some of the hunters killed a brown bear in a small botton on the South side, and having come 18 miles, we encamped just above the bottom on the same side, at the mouth of a large river.[2]

1. Again Gass notices streams the captains did not think worthy of mention. Spring and Sixmile coulees are found on the north side, and Crow Coulee on the south, all in Chouteau County, Montana. Spring and Crow coulees are probably the ones appearing nameless on expedition maps.
2. They had arrived at the confluence of the Missouri and the Marias, and camped in Chouteau County, opposite the mouth of the latter stream, which was perhaps a mile below the present mouth. Lewis named the Marias after his cousin, Maria Wood.

Monday 3rd.   We crossed over to the point between the two rivers and encamped[1] there. The commanding officers could not determine which of these rivers or branches, it was proper to take; and therefore concluded to send a small party up each of them. Myself and two men went up the South branch, and a serjeant and two more up the North.[2] The parties went up the two branches about 15 miles. We found the South branch rapid with a great many islands and the general course South West. The other party reported the North branch as less rapid, and not so deep as the other. The North branch is 186 yards wide and the South 372 yards. The water of the South branch is clear, and that of the North muddy. About a mile and an half up the point from the confluence, a handsome small river falls into the North branch, called Rose river.[3] Its water is muddy, and the current rapid. Captain Lewis took a meridian altitude at the point, which gave 47° 24 12 North latitude. Captain Lewis and Captain Clarke were not yet satisfied with respect to the proper river to ascend.

1. In Chouteau County, Montana, below the present mouth of the Marias, where they remained until June 12 to determine which branch was the true Missouri.

2. Gass went up the Missouri (the south fork), while Pryor, with a party including White-house, went up the Marias.

3. Teton River, a tributary of the Marias; the captains also used the name Tansey River, after a plant growing on its banks.

Tuesday 4th.   Captain Lewis with six men[1] went up the North branch, to see if they could find any certain marks to determine whether that was the Missouri or not; and Captain Clarke myself and four others[2] went up the South branch, for the same purpose with regard to that branch. About eight miles above the confluence, the South branch and the small river which falls into the North branch, are not more than 200 yards apart. Near this place and close on the bank of the South branch is a beautiful spring where we refreshed ourselves with a good drink of grog;[3] and proceeded on through the high plains. Here nothing grows but prickly pears,[4] which are in abundance, and some short grass. We sent on about thirty miles and found the river still extending in a South West direction. We saw a mountain[5] to the South about 20 miles off, which appeared to run East and West, and some spots on it resembling snow. In the evening we went towards the river to encamp, where one of the men[6] having got down to a small point of woods on the bank, before the rest of the party, was attacked by a huge he-bear, and his gun missed fire. We were about 200 yards from him, but the bank there was so steep we could not get down to his assistance: we, however, fired at the animal from the place where we stood and he went off without injuring the man. Having got down we all encamped[7] in an old Indian lodge for the night.

1. Lewis's party included Pryor, Drouillard, Shields, Cruzatte, Jean Baptiste Lepage, and Windsor.

2. With Clark, besides Gass, were Joseph and Reubin Field, Shannon, and York.

3. The "Grog Spring" does not appear on any *Atlas* maps, but is mentioned by Clark on June 12; the site, as Gass says, is where the Teton and Missouri rivers approach very closely, in Chouteau County, Montana. Grog is generally taken to be a mixture of rum and water.

4. Probably plains prickly pear, *Opuntia polyacantha* Haw.

5. The Highwood Mountains, Chouteau County.

6. Joseph Field.

7. About a mile and a half upstream from Carter Ferry, Chouteau County.

Wednesday 5th.   Some light showers of rain fell in the night, and the morning was cloudy. When preparing to set out we discovered three bears coming up the river towards us; we therefore halted a while and killed the whole of them. About 7 we set out along the plains again, and discovered the mountain South of us covered with snow, that had fallen last night. When we had gone about 11 miles we saw a large mountain[1] to the West of us also covered with snow. This mountain appeared to run from North to South, and to be very high. The bearing of the river is still South West. Captain Clarke thought this a good course for us to proceed on our voyage, and we turned back towards the camp again. We went about 15 miles and struck the small river[2] about 20 miles from its mouth. Here we killed some elk and deer and encamped[3] all night. There is a great deal of timber in the bottoms of this little river, and plenty of different kinds of game. In these bottoms I saw the stalks of a plant[4] resembling flax in every particular.

1. The Little Belt Mountains, perhaps with the Big Belt Mountains behind.

2. Teton River, Chouteau County, Montana.

3. Gass gives the impression that they camped where they reached Teton River, but Clark indicates they went down the river a few miles. They camped west or west-northwest of Fort Benton, Chouteau County.

4. Perhaps blue flax, *Linum perenne* L., or roundleaf harebell, *Campanula rotundifolia* L., which resembles flax. See Lewis's entry of July 18.

Thursday 6th.   We proceeded down the small river and killed some deer. About 1 o'clock we went on the plains again, which we kept on till we came to the point in the evening.[1] Captain Lewis and his party had not returned. Some light rain fell this afternoon.

1. They returned to the main party's camp of June 3, at the then-mouth of the Marias River, Chouteau County, Montana.

Friday 7th. It rained all day: Captain Lewis and party did not return.

Saturday 8th. A fine cool morning. About 10 o'clock A. M. the water of the South river, or branch, became almost of the colour of claret,[1] and remained so all day. The water of the other branch has the appearance of milk when contrasted with the water of this branch in its present state. About 4 in the afternoon Captain Lewis and his party came to camp. They had been up the North branch about 60 miles, and found it navigable that distance; not so full of islands as the other branch and a greater quantity of timber near it and plenty of game, which is not the case on the South branch. Its bearing something north of west a considerable distance, and then to the south of west. The party while out killed 18 deer and some elk. From the appearance of the river where they left it to return, they supposed it might be navigable a considerable distance further. They saw no mountains ahead, but one off towards the north:[2] it was not covered with snow like those we had seen. Both these rivers abound in fish; and we caught some of different kinds, but not large. About five o'clock in the afternoon the weather became cloudy and cold, and it began to rain. The officers concluded that the south branch was the most proper to ascend, which they think is the Missouri.[3] The other they called Maria's river. At dark the rain ceased.

    1. A reddish-brown color, according to Clark.
    2. Lewis's Tower Mountain (see his entry of June 5, 1805); the southern end of Sweetgrass Hills, on the Montana-Alberta border.
    3. For the captains' reasoning, see Lewis's entry of June 9, 1805.

Sunday 9th. A fine morning. It was thought adviseable to leave the large periogue[1] here and part of the stores and baggage, and some of the men were engaged in digging a case[2] to bury them in. The water of the Missouri changed this morning to its former colour. The day was fine, but the wind blew hard from the northwest. One of the men killed an excellent fat buffaloe. There is a quantity of gooseberry and choak-cherry bushes on the point, and also some rabbit berries.[3]

    1. The red pirogue.
    2. A cache. Cruzatte supervised the construction; see Lewis's entry of this day for details.

3. The gooseberry may be bristly gooseberry, *Ribes setosum* Lindl., choke cherry is the familiar species, and rabbit berries are again buffaloberry.

Monday 10th. We hauled our large periogue on an island in the mouth of Maria's river, and covered it over with brush. We then began to examine and assort our effects to see what would be least wanted and most proper to leave; but about two it began to rain and blow so hard, we were obliged to desist. The rain continued only an hour, and in the evening we loaded the rest of the craft, and left the remainder of our stores and baggage to be buried, consisting of corn, pork, flour, some powder and lead, and other articles amounting to about one thousand pounds weight.[1]

1. Lewis gives a more detailed list of the cached items in his entry of this date.

Tuesday 11th. A fine day. Captain Lewis and four men[1] set out this morning to go to the mountains, which we had discovered towards the west. The rest of the party were engaged in burying the baggage and goods which had been left, and preparing to start the following morning.

1. Drouillard, Joseph Field, Gibson, and Goodrich.

Wednesday 12th. The morning was fine; we set out from the mouth of Maria's river, and went on very well. In the forenoon we passed 12 islands. At 1 o'clock the weather became cloudy and threatened rain; at 2 there was a light shower, and the day became clear. We passed three islands this afternoon and some handsome bluffs on both sides of the river. We went 18 miles and encamped[1] in a small bottom on the north side, where we killed 2 elk and some deer.

1. In Chouteau County, Montana, in the vicinity of Evans Bend, about five miles downstream from Fort Benton.

Thursday 13th. We set out early in a fine morning. Some dew fell last night. We passed a large creek on the south side, called Snow creek.[1] The water of the river is very clear and the current very rapid. We passed a number of islands covered with timber; but there is none to be seen on the hills on either side. We went 14 miles and encamped[2] on the south side.

1. Shonkin Creek, Chouteau County, Montana.
2. In Chouteau County, perhaps in the vicinity of Bird Coulee.

Friday 14th.   We embarked early, and the morning was pleasant. About 7 o'clock A. M. we passed a place where Captain Lewis and his men had killed two bears, and had left a note directing us where to find them. About 2 one of Captain Lewis's men met us,[1] and informed us that the falls were about 20 miles above; and that Captain Lewis and the other three men, were gone on to examine what the distance was above the falls, before we could take the water again. We went 10 miles and encamped[2] in a small bottom on the south side.

1. Joseph Field; Clark puts the time at four o'clock.
2. In Chouteau County, Montana, near the entrance of Black Coulee.

Saturday 15th.   We proceeded on as usual, but had the most rapid water, I ever saw any craft taken through. At noon we stopped at the mouth of a creek on the south side called Strawberry creek,[1] handsome rapid stream, but not large. On a point above, there is a great quantity of strawberry,[2] gooseberry and choak-cherry bushes; and there appears to be a good deal of small cotton-wood on the banks of this creek. In the afternoon we passed red bluffs on both sides of the river, and at night came to a large rapid which we did not venture to pass so late; and therefore encamped[3] below on the north side, after going 12 miles.

1. Clark called it Shields River, after John Shields of the party; it is present Highwood Creek, Chouteau County, Montana. Ordway and Whitehouse agree with Gass about the name.
2. Probably either wild strawberry, *Fragaria virginiana* Duchn. var. *glauca* Wats., or woodland strawberry, *F. vesca* L. var. *americana* Porter.
3. The camp was in Cascade County, Montana, a little below and opposite the mouth of Belt Creek, the captains' Portage Creek.

Sunday 16th.   In the morning all hands were engaged in taking the canoes over the rapid about a mile in length, which having accomplished they returned and took up the periogue, where we halted to examine another great rapid close ahead. One man[1] had been sent on last night to Captain Lewis, to find out what discoveries he had made. We remained here some time, and a few of the men went out to hunt. About noon Captain Lewis and the party with him joined us, and the hunters came in. Captain Lewis had been up the falls 15 miles above the first shoot or pitch, and found the falls continue all that distance, in which there were 5 different shoots 40 or 50 feet perpendicular each, and very rapid water between them.[2] As we found the south side the best to carry our canoes up, we crossed over and unloaded our craft. We then had to take the empty canoes to the side we had left, and to tow them up by a line about a mile, in order to get them up to the mouth of a small river on the south side,[3] as a more convenient place to take them up the bank. This business was attended with great difficulty as well as danger, but we succeeded in getting them all over safe.

1. Joseph Field.
2. The Great Falls of the Missouri River consists of a series of five falls in Cascade County, Montana. For a more accurate measure of the various heights, see Clark's survey notes of June 17–19, 1805.
3. Belt Creek, the party's Portage Creek, the boundary between Cascade and Choteau Counties.

Monday 17th.   Part of the men were employed in taking the canoes up the small river about a mile and an half; and some engaged in making small waggons to haul the canoes and loading above the falls. Captain Clarke and 4 men[1] went to view and survey our road to the place where we were to embark above the falls. Opposite the mouth of the small river, a beautiful sulphur spring[2] rises out of the bank, of as strong sulphur water as I have ever seen. On the bottoms of this small river and also on the Missouri is a great quantity of flax growing, and at this time in bloom. Two men went out this morning to hunt for elk, in order to get their skins for covering to the iron frame of a boat, which we had with us. In the evening the men got the canoes to a proper place to take them upon land.

1. Actually five men, including Alexander Willard, Colter, and perhaps Joseph Field.
2. Sulphur, or Sacagawea, Springs still exists about three hundred yards from the Missouri, opposite the mouth of Belt Creek, Cascade County, Montana.

Tuesday 18th.   The periogue[1] was hauled out of the water and laid safe; and some men went to dig a place for depositing more of our baggage.

About 12 the two hunters came in, and could find no elk, but killed 10 deer. In the evening we compleated our waggons, which were made altogether of wood, and of a very ordinary quality; but it is expected they will answer the purpose.

1. The white pirogue.

Wednesday 19th. A fine day, but the wind very high. Three hunters set out for Medicine river,[1] a large river above the falls, which comes in on the north side, to hunt for elk. We finished the burying place, so that we will be ready to start as soon as Capt. Clarke returns. All our people are making mockasons to go through the prairie.

1. Sun River, meeting the Missouri at the town of Great Falls, Cascade County, Montana.

Thursday 20th. A cloudy morning: four hunters went out to kill some fat buffaloe. About 4 o'clock one of them came in for men to carry the meat to camp; as they had 14 down ready to butcher. We went out about a mile and an half, and brought in a load, leaving three men to dress the rest. Captain Clarke and his party returned, having found a tolerable good road except where some draughts crossed it. They had left their blankets and provision at the place where they expect we will again embark.[1]

1. At the upper portage camp, Cascade County, Montana, on the Missouri about three-quarters of a mile north of Sand Coulee Creek.

Friday 21st. This morning was also fine, but there was a high wind. The remainder of the meat was brought in, and one of the men killed 2 deer.

Saturday 22nd. All hands, except two and the interpreter and his wife,[1] set out through the prairie, with one canoe on a waggon loaded heavy with baggage. We went on slowly as our axletrees were weak; and about 12 o'clock one of them broke; when we had to halt and put in a new one. This accident happened at a draught[2] where there was some willow, and we put in an axletree of that; which I believe is the best this country affords for the purpose.

It was late in the evening before we got to the intended place of embarkation on the river.[3]

1. Ordway and Goodrich with Charbonneau and Sacagawea (and her baby, Jean Baptiste).
2. Gass's version of "draw"; Box Elder Creek in Cascade County, Montana.
3. The upper portage camp.

Sunday 23rd. The morning was cloudy. When I awoke this morning I found a material difference between the river and country here and below the falls. Here the river is wide and the current gentle. There are three small islands at this place and some timber on the banks, but not much, and what is there is cotton-wood and willow. The banks are very low, and the country rising in plains a considerable distance on both sides of the river; and far off mountains covered with snow on both sides and ahead. Two of the men[1] and myself remained with Captain Lewis here to assist him in putting together his iron boat, the rest went back for another load. The iron boat-frame is to be covered with skins and requires a quantity of thin shaved strips of wood for lining. In the forenoon we put the frame together, which is 36 feet long, 4½ wide, and 2 feet 2 inches deep. In the afternoon Capt. Lewis and one of the men[2] went down to Medicine river, which is about two miles distant; to see whether the three men[3] sent there to hunt had procured any elk skins. In the evening they found one of the hunters,[4] and encamped with him all night.

1. Joseph Field and Shields.
2. Joseph Field.
3. Drouillard, Reubin Field, and Shannon.
4. Shannon; he was encamped at the mouth of Sun River.

Monday 24th. In the morning Capt. Lewis came up to our camp. We found it very difficult to procure stuff for the boat.[1] The two men[2] which Captain Lewis had left in the morning came to our camp in the afternoon, but had seen nothing of the other two hunters.[3] In the evening there was a very heavy shower of rain; at night the weather cleared up, and the men arrived with two more canoes. The two hunters which Captain Lewis could not find, had killed some buffaloe below the mouth of the Medicine river, where one remained, and the other had gone across to the camp below the falls again, but had found no elk.[4]

1. Items needed for the iron-frame boat included straight sticks four and one-half feet long, for the framework of the boat, and pine logs from which to extract pitch to make the covering waterproof.

2. Joseph Field and Shannon; see June 23 and Lewis's entry for this day.

3. Drouillard and Reubin Field.

4. Drouillard remained at the Sun (Medicine) River camp, while Reubin Field returned.

Tuesday 25th. A cloudy morning. The men went back for more canoes and baggage; and one[1] went down to the hunter's camp below Medicine river to bring him up in a canoe. Another[2] went up the river to look for elk. When he had gone about three miles, he was attacked by 3 brown bears, that were near devouring him; but he made his escape by running down a steep bank into the water. In this adventure he fell, injured his gun, and hurt one of his hands; therefore returned to camp. One of the men[3] and myself went over to an island to look for stuff for the canoe, but could find nothing but bark, which perhaps will answer. We killed two elk on the island. There is in the bottoms a great quantity of spear-mint and currant bushes.[4] Also multitudes of blackbirds.[5] The musquitoes[6] are very troublesome, though the snow is on the mountains so near. In the evening the two men[7] came up the river with a quantity of good meat and 100 pounds of tallow.

1. Frazer, to pick up Drouillard.

2. Joseph Field.

3. Shields.

4. Gass's spearmint is probably field mint, *Mentha arvensis* L., while the currants could be any of a number of species.

5. Perhaps rusty blackbird, *Euphagus carolinus,* or Brewer's blackbird, *E. cyanocephalus.* The party also apparently called the common grackle, *Quisculus quiscula,* a blackbird.

6. Probably *Aedes vexans.*

7. Drouillard and Frazer.

Wednesday 26th. A fine morning. Two hunters[1] went up the river, and myself and another[2] went over the river to collect bark; where a great gang of buffaloe came near us, and we killed 7 of them. In the evening the men returned over the plains with two more canoes and baggage. One man fell very sick,[3] and Captain Lewis had to bleed him with a penknife, having no other instrument at this camp. Captain Clarke measured the length of this portage accurately and found it to be 18 miles.[4] He also measured the height of the falls, and found them in a distance of 17 miles 362 feet 9 inches. The first great pitch 98 feet, the second 19 feet, the third 47 feet 8 inches, the fourth 26 feet; and a number of small pitches, amounting altogether to 362 feet 9 inches.[5]

1. Drouillard and Joseph Field.
2. Shields.
3. Whitehouse.
4. Seventeen and three-fourths miles according to Lewis's entry on this day.
5. See Clark's survey notes of June 17–19, 1805, for the heights of the falls.

Thursday 27th. A fine day. The men went back for the remaining canoe and baggage. The sick man[1] is become better. This morning some elk came close to camp and we killed two of them. In the afternoon a dreadful hail storm came on, which lasted half an hour. Some of the lumps of ice that fell weighed 3 ounces, and measured 7 inches in circumference. The ground was covered with them, as white as snow. It kept cloudy during the evening and some rain fell. At night the two hunters[2] that went up the river returned. They had killed while out 9 elk and 3 bears.

1. Whitehouse.
2. Drouillard and Joseph Field.

Friday 28th. A fine morning. There are but 6 persons[1] now at this camp, but all busy about the boat; some shaving skins, some sewing them together; and some preparing the wood part.

1. Lewis, Gass, Drouillard, Joseph Field, Frazer, Whitehouse, and Shields were all there; perhaps Gass did not count himself. For their duties, see Lewis's entry.

Saturday 29th. We had a very hard gust of wind and rain in the morning; but a fine forenoon after it. Captain Lewis and a hunter[1] went down the river about 7 miles, to see a very large spring[2] which rises out of the bank of the Missouri on the south side. In the afternoon there was another heavy shower of rain, and after it a fine evening. Captain Lewis came to camp, but drenched with rain.

1. Drouillard.

2. Giant Springs, now in a park northeast of the city of Great Falls, Cascade County, Montana.

Sunday 30th.   A fine morning and heavy dew, which is very rare in this country. The men with the canoe and baggage did not return, as we expected.

Monday 1st July, 1805.   A fine day. In the afternoon, Captain Clarke and the men came with all the baggage except some they had left six miles back. The hail that fell on the 27th hurt some of the men very badly. Captain Clarke, the interpreter, and the squaw and child, had gone to see the spring at the falls; and when the storm began, they took shelter under a bank at the mouth of a run; but in five minutes there was seven feet water in the run; and they were very near being swept away. They lost a gun, an umbrella and a Surveyor's compass, and barely escaped with their lives.[1]

1. See Clark's account of this incident in his entry of June 29. York was also with this group.

Tuesday 2nd.   A fine morning. The Surveyer's compass, which had been lost was found to day.[1] The men went out for the baggage which had been left on the way, and got in with the whole of it, and canoes safe.

In the evening, the most of the corps crossed over to an island, to attack and rout its monarch, a large brown bear, that held possession and seemed to defy all that would attempt to besiege him there. Our troops, however, stormed the place, gave no quarter, and its commander fell. Our army returned the same evening to camp without having suffered any loss on their side.

1. Clark in his entry of June 30 says it was found that day.

Wednesday 3rd.   A fine morning. I was so engaged with the boat, that I had not visited the falls. I therefore set out with one of the men[1] to day for that purpose. I found the 2nd pitch the most beautiful, though not the high-est.[2] About a mile below the upper pitch,[3] the largest and most beautiful spring[4] rises out of the bank of the Missouri on the south side that I ever beheld. We had a light shower of rain. During this excursion I saw more buffaloe than I had seen in any day previous: we killed 7 of them before we returned to camp. We also saw 25 wolves in one gang or pack.

1. Apparently Hugh McNeal, although Lewis says "several others" also went to view the falls. Whitehouse counts two others, Ordway four.
2. Crooked Falls, Cascade County, Montana, if Gass ordered the different falls in the same way as the captains.
3. Black Eagle Falls, Cascade County.
4. Giant Springs; see Gass's entry of June 29.

Thursday 4th.   A fine day. A part of the men were busily engaged at the boat, and other in dressing skins for clothing, until about 4 o'clock in the afternoon, when we drank the last of our spirits in celebrating the day, and amused ourselves with dancing till 9 o'clock at night, when a shower of rain fell and we retired to rest.

Friday 5th.   A fine morning. All the men, except five of us who were en-gaged at the boat, went to hunt; at night they came in and had killed several buffaloe and some cabres or antelopes.

Saturday 6th.   As many of the hands as could find room to work were engaged at the boat; and four went down the river to hunt buffaloe, in order to get their skins to cover our craft. This was a beautiful and pleasant day.

Sunday 7th.   The morning was fine. The hunters had remained out all night. In the evening some few drops of rain fell; and the hunters came in; but had not had good luck, the buffaloe being mostly out in the plains. At night we got our boat finished, all but greasing; and she was laid out to dry.

Monday 8th.   Again we had a fine morning, and a number of the party went out to hunt. In the evening they all came in, and had killed but three buffaloe, a deer and a cabre; and caught a small animal almost like a cat, of a light colour.[1] Yesterday one of the men caught a small squirrel,[2] like a ground squirrel, but of a more dun colour, and more spotted. We finished the boat this evening, having covered her with tallow and coal-dust. We called her the Experiment, and expect she will answer our purpose.

1. The swift fox, *Vulpes velox.*
2. The thirteen-lined ground squirrel, *Spermophilus tridecemlineatus.*

Tuesday 9th.   A fine morning, and heavy dew. In the forenoon we loaded our canoes, and put the Experiment into the water. She rides very light but leaks some. In the afternoon a storm of wind, with some rain came on from the north west, and we had again to unload some of our canoes, the waves ran so high. After the storm we had a fine evening. The tallow and coal were found not to answer the purpose; for as soon as dry, it cracked and scaled off, and the water came through the skins. Therefore for want of tar or pitch we had, after all our labour, to haul our new boat on shore, and leave it at this place.

Wednesday 10th.   A fine cool morning. Captain Lewis and Captain Clarke thought it would be best to make two canoes more, if we could get timber large enough. So Captain Clarke and 10 men set out in search of it.[1] Some of the hunters having seen large timber about 20 miles up the river, the canoes were sent on loaded, and a party went by land; the distance that way being only 6 or 7 miles. If timber is found the canoes are to unload and return for the remainder of the baggage. Captain Lewis, myself and nine men staid to take the boat asunder and bury her; and deposited her safely under ground. Captain Lewis had an observation at 12 which gave 47° 3 10 N. Latitude. In the afternoon I went out to see if there were any buffaloe near, but found none: they appear to have all left the river. On the bank of a run where there are high rocks, I found a great quantity of sweet gooseberries, all ripe.

1. Ordway took four canoes and eight men, including Whitehouse, while Clark went by land with Pryor, "four Choppers two Involids & one man to hunt." Bratton may have been one of the "Involids."

Thursday 11th. We continued here waiting for the return of the canoes until 2 o'clock; then four of us went out and killed a buffaloe and brought in part of the meat. The canoes did not come back this evening.

Friday 12th. A fine morning. Myself and three of the men went up the river to assist Captain Clarke's party. In our way we passed a small bottom on the north side of the river, in which there is an old Indian lodge 216 feet in circumference.[1] Here we saw some wild pigeons[2] and turtle doves.[3] Having gone about 7 miles we found Captain Clarke's party,[4] who had cut down two trees and taken off logs for canoes, one 25 and the other 30 feet in length. The canoes had returned to our old camp, where Captain Lewis was.

  1. See Lewis's description at his entry of July 13. Probably a Blackfeet sun dance lodge.
  2. The now-extinct passenger pigeon, *Ectopistes migratorius.*
  3. The name of a Eurasian species commonly given to the mourning dove, *Zenaida macroura.*
  4. At Clark's canoe-making camp in Cascade County, Montana, southeast of Antelope Butte and a few miles east of the town of Ulm (see Lewis's entry of July 10).

Saturday 13th. A fine day, but high wind. Captain Lewis came up here accompanied by the squaw. He informed us that the canoes had started with all the baggage from the former encampment, which we had called White-bear camp.[1] The musquitoes are very troublesome. This evening the canoes were finished except the putting in some knees.

  1. White Bear Islands camp was an alternate name for the upper portage camp (see June 20). The islands themselves have virtually disappeared.

Sunday 14th. A fine morning. About 11 o'clock the men came up with the canoes and baggage. The distance by water was found to be 22 miles, and by land only 6 miles. In the afternoon some rain fell but we continued to work at the canoes, and finished them ready for loading.

Chapter Fifty-Two

Across the Rockies

July 15–October 10, 1805

Monday 15th. After a night of heavy rain, we had a pleasant morning, and loaded the canoes. About 11 o'clock we set out from this place, which we had called Canoe camp; had fine still water, and passed some handsome small bottoms on both sides of the river. We also passed a handsome river[1] on the south side about 100 yards wide, which seemed to have its source in a large mountain on the same side.[2] The snow appears to have melted from all the mountains in view. The country around is composed of dry plains, with short grass. We passed two small creeks,[3] one on each side of the river; made 26 miles, and encamped[4] on the north side.

1. Smith River, named by the party for Robert Smith, Jefferson's secretary of the navy, meeting the Missouri in Cascade County, Montana.
2. The sources of Smith River are in the Little Belt Mountains.
3. The captains took little notice of these watercourses in Cascade County, although Clark named the one on the north Fort Mountain Creek. They seem to remain without official names.
4. In Cascade County, a few miles southwest of Ulm.

Tuesday 16th. We embarked early and had a fine morning. Captain Lewis and two men[1] went on ahead to the mountain to take an observation. We passed the channel of a river on the south side without water, about 60 yards wide.[2] We had fine water until about 1 o'clock, when we came within about two miles of the mountain; when the water became more rapid; but the current not so swift as below the falls. At this place there are a number of small islands. One of our men has been taken unwell. In the afternoon we continued our voyage, and the water continued very rapid. We got about 3 miles into the first range of the Rock mountains, and encamped[3] on the north side of the river on a sand beach. There is some fine timber on the mountains, but not much in this part. There are great hills of solid rock of a dark colour. This day we went about 20 miles.

1. Three, according to Lewis: John Potts, Lepage, and Drouillard.
2. They were setting out for the point where the Missouri emerged from the mountains. Apparently Bird Creek, Cascade County, Montana; perhaps the nameless "bayou" noted in Clark's courses for the day.
3. Near Tintinger Slough, Cascade County.

Wednesday 17th.   We set out early, and the morning was fine and pleasant. At 8 o'clock we came to Captain Lewis's camp,[1] at a very rapid place of the river, and took breakfast. We had here to join the crews of two canoes together, to go up the rapids which were about half a mile long. The Missouri at this place is very narrow. At the head of these rapids a fine spring comes in on the south side,[2] which rises about a quarter of a mile from the river; and has a good deal of small cotton-wood[3] and willows[4] on its banks. There is also another spring below the rapids, but it sinks before it reaches the river. We proceeded on through the mountains, a very desert looking part of the country. Some of the knobs or peaks of these mountains, are 700 (perhaps some nearly 1200) feet high, all rock; and though they are almost perpendicular, we saw mountain sheep on the very tops of them. We saw few other animals to day. The general breadth of the river is 100 yards. We went 11 miles and encamped[5] in a small bottom on the north side.

1. Probably near later Half-Breed, or Lone Pine, Rapids, Cascade County, Montana.
2. Perhaps the "small run" noted in passing by Clark.
3. In this area the eastern cottonwood species, *Populus deltoides,* gives way to the western variety, narrowleaf cottonwood, *P. angustifolia.*
4. There are many species of willow in this area.
5. In Lewis and Clark County, Montana, a few miles below the mouth of Dearborn River, near where Interstate Highway 15 crosses the Missouri River.

Thursday 18th. The morning was fair and we proceeded on early: passed Clear-water river[1] on the north side about 50 yards wide, rapid and shallow. There are a great quantity of currants[2] all along the river on both sides in the small bottoms. At breakfast time Captain Clarke with three men[3] went on ahead. About 11 we got through the higher part of the mountains, and to where there is less timber and the rocks not so large. In the forenoon we passed two small creeks on the north side,[4] and in the afternoon a small river on the same side;[5] above the mouth of which we got a deer skin, that Captain Clarke's man[6] had hung up. The country continues much the same. We made 20 miles this day.[7]

1. Dearborn River, named by the captains for Henry Dearborn, Jefferson's secretary of war, forms the boundary between Cascade and Lewis and Clark counties, Montana, for a short distance above its mouth.

2. See Lewis's entry of July 17, 1805, for a discussion of the currants of the region.

3. Joseph Field, Potts, and York.

4. The two small creeks should be Stickney and Werner creeks, Lewis and Clark County, except it is hard to see how Gass places them on the north side of the Missouri, or on the same side of the river as the "small river" which follows. Perhaps this is an error by McKeehan.

5. Named by the captains Ordway's Creek, for Sergeant John Ordway of the party, later Little Prickly Pear Creek, Lewis and Clark County.

6. Presumably York.

7. Camp was in Lewis and Clark County, above Holter Dam.

Friday 19th. A fine morning. At 9 we came to high parts of the mountains, which had a good deal of pine, spruce and cedar[1] on them, and where there were not so many rocks; but no timber in the bottoms except some small willows. About 1 o'clock we had thunder, lightening and rain, which continued an hour or two, and then the weather became clear. This afternoon we passed parts of the mountains, that were very high, and mostly of solid rock of a light colour.[2] The mountains are so close on the river on both sides that we scarcely could find room to encamp. We went 20 miles and encamped[3] on the south side. After night some rain fell.

1. The pine is probably ponderosa pine, the spruce is probably Engelmann spruce, *Picea engelmannii* (Parry) Engelm., and the cedar is probably Rocky Mountain red cedar.

2. The Gates of the Mountains, still as named by Lewis, Lewis and Clark County, Montana.

3. In Lewis and Clark County, a short distance downstream from Upper Holter Lake.

Saturday 20th. We had a fine morning, and embarked early. About 8 we got out of the high part of the mountains, and came to where they are lower and not so rocky; and where there are the finest currants I ever saw of different kinds, red, yellow and black: the black are the most pleasant and palatable.[1] There is also a good portion of timber on the mountains all along this part. We killed an elk in our way, and found the skin of one which Captain Clark had left on the bank with a note, informing us he would pass the mountain he was then on, and wait for the canoes. We passed a small creek on the south side,[2] and about 2 o'clock came to a level plain on the north side, from which we saw a strong smoke rising, and supposed it was from a fire made by Capt. Clarke. The river is very crooked in general, and here is a great bend to the southeast; and in the afternoon it turned so far that our course was north of east. We proceeded on through a valley between two mountains, one of which we passed, and the other is in view ahead.[3] We went 15 miles and encamped[4] at the mouth of a small run on the south side.

1. All are the golden currant, *Ribes aureum* Pursh. Gass agrees with Lewis and Ordway in finding the black individuals the best-tasting.

2. Gass's use of "north" and "south" is especially confusing here. Among the various streams passed this day, this is probably Beaver Creek, Lewis and Clark County, Montana, which is on the east side of that particular stretch of the Missouri.

3. The Big Belt Mountains lie east of the Missouri in this area; the Spokane Hills and Elkhorn Mountains lie to the west of the river, and ahead of the point they reached on July 20.

4. In Lewis and Clark County, on the point of a bend between Soup and Trout creeks.

Sunday 21st. We set out at sunrise and had a pleasant morning; passed some middling high hills on the river, and rocks of a red purple colour; also two small creeks one on each side.[1] There are a few pines on the hills. At noon our course began to change more to the southwest again; the wind blew very hard and some drops of rain fell. In the afternoon we passed through a ridge,[2] where the river is very narrow; and close above a large cluster of small islands, where we had some difficulty to get along, the water being so much separated. We went 15 miles and an half and encamped[3] on the south side, on a beautiful prairie bottom. One of our hunters killed a fine deer.

1. Lewis notices one of these, Spokane Creek, Lewis and Clark County, Montana, which he called Pryor's Creek, after Sergeant Nathaniel Pryor of the party. There are various creeks

on the other side of the Missouri, of which the first in the day's course, and the closest to Spokane Creek, is Trout Creek.

2. They passed the Spokane Hills into the valley, in Lewis and Clark and Broadwater counties, now largely covered by Canyon Ferry Reservoir.

3. In Lewis and Clark County, a few miles east of Helena and about five miles above Canyon Ferry Dam, near the Lewis and Clark–Broadwater county line.

Monday 22nd. We embarked early, the weather being pleasant: passed some fine springs on the southern shore, and a large island near the northern: On the south side the country is level to a good distance, but on the north the hills come close to the river. At breakfast our squaw informed us she had been at this place before when small. Here we got a quantity of wild onions.[1] At half past 9, we proceeded on again; passed a large island at noon; and in the afternoon, more islands: and came to a place where Captain Clarke and his party were encamped. They told us they had seen the same smoke, which we had discovered a few days ago, and found it had been made by the natives, who they supposed had seen some of us, and had fled, taking us for enemies. We went 17 miles and an half and encamped[2] on an island; where we found the musquitoes very bad. We saw to day several banks of snow on a mountain west of us.[3]

1. Possibly nodding onion, *Allium cernuum* Roth, or Geyer's onion, *A. geyeri* S. Wats.
2. In Broadwater County, Montana, a few miles upstream from Beaver (the party's White Earth) Creek, on a site now under Canyon Ferry Lake.
3. Elkhorn Mountains.

Tuesday 23rd. A cloudy morning. We embarked early, and at the same time Captain Clarke and four men[1] went on again to endeavour to meet with some of the natives. We had rapid water, and passed a great number of islands. Capt. Clarke and his men killed four deer and a cabre, and left the skins and meat on the shore, where we could easily find them. The course of the river all day was nearly from the south, through a valley of 10 or 12 miles wide. The mountains are not so high nor so rocky, as those we passed. Large timber is not plenty, but there are a great quantity of small shrubs and willows. We passed a small river on the south side,[2] and some banks of very white clay. We encamped[3] on an island, having made 24 miles.

1. Joseph and Reubin Field, Frazer, and Charbonneau. They overtook Drouillard hunting several miles ahead.

2. Lewis named it Whitehouse's Creek, after Joseph Whitehouse of the party; it is later Duck, or Gurnett, Creek, Broadwater County, Montana.

3. In Broadwater County, near the south end of Canyon Ferry Lake, a little north of Townsend.

Wednesday 24th. The morning was fine, and we early prosecuted our voyage; passed a bank of very red earth, which our squaw told us the natives use for paint.[1] Deer are plenty among the bushes, and one of our men killed one on the bank. We continued through the valley all day: Went 19 miles and encamped on the north side.[2]

1. The red earth is shale, formerly a lateritic soil horizon.
2. About seven miles north of Toston, Broadwater County, Montana.

Thursday 25th. We embarked and proceeded on at the usual time, in a fine morning; we passed a beautiful plain on the north side, and at 2 o'clock we came to the entrance of another chain of mountains;[1] where we took dinner and again went on. Passing through this chain we found some difficult rapids, but good water between them. This chain of mountains are not so high, nor so rocky as those we passed before. Six very fine springs rise on the southern shore, about four miles above the entrance of this range. We went 16 miles and encamped[2] on the north side.

1. Apparently the cliffs Clark labeled "Little Gate of the Mountains," Broadwater County, Montana, between Toston and Lombard. Gass does not mention the stream the captains named Gass's Creek for him, now Crow Creek, Broadwater County.
2. In Broadwater County, immediately above Toston Dam.

Friday 26th. The morning was fine and we continued our course through the mountains. There are some cedar and spruce trees on the shore; but very little of any kind on the mountains. About 11 o'clock we got through this range into a valley: About 2 came to a large island and halted on it for dinner. A rattle-snake[1] came among our canoes in the water, of a kind different from any I had seen. It was about two feet long, of a light colour, with small spots all over. One of our hunters went on ahead in the morning, and at this place killed 4 deer. While we remained here it became cloudy and some rain fell. At 4 o'clock we proceeded on through the valley; passed a creek on the south side,[2] and having gone 18 miles and an half encamped[3] on the same side, where a small mountain comes in to the river.

1. Probably the prairie rattlesnake, *Crotalus viridus viridus*. The species was new to science but not to the party. One was killed and then described by Lewis on May 17.

2. Lewis called it Howard's Creek, after Thomas P. Howard of the party. It is now Sixteen-mile Creek, on the Broadwater-Gallatin county line, Montana, at this point. However, Gass's suggested time seems rather late for passing this creek, or Garden Gulch, Gallatin County, mislabeled "Howard's Creek" by Clark on *Atlas* map 64.

3. In Gallatin County, near the landmark of Eagle Rock.

Saturday 27th.   We continued our voyage early, and had a pleasant morning; proceeded on, and at 9 o'clock got through the small mountain. At the entrance of the valley, a branch of the Missouri comes in on the south side, about 60 yards wide; the current rapid but not very deep. Here we took breakfast, and having proceeded on a mile, came to another branch of the same size. There is very little difference in the size of the 3 branches.[1] On the bank of the north branch[2] we found a note Captain Clarke had left informing us, he was ahead and had gone up that branch. We went on to the point, and, as the men were much fatigued, encamped in order to rest a day or two.[3] After we halted here, it began to rain and continued three hours. About 12 o'clock Capt. Clarke and his men[4] came to our encampment, and told us they had been up both branches[5] a considerable distance, but could discover none of the natives. There is a beautiful valley at these forks; and a good deal of timber on the branches, chiefly cotton-wood. Also currants, goose and service berries,[6] and choak-cherries on the banks. The deer are plenty too; some of the men went out and killed several to day. Capt. Clarke was very unwell and had been so all last night. In the evening the weather became clear and we had a fine night.

1. The Three Forks of the Missouri meet near the Broadwater-Gallatin county line, Montana, about four miles northeast of the town of Three Forks. The first branch they encountered was the Gallatin, and then they proceeded on to the junction of the Jefferson and the Madison. Clark's advance party had reached the confluence on July 25.

2. The Jefferson.

3. Apparently on later Barkers Island, between two branches of the Jefferson, northeast of the town of Three Forks, Gallatin County.

4. Frazer, Joseph and Reubin Field, and Charbonneau.

5. The Jefferson and the Madison.

6. Serviceberry, *Amerlanchier alnifolia* Nutt.

Sunday 28th. As this was a fine day, the men were employed in airing the baggage, dressing skins and hunting. Capt. Clark still continued unwell. Our squaw informed us, that it was at this place she had been taken prisoner by the Grossventers 4 or 5 years ago.[1] From this valley we can discover a large mountain with snow on it, towards the southwest;[2] and expect to pass by the northwest end of it. Capt. Lewis had a meridian altitude here, which gave 45° 22 34.5″ north latitude. We also remained here the 29th, which was a fine day, and the men chiefly employed in the same way. Capt. Clarke is getting better.

1. See Lewis's reflections on this information on this date.
2. The Tobacco Root Mountains.

Tuesday 30th. We left our encampment at the forks, and proceeded on about 7 o'clock A. M. up the north branch.[1] This branch is about 60 yards wide and 6 feet deep, with a rapid current. We passed a number of islands. The valley continued on the south side all this day; but the spur of a mountain, about 5 or 6 miles from the forks came in close on the north side with very high cliffs of rocks. We encamped[2] where it terminated, having made 13 miles and an half.

1. Up the Jefferson River. Gass fails to mention that Lewis went ahead with Charbonneau, Sacagawea, the baby Jean Baptiste, and "two invalleds."

2. In Jefferson County, Montana, just below the mouth of Willow Creek (the party's Philosophy River), and about two miles north of the town of Willow Creek.

Wednesday 31st. We set out early, and had a fine cool morning with dew. Last night Capt. Lewis went on ahead, and the canoes being unable to get on to him, he was obliged to encamp out alone in this howling wilderness. We passed a small creek[1] this morning on the south side, which empties into the river, through 2 or 3 mouths, on account of its being much dammed up by the beaver, which are very plenty. At breakfast time we came up to Capt. Lewis; and having made 17 miles and three quarters, encamped[2] on an island.

1. Willow Creek, which they named Philosophy River, joining the Jefferson in Gallatin County, Montana.

2. Near the mouth of Antelope Creek, in either Gallatin or Madison County, a little down-stream from the entrance of Lewis and Clark Caverns State Park, and some two miles above where U.S. Highway 287 crosses the Jefferson. Gass does not mention that he injured his back this day by falling on the gunwale of a canoe; see Lewis's entry.

Thursday 1st August, 1805. We set out early in a fine morning and pro-ceeded on till breakfast time; when Capt. Lewis, myself and the two interpre-ters[1] went on ahead to look for some of the Snake Indians. Our course lay across a large mountain on the north side,[2] over which we had a very fatigu-ing trip of about 11 miles. We then came to the river again, and found it ran through a handsome valley of from 6 to 8 miles wide. At the entrance of this valley, which is covered with small bushes, but has very little timber, we killed two elk and left the meat for the canoes to take up, as the men stood much in need of it, having no fresh provisions on hand. We crossed a small creek[3] on the north shore, and encamped[4] on the same side.

1. Drouillard and Charbonneau, all seeking the Shoshone Indians, Sacagawea's people.

2. The Bull Mountains, Jefferson County, Montana.

3. Labeled "R. Fields Valley Creek," by the captains, for Reubin Field of the party, now Boulder River, Jefferson County.

4. In Jefferson County, somewhere above Cardwell.

Friday 2nd. The morning was fine and we went on at sunrise, proceeded 4 or 5 miles and crossed the river. In the middle of the day it was very warm in the valley, and at night very cold; so much so that two blankets were scarce a sufficient covering. On each side of the valley there is a high range of mountains,[1] which run nearly parallel, with some spots of snow on their tops. We killed a deer; went about 24 miles and encamped[2] on the south side.

1. The Bull and then the Highland Mountains to their right going up the Jefferson, and the Tobacco Root Mountains to their left.

2. In the vicinity of Waterloo, Madison County, Montana.

Saturday 3rd.   A fine cool morning. We left a note for Capt. Clarke, continued our route along the valley; and passed several fine springs that issue from the mountains. Currants and service berries are in abundance along this valley, and we regaled ourselves with some of the best I had ever seen. We went about 22 miles and encamped.[1] The night was disagreeably cold.

1. In Madison County, Montana, above the mouth of the Big Hole River, the party's Wisdom River, which Gass does not mention.

Sunday 4th.   At sunrise we continued our march, in a fine morning; went about 6 miles when we came to a fork of the river;[1] crossed the south branch and from a high knob discovered that the river had forked below us, as we could see the timber on the north branch about 6 or 7 miles from the south and west branches. We therefore crossed to the north branch, and finding it not navigable for our canoes, went down to the confluence and left a note for Capt. Clarke directing him to take the left hand branch. We then went up the north branch about 10 miles and encamped[2] on it.

1. The forks of the Jefferson, where Ruby River (the party's Philanthropy River) comes from the east to join the Beaverhead and form the Jefferson. They had passed the Big Hole (Wisdom) River, Gass's "north branch," the previous day without knowing it.

2. They went up the Big Hole River and camped near the Madison-Beaverhead county line, above the mouth of the Nez Perce Creek.

Monday 5th.   This morning Capt. Lewis thought it would be best for me and one of the interpreters[1] to go over to the west branch,[2] and remain there, until he and the other[3] should go higher up the north, cross over in search of Indians and then go down and join us. At night they came to our camp,[4] but had not seen any of the natives, nor any fresh signs.

1. Charbonneau, who was having trouble marching because of his ankle.

2. The Beaverhead River, which the party called the Jefferson.

3. That is, the other interpreter, Drouillard.

4. On the Beaverhead River, in Madison County, Montana, a few miles above the mouth of Ruby River.

Tuesday 6th. We started early to go down to the point to see if the canoes had come up that far, and came upon the north branch about 2 miles above it. Here we discovered that the people in the canoes had not found the note,[1] and with great difficulty, had proceeded 5 or 6 miles up the north branch. In their return down one of the canoes was overturned; a knapsack, shot-pouch and powder-horn lost, and all the rest of the loading wet. We got down to the forks about 12 o'clock, put all our baggage out to dry, and en-camped[2] for the night. Some hunters went out and killed 3 deer.

1. A beaver had chewed down the pole on which Lewis had left a note telling Clark to go up the Beaverhead (the middle fork); instead his party went up the Big Hole River.

2. On the Jefferson opposite the mouth of the Big Hole River, Madison County, Montana, just north of Twin Bridges.

Wednesday 7th. We remained here during the forenoon,[1] which was fair and clear, and where Capt. Lewis took a meridian altitude, which made the latitude of this place 45° 2 53 north. At 3 o'clock in the afternoon, we were ready to continue our voyage. In the evening a heavy cloud came up, and we had hard thunder with lightening and rain. We went on 7 miles and en-camped[2] on the north side, when the weather cleared, and we had fine night. The canoes came 62 miles and three quarters while we were out.

1. Gass remained with Lewis at the previous night's camp to take an observation, while Clark took the rest of the party up the Jefferson River.

2. In Madison County, Montana, just above Twin Bridges.

Thursday 8th. We proceeded on early and had a pleasant morning. The west branch which we went up is about 30 yards wide, and the south, which we passed, about 15 yards.[1] Three hunters went by land to day, and at noon had killed 2 deer and a goat or cabre. The river is very crooked in this valley. The hunters again went out in the afternoon and killed 2 deer more. There are no buffaloe in this part of the country, and other game is not plenty. We went this day 19 miles.[2]

We found out the reason why Capt. Clarke did not get the note left at the point, which was that a beaver had cut down and dragged off the pole, on which I had fixed it.

1. The west branch is the Beaverhead River, which the party continued to call the Jefferson; the south branch is Ruby River, their Philanthropy River.

2. They camped on the Beaverhead, a few miles above the mouth of Ruby River, Madison County, Montana.

Friday 9th. We set out at sunrise, and had a fine morning with some dew; proceeded on till 9 o'clock when we halted for breakfast. Here one of the hunters[1] came to us who had been out since the morning the canoes went up the north branch by mistake, and who had that morning proceeded them by land. Here also Captain Lewis and three men[2] started to go on ahead; and at 10 we proceeded on with the canoes. The river is narrow and very crooked, and the valley continues about the same breadth. There is some timber on the mountain on the south side, and white earth or rocks appearing through the pines. At noon we halted for dinner, and hauled out one of the canoes, which had sprung a leak and caulked her.

This morning our commanding officers thought proper that the Missouri should lose its name at the confluence of the three branches we had left on the 30th ultimo.[3] The north branch, which we went up, they called Jefferson; the west or middle branch, Madison; the south branch, about 2 miles up which a beautiful spring comes in, Gallatin! and small river above the forks they called *Philosophy*. Of the 3 branches we had just left, they called the north *Wisdom*, the south *Philanthropy*, and the west or middle fork, which we continued our voyage along, retained the name of Jefferson. We went 14 miles and encamped[4] on the south side. Our two hunters killed but one goat.

1. Shannon, who had been up the Big Hole (Wisdom) River; see Lewis's entry for this day.

2. Lewis took Drouillard, Shields, and McNeal.

3. Lewis gives the names of the Forks of the Missouri in his entry of July 28, 1805, and names the forks of the Jefferson on August 6. If Gass is correct, Lewis's entries could not have been written until August 9 or later. Both Ordway and Whitehouse wrote that the names were decided on "back at the 3 forks," then both crossed out their material relating to the naming of the rivers. It may be that Gass only learned of their decisions about nomenclature on this date, or that McKeehan made some mistake in putting his version together.

4. In Madison County, Montana, a little downstream from the Beaverhead County line and the crossing of Montana Highway 41 over the Beaverhead River.

Saturday 10th.   We set out early in a fine morning, and proceeded on through the valley, until breakfast time, when we came to a place where the river passes through a mountain.[1] This narrow passage is not more than a quarter of a mile in length. At the upper end another valley commences, but not so wide as the one below. There is no timber in the lower end of this valley; and the river very crooked, narrow, and in some places so shallow, that we were obliged to get into the water and drag the canoes along. At 1 o'clock we halted to dine, when a shower of rain came on with thunder and lightening, and continued an hour, during which some hail fell. Two hunters were out to day and killed but one deer. We came 13 miles and encamped[2] on the North side. Here the valley begins to be more extensive.

1. At Beaverhead Rock, Madison County, Montana, near the Beaverhead County line, along Montana Highway 41, about twelve miles southwest of Twin Bridges and fourteen miles northeast of Dillon. See note to Lewis's entry of August 8 and Clark's description of August 10.
2. Above the Madison-Beaverhead county line and near Beaverhead Rock.

Sunday 11th.   This morning was cloudy and we did not set out until after breakfast. Three hunters were sent out and we proceeded on about 3 miles, when we came to a large island, which is 3000 miles from the river Du Bois at the mouth of the Missouri. We therefore called it *3000 mile Island.*[1] We took up the South side of it, and had difficulty in passing the water being shallow. About 2 some rain fell.— Our hunters killed 3 deer and a goat. We went 14 miles and encamped[2] on the North side.

1. The island, in Beaverhead County, Montana, has apparently since disappeared.
2. About halfway between Beaverhead Rock and Dillon, Beaverhead County.

Monday 12th.   We proceeded on at the usual time, and three hunters were again sent out. A few drops of rain fell to day. Our hunters killed 4 deer; and after making 12 miles we encamped[1] on the North side.

1. There is some question about which side of the Beaverhead this camp was on; see Lewis's entry for the date. It was in Beaverhead County, Montana, a few miles below the mouth of Blacktail Deer Creek, north of Dillon, and a few miles downstream from where Interstate Highway 15 crosses the river.

Tuesday 13th. A cloudy morning. We set out early, through rapid water; the river being crooked and narrow, and passed a small creek[1] on the south side. The weather was cold during the whole of this day. We went 16 miles and encamped[2] in a beautiful plain on the South side.

1. Blacktail Deer Creek, which they named McNeal's Creek after Hugh McNeal of the party, reaches the Beaverhead River at Dillon, Beaverhead County, Montana.
2. A few miles southwest of Dillon, and north of where Montana Highway 41 crosses the Beaverhead River and joins Interstate Highway 15.

Wednesday 14th. The morning was clear and cold. We embarked after breakfast; passed a small creek[1] on the north side and a beautiful valley on the same side. Timber is very scarce, and only some few scattering trees along the river. Our hunters[2] came in at noon, who had been out all day yesterday: they had killed 5 deer and a goat. There are a few deer and goats in this part of the country; and otter and beaver in plenty along the river, but no other kind of game that we could discover. There are some fish in the river and trout of a large size, and of the black kind.[3] We went 15 miles and encamped[4] on the South side where we had great difficulty in procuring a sufficient quantity of wood to cook with.

1. The party's Track Creek, apparently later Rattlesnake Creek, Beaverhead County, Montana.
2. The Field brothers.
3. Probably one species, the cutthroat trout, *Oncorhynchus clarki* (formerly *Salmo clarkii*).
4. In Beaverhead County, about ten miles southwest of Dillon and just downstream from Barretts siding.

Thursday 15th. We had a fine morning and proceeded on about 8 o'clock. Having gone 2 miles, we came to the entrance of a mountain, where Captain Lewis and his party on the second day after their departure had taken dinner; and had left 4 deer skins. At the entrance of the mountain there are two high pillars[1] of rocks, resembling towers on each side of the river. The mountains are not very high and do not approach so near the river as some we have passed; they are about a quarter of a mile distant, and the river meanders along between them through the bushes and is not more than 20 yards wide, and about a foot and a half deep. The water is very cold, and severe and disagreeable to the men, who are frequently obliged to wade and drag the canoes. We went 15 miles and encamped[2] on the South side.

1. Rattlesnake Cliffs, so named by the captains, about ten miles southwest of Dillon, Beaverhead County, Montana, near Barretts siding on Interstate Highway 15.
2. Apparently just below the mouth of Gallagher's Creek, Beaverhead County.

Friday 16th. We did not set out till after breakfast, and while here one of the men went out and killed a fine buck. We proceeded through rapid water; the river is very narrow, crooked and shallow. This morning we passed a place where the hills come close to the river for a short distance, and then open on each side of a small valley, which, on account of the great quantity of service berries in it, we called Service-berry valley. We passed over a rapid of about a quarter of a mile, and encamped[1] on the South side, having come 15 miles.

1. In Beaverhead County, Montana, about four miles below the forks of the Beaverhead and Clark Canyon Dam.

Saturday 17th. A fine morning. We proceeded on about 2 miles, and discovered a number of the natives, of the Snake nation, coming along the bank on the South side. Captain Lewis had been as far as the waters of the Columbia river and met them there.[1] We continued on about two miles further to a place where the river forks, and there halted and encamped,[2] after much fatigue and difficulty. The water is so shallow that we had to drag the canoes, one at a time, almost all the way. The distance across from this place to the waters of the Columbia river is about 40 miles, and the road or way said to be good. There were about 20 of the natives came over with Captain Lewis and had the same number of horses. Here we unloaded the canoes, and had a talk with the Indians; and agreed with them that they should lend us some of their horses to carry our baggage to the Columbia river.

1. Lewis's party had crossed the Continental Divide and met the Shoshones on the Lemhi River in Idaho.

2. The junction of Horse Prairie Creek and Red Rock River to form Beaverhead River. Here, in Beaverhead County, Montana, they formed Camp Fortunate just below the forks on a site now under Clark Canyon Reservoir.

Sunday 18th. A fine morning. We bought three horses of the Indians. Captain Clarke and 11 more, with our interpreter and his wife, and all the Indians set out at 11 o'clock to go over to the Columbia.— The Indians went for horses to carry our baggage, and we to search for timber to make canoes for descending the Columbia. We proceeded up the north branch which is the largest and longest branch of Jefferson river,[1] through a handsome valley about 5[2] miles wide. In this we found a number of springs and small branches, but no timber. There is plenty of grass and clover, and also some flax all along it. The Indians all except 5 went on ahead. We travelled 15 miles and encamped[3] close on the branch which is about 5 yards wide. Here we killed two small deer. The country all around is very mountainous, with some few pine trees on the mountains. At three o'clock this afternoon there was a violent gust of wind, and some rain fell. In about an hour the weather became clear, and very cold, and continued cold all night.

1. They went up Horse Prairie Creek, not the main branch of Beaverhead (Jefferson to the party) River, but the best for their purposes, into Shoshone Cove, Beaverhead County, Montana.

2. The numeral in McKeehan's edition is nearly illegible, and the interpretation could be debatable.

3. Near Red Butte, some eight miles west of Grant, Beaverhead County.

Monday 19th. A fine morning, but cold. We proceeded on at 8 o'clock along the valley for six miles, when the hills came more close on the branch, which here divides into three parts or other small branches, and two miles further the principal branch again forks,[1] where the mountains commence with a thick grove of small pines on our left, and large rocks on our right. At 1 o'clock we dined at the head spring of the Missouri and Jefferson river,[2] about 25 miles from the place, where we had left the canoes, and from which the course is nearly west. About 5 miles South of us we saw snow on the top of a mountain, and in the morning there was a severe white frost: but the sun shines very warm where we now are. At three o'clock we proceeded on, and at the foot of the dividing ridge,[3] we met two Indians coming to meet us, and who appeared very glad to see us. The people of this nation instead of shaking hands as a token of friendship, put their arms round the neck of the person they salute. It is not more than a mile from the head spring of the Missouri to the head of one of the branches of the Columbia. We proceeded on through the mountain; passed some fine springs and encamped[4] about 36 miles from our camp, where the canoes are. Here we were met by a number of the natives.

1. Clark's party went up Horse Prairie Creek, Bloody Dick Creek, and Trail Creek, all in Beaverhead County, Montana, heading for Lemhi Pass.

2. The headwaters of Trail Creek, Beaverhead County, just below the Continental Divide. Modern geographers do not agree with the party's view of this spring as "the most distant fountain of the waters of the mighty Missouri" (see Lewis's entry for August 12, 1805).

3. They crossed the Continental Divide at Lemhi Pass, into Lemhi County, Idaho, as Lewis's advance party had done on August 12.

4. That is, from Camp Fortunate, at the forks of the Beaverhead. Clark's camp this day was perhaps on Pattee Creek, Lemhi County.

Tuesday 20th. A fine cool frosty morning. We set out early and travelled about 4 miles, to a village of the Indians on the bank of a branch[1] of the Columbia river, about ten yards wide and very rapid. At this place there are about 25 lodges made of willow bushes. They are the poorest and most miserable nation I ever beheld; having scarcely any thing to subsist on, except berries and a few fish, which they contrive by some means, to take. They have a great many fine horses, and nothing more; and on account of these they are much harassed by other nations. They move about in any direction where the berries are most plenty. We had a long talk with them, and they gave us very unfavourable accounts with respect to the rivers. From which we understood that they were not navigable down, and expect to perform the route by land. Here we procured a guide,[2] and left our interpreters[3] to go on with the natives, and assist Captain Lewis and his party to bring on the baggage.

Captain Clarke and our party proceeded down the river with our guide, through a valley about 4 miles wide, of a rich soil, but almost without timber.— There are high mountains on both sides, with some pine trees on them. We went about 8 miles and encamped[4] on a fine spring. One of our men[5] remained behind at the village to buy a horse, and did not join us this evening. Five of the Indians came and stayed with us during the night. They told us that they were sometimes reduced to such want, as to be obliged to eat their horses.

1. On the Lemhi River, about four miles north of Tendoy, Lemhi County, Idaho.
2. Toby or Old Toby; see the captains' entries for this day.
3. Charbonneau and Sacagawea.
4. On the west side of the Lemhi River, in the vicinity of Baker, Lemhi County, apparently on Withington Creek.
5. Cruzatte.

Wednesday 21st. About 7 o'clock in the morning we continued our journey down the valley, and came to a few lodges of Indians where our guide lives. We remained here about two hours, during which time a number of Indians passed us, going to fish. We proceeded on the way the Indians had gone; and one of our men went with them to the fishing place. The valley becomes very narrow here, and a large branch of the river comes in a short distance below.[1] Here we had to ascend high ground, the bottom is so narrow; and continued on the high ground about six miles when we came again to the river, where a fine branch flows in, the valley 4 or 5 miles wide.[2] In this branch we shot a salmon[3] about 6 pounds weight. We travelled 20 miles this day, and encamped[4] at a place where the mountains come close to the river. In the valley through which we passed and all along the river, there are cherries, currants and other small fruit. The man[5] who had remained behind at the first village and the other who had gone with the Indians to their fishing place, both joined us here. The Indians gave them five salmon to bring to us: and he that had stayed for a horse, brought one with him. At this place the river is about 70 yards wide.

1. Going down the Lemhi River, Clark's party arrived at its junction with the Salmon River, Lemhi County, Idaho. For the party these were the East and West Forks, respectively, of Lewis's River.
2. The valley, not the creek, is four or five miles wide. The stream may be Carmen Creek, their Salmon Run, Lemhi County.

3. An unknown salmon or trout, *Oncorhynchus* sp.

4. On the east side of the Salmon River, Lemhi County, a few miles north of Carmen, and below the mouth of Tower Creek.

5. Cruzatte.

Thursday 22nd.   The morning was fine, with a great white frost. We began our journey at 7 o'clock; and having travelled about a mile, crossed a branch of the river. Here the mountains come so close on the river, we could not get through the narrows, and had to cross a very high mountain about 3 miles over, and then struck the river again, where there is a small bottom and one lodge of the natives in it, gathering berries, haws[1] and cherries for winter food. We soon had to ascend another large mountain, and had to proceed in the same way until we crossed 4 of them, when we came to a large creek,[2] where there is a small bottom and 3 lodges of Indians. Three of our men having gone through the bottom to hunt, came first upon the lodges which greatly alarmed the unhappy natives, who all fell a weeping and began to run off; but the party coming with the guide relieved them from their fears. They then received us kindly, and gave us berries and fish to eat. We remained with them about two hours and gave them some presents. Those of the natives, who are detached in small parties, appear to live better, and to have a larger supply of provisions, than those who live in large villages. The people of these three lodges have gathered a quantity of sunflower seed, and also of the lambs-quarter,[3] which they pound and mix with service berries, and make of the composition a kind of bread; which appears capable of sustaining life for some time. On this bread and the fish they take out of the river, these people, who appear to be the most wretched of the human species, chiefly subsist. They gave us some dried salmon, and we proceeded down the river; but with a great deal of difficulty: the mountains being so close, steep and rocky. The river here is about 80 yards wide, and a continual rapid, but not deep. We went about 15 miles to day, and encamped[4] on a small island, as there was no other level place near. Game is scarce, and we killed nothing since the 18th but one deer; and our stock of provisions is exhausted.

1. Columbia hawthorn, *Crataegus columbiana* How.

2. North Fork Salmon River, the party's Fish Creek; the hamlet of North Fork, Lemhi County, Idaho, is found at the junction today.

3. The sunflower is either common sunflower, *Helianthus annuus* L., or Nuttall sunflower, *H. nuttallii* T. & G., while lambsquarter is *Chenopodium album* L. Lewis provides an extensive discussion of regional ethnobotany for this day, but it differs considerably with Gass. No one but Gass gives this ethnobotanical information on the Shoshone method of making bread. See also Paul Russell Cutright, *Lewis and Clark: Pioneering Naturalists* (Urbana: University of Illinois Press, 1969), 188.

4. Clark's party continued down the Salmon and camped a few miles southwest of North Fork, Lemhi County.

Friday 23rd. We proceeded down the river through dreadful narrows, where the rocks were in some places breast high, and no path or trail of any kind. This morning we killed a goose, and badly wounded a large buck in the water. One of our sergeants[1] is very unwell. We went on 3 miles, when Captain Clarke did not think proper to proceed further with the horses, until he should go forward and examine the pass. So we halted on a small flatt[2] and breakfasted on some fish the natives had given us. Captain Clarke, our guide, and three men then went on. Another Indian who had come on from the last Indian camp remained with us. We had yet seen no timber large enough to make canoes. Two of the hunters went in search of the buck, which had been wounded; and the rest staid at the camp to fish. In the afternoon the men came in from hunting the wounded deer, but could not find him. They killed three prairie hens, or pheasants.[3] At night the sergeant who had been sick, became better. We caught some small fish in the night. The natives take their fish by spearing them; their spears for this purpose are poles with bones fixed to the ends of them, with which they strike the fish. They have but four guns in the nation, and catch goats and some other animals by running them down with horses. The dresses of the women are a kind of shifts made of the skins of these goats and mountain sheep, which come down to the middle of the leg. Some of them have robes, but others none. Some of the men have shirts and some are without any. Some also have robes made of beaver and buffaloe skins; but there are few of the former. I saw one made of ground hog skins.[4]

1. This must be Pryor, since Ordway was with Lewis's party.

2. On the Salmon River, Lemhi County, Idaho, perhaps near the mouth of Dump Creek or of Moose (otherwise Little Moose) Creek. Here Gass was left with the horses and seven other men, including the ailing Pryor.

3. Perhaps sage grouse, *Centrocercus urophasianus.*

4. Probably the yellow-bellied marmot, *Marmota flaviventris,* which Lewis called a "monax" when he saw robes of its skin on August 20, 1805.

Saturday 24th. We had a pleasant morning and some of the men went out to hunt. The river at this place is so confined by the mountains that it is not more than 20 yards wide, and very rapid. The mountains on the sides are not less than 1000 feet high and very steep. There are a few pines growing on them. We caught some small fish to day, and our hunters killed 5 prairie fowls. These were all we had to subsist on. At 1 o'clock Captain Clarke and his party returned, after having been down the river about 12 miles.[1] They found it was not possible to go down either by land or water, without much risk and trouble. The water is so rapid and the bed of the river so rocky, that going by water appeared impracticable; and the mountains so amazingly high, steep and rocky, that it seemed impossible to go along the river by land. Our guide speaks of a way to sea, by going up the south fork of this river,[2] getting on to the mountains that way, and then turning to the south west again. Captain Clarke therefore wrote a letter to Captain Lewis, and dispatched a man on horseback to meet him; and we all turned back up the river again, poor and uncomfortable enough, as we had nothing to eat, and there is no game. We proceeded up about 3 miles, and supperless went to rest for the night.[3]

1. On August 23 Clark reached a point perhaps three miles above Shoup, Lemhi County, Idaho. See the captains' descriptions for that date.

2. This could refer to the Snake River, into which the Salmon flows. However, Gass may mean the North Fork Salmon River, up which the party did indeed travel to reach the Bitterroot valley in Montana, and then travel southwest on the Lolo Trail to the Nez Perce country on the Clearwater River.

3. About two or three miles up the Salmon (northeast) from the spot where Gass had remained with the enlisted men, in Lemhi County, Idaho, a few miles southwest of North Fork and the mouth of the North Fork Salmon River.

Sunday 25th. We set out early and had a fine morning; passed the Indian camp, where they gave us a little dried salmon, and proceeded back again over the mountains. Some hunters went on ahead and about 4 o'clock we got over the four mountains, and encamped[1] in the valley. Two men went to hunt, and all the rest to fish. We soon caught as many small fish as made, with two salmon our guide got from some Indians, a comfortable supper. At dark our hunters[2] came in and had killed but one beaver.

1. At Clark's camp of August 21, 1805, Lemhi County, Idaho, a few miles north of Carmen.
2. Including Shannon.

Monday 26th. We had again a pleasant morning; and four hunters went on early ahead, and one man to look for the horses. We breakfasted on the beaver and a salmon, which had been saved from supper the preceding evening. The man, who had gone for the horses, having returned without finding them, 4 or 5 more went out, and our guide immediately found them. We then about 10 o'clock, proceeded on to the forks,[1] where we found our hunters; but they had killed nothing. So we went up to a small village of the natives, got some fish from them, and lodged there all night.[2]

1. The junction of the Salmon and Lemhi rivers at Salmon, Lemhi County, Idaho.
2. At the fish weir on the Lemhi River, about five miles southeast of Salmon, Lemhi County.

Tuesday 27th. A fine morning with frost; and eight of us went out to hunt. I observed some flax[1] growing in the bottoms on this river, but saw no clover or timothy, as I had seen on the Missouri and Jefferson river.[2] There is a kind of wild sage or hyssop,[3] as high as a man's head, full of branches and leaves, which grows in these bottoms, with shrubs of different kinds. In the evening we all came in again, and had killed nothing but a fish. We got some more from the natives, which we subsisted on. We lodged here again all night, but heard nothing from Captain Lewis.

1. Probably blue flax again.
2. See Lewis's discussion of clover and timothy on August 8.
3. Big sagebrush, *Artemisia tridentata* Nutt; see Lewis's entry of August 10.

Wednesday 28th. The morning again was pleasant, and I went on to the upper village,[1] where I found Captain Lewis and his party buying horses. They had got 23, which with 2 we had, made in the whole 25. I then returned to our camp, a distance of 15 miles, and arrived there late. I found the weather very cold for the season.

1. The Shoshone camp was now apparently about four miles north of Tendoy, Lemhi County, Idaho, near where Kenney Creek joins the Lemhi River.

Thursday 29th. There was a severe white frost this morning. Captain Clarke and all the men except myself and another, who remained to keep camp and prepare packsaddles, went up to Captain Lewis's camp. While I lay here to day, one of the natives shewed me their method of producing fire, which is somewhat curious. They have two sticks ready for the operation, one about 9 and the other 18 inches long: the short stick they lay down flat and rub the end of the other upon it in a perpendicular direction for a few minutes; and the friction raises a kind of dust, which in a short time takes fire. These people make willow basket so close and to such perfection as to hold water, for which purpose they make use of them. They make much use of the sunflower and lambs-quarter seed, as before mentioned; which with berries and wild cherries pounded together, compose the only bread they have any knowledge of, or in use. The fish they take in this river are of excellent kinds, especially the salmon, the roes of which when dried and pounded make the best of soup.

Friday 30th. We remained here all day, and in the evening the whole of the corps came down within a mile of our camp,[1] and remained there all night, being a good place for grass.

1. Above the fish weir, somewhat below Baker, on the Lemhi River, Lemhi County, Idaho.

Saturday 31st. They all came down to our camp, and we proceeded on with 27 horses and one mule. Our old guide after consulting with the rest of the Indians, thought it was better to go along the north side of the Columbia, than on the south side.[1] We therefore proceeded down, the same way Captain Clarke had been before, 30 miles, and then turned up a creek[2] that comes in from the north, and encamped[3] on it about 3 miles and an half from the mouth. Two hunters had gone on ahead this morning, and at night joined us, having killed one deer. The first cost of the articles, which had been given for each horse, did not amount to more than from three to five dollars; so that the whole of them only cost about one hundred dollars.

1. Although this passage is obscure, the "south side" may refer to a proposed route along the Snake River in southern Idaho, with the "north side" referring to the route they actually took, up the North Fork Salmon River, down the Bitterroot River, and along the Lolo Trail to the Clearwater River. See Gass's entry of August 24, 1805, and also Lewis's entry of June 20, 1806. Possibly Gass, or McKeehan, is referring to the Lemhi and the Salmon rivers as the Columbia, and their route along the "north" (actually the east) side on this day.

2. Tower Creek, flowing into the Salmon River, Lemhi County, Idaho.

3. A few miles above the mouth of Tower Creek, Lemhi County.

Sunday 1st Sept. 1805.   We set out early in a fine morning, and travelled on nearly a west course. We found here the greatest quantity and best service berries, I had ever seen before; and abundance of choak-cherries. There is also a small bush grows in this part of the country, about 6 inches high, which bears a bunch of small purple berries. Some call it mountain holly;[1] the fruit is of an acid taste. We are much better supplied with water than I expected; and cross several fine springs among the mountains through which we pass. At noon some rain fell, and the day continued cloudy. About the middle of the day Capt. Clarke's blackman's feet became so sore that he had to ride on horseback. At 3 o'clock we came to a creek,[2] where there was fine grass and we halted to let our horses eat. There are a great number of fish in this creek. After we halted the weather became cloudy, and a considerable quantity of rain fell. We therefore concluded to remain where we were all night, having come this day 18 miles. Our hunters killed a deer, and we caught 5 fish.

1. This may be creeping Oregon grape, *Mahonia repens* (Lindl.) G. Don. Gass is the only expedition journalist to mention this plant.

2. North Fork Salmon River. They camped on the stream, a few miles south of Gibbonsville, Lemhi County, Idaho, near the mouth of Hull Creek.

Monday 2nd.   The morning was cloudy. We set out early; proceeded up the creek, and passed some part closely timbered with spruce and pine. We went on with difficulty on account of the bushes, the narrowness of the way and stones that injured our horses feet, they being without shoes. In the forenoon we killed some pheasants[1] and ducks, and a small squirrel. In the afternoon we had a good deal of rain, and the worst road (if road it can be called) that was ever travelled. The creek is become small and the hills come close in upon the banks of it, covered thick with standing timber and fallen trees; so that in some places we were obliged to go up the sides of the hills, which are very steep, and then down again in order to get along at all. In going up these ascents the horses would sometimes fall backwards, which injured them very much; and one was so badly hurt that the driver was obliged to leave his load on the side of one of the hills. In the low ground there are most beautiful tall straight pine trees of different kinds, except of white pine.[2] Game is scarce; and a small quantity of dried salmon, which we got from the natives is almost our whole stock of provisions. A son of our guide joined us to day and is going on. We went 13 miles and encamped;[3] but some of the men did not come up till late at night.

1. The party noted three species of "pheasants" in the mountains, all species of grouse. They include blue grouse, *Dendragapagus obscurus,* spruce grouse, *D. canadensis,* and Oregon ruffed grouse, *Bonasa umbellus sabini,* now classified under *B. umbellus.*

2. Gass may be using the term "pine" as a generic designation for evergreen conifers. See listings of area trees at the captains' entries of September 9, 14, and 16.

3. Northwest of Gibbonsville, Lemhi County, Idaho, near U.S. Highway 93. See Clark's entry for this day for a discussion of the exact location.

Tuesday 3rd.   The morning of this day was cloudy and cool. Two men went back with a horse to bring on the load, which had been left behind last night; and we breakfasted on the last of our salmon and waited their return. Two hunters were sent on ahead, and on the return of the two men, who had been sent back, we pursued our journey up the creek, which still continued fatiguing almost beyond description. The country is very mountainous and thickly timbered; mostly with spruce pine.[1] Having gone nine miles we halted for dinner, which was composed of a small portion of flour we had along and the last of our pork, which was but a trifle:— Our hunters had not killed any thing. We staid here about two hours, during which time some rain fell, and the weather was extremely cold for the season. We then went on about 3 miles over a large mountain, to the head of another creek and encamped[2] there for the night. This was not the creek our guide wished to have come upon; and to add to our misfortunes we had a cold evening with rain.

1. Clark uses this same term for Engelmann spruce.

2. The party's route and camp this day are particularly "obscure and enigmatic"; see Clark's entry. Those who have studied the matter disagree whether the camp was in Lemhi County, Idaho, or in Ravalli County, Montana, to say nothing of the exact location. Most likely they crossed the Continental Divide near Lost Trail Pass and entered Montana.

Wednesday 4th. A considerable quantity of snow fell last night, and the morning was cloudy. After eating a few grains of parched corn, we set out at 8 o'clock; crossed a large mountain and hit on the creek and small valley, which were wished for by our guide.[1] We killed some pheasants on our way, and were about to make use of the last of our flour, when, to our great joy, one of our hunters killed a fine deer. So we dined upon that and proceeded down a small valley about a mile wide, with a rich black soil; in which there are a great quantity of sweet roots and herbs, such as sweet myrrh,[2] angelica[3] and several other, that the natives make use of, and of the names of which I am unacquainted. There is also timothy grass[4] growing in it; and neither the valley nor the hills are so thickly timbered, as the mountains we had lately passed. What timber there is, is mostly pitch pine.[5] We kept down the valley about 5 miles, and came to the Tussapa band of the Flathead nation of Indians,[6] or a part of them. We found them encamped[7] on the creek and we encamped with them.

Captain Clarke in his letter to his brother, calls them the Oleachshoot band of the Tucknapax. It is of no very great importance, at present, to know by what names the several tribes and bands are distinguished; and Mr. Gass says, that without an interpreter it was very difficult to ascertain them with any degree of certainty.[8]

1. They apparently ascended Saddle Mountain and came down the valley between the forks of Camp Creek, Ravalli County, Montana.

2. Among several *Osmorhiza* species, it may be western sweet cicely, *O. occidentalis* (Nutt.) Torr. None of the other journalists noted this plant. Gass recalls an imported European herb that he knew from the East, sweet cicely, *Myrrhis odorata* Scop. C. Leo Hitchcock, Arthur Cronquist, Marion Ownbey, and J. W. Thompson, *Vascular Plants of the Pacific Northwest* (5 vols. Seattle: University of Washington Press, 1955–69), 3:573–74; L. H. Bailey, *Manual of Cultivated Plants* (Rev. ed. New York: Macmillan, 1949), 752.

3. Of several possible *Angelica* species, it probably is small-leafed angelica, *A. pinnata* Wats. Hitchcock et al., *Vascular Plants of the Pacific Northwest*, 3:517. Another singular sighting by Gass.

4. Another identification unique to Gass. It is alpine timothy, *Phleum alpinum* L. Gass was acquainted with a European timothy species grown in the East, *P. pratense* L. Ibid., 1:645.

5. Pitch pine at this point is probably lodgepole pine, *Pinus contorta* Dougl. ex Loud. (see Clark's entry for September 14, 1805).

6. The Flathead (Salish) Indians. "Tussapa," or Tushepaw, as spelled variously by the captains, represents the Shoshone term *tatasiba*, "the people with shaved heads," meaning the Flatheads. See Clark's entry for this day.

7. In the valley now called Ross, or Ross's, Hole, east of Sula, Ravalli County, probably on Camp Creek near its entrance into the East Fork Bitterroot River.

8. McKeehan refers to Clark's letter to his brother on returning to St. Louis, dated September 23, 1806, which became the first published report of the expedition. As Clark indicated on September 5, 1805, communication with the Flatheads was through several interpreters, probably in this sequence: Toby or his son, Sacagawea, Charbonneau, Labiche, and the captains.

Thursday 5th.   This was a fine morning with a great white frost. The Indian dogs are so hungry and ravenous, that they eat 4 or 5 pair of our mockasons last night. We remained here all day, and recruited our horses to 40 and 3 colts; and made 4 or 5 of this nation of Indians chiefs. They are a very friendly people; have plenty of robes and skins for covering, and a large stock of horses, some of which are very good; but they have nothing to eat, but berries, roots and such articles of food. This band is on its way over to the Missouri or Yellow-stone river to hunt buffaloe. They are the whitest Indians I ever saw.

Friday 6th.   A cloudy morning. We exchanged some of our horses, that were fatigued, with the natives; about 12 o'clock some rain fell; and we prepared to move on. At 1 we started, when the Indians also set out. We proceeded over a mountain to a creek, and went down the creek,[1] our course being northwest; found the country mountainous and poor; and the game scarce. Having travelled about 7 miles we encamped.[2] Four hunters had been out to day, but killed nothing; we therefore supped upon a small quantity of corn we had yet left.

1. The East Fork Bitterroot River, Ravalli County, Montana.

2. In Ravalli County, a few miles northwest of Sula, on the East Fork Bitterroot River, apparently above and opposite Warm Springs Creek.

Saturday 7th.   We set out early in a cloudy cool morning; and our hunters went on as usual. We proceeded down the creek,[1] and in our way we were met by a hunter, who had not come in last night, and who had lost his horse. We halted at 12 o'clock, and one of the hunters killed 2 deer; which was a subject of much joy and congratulation. Here we remained to dine, and some rain fell. On the south of this place there are very high mountains covered with snow and timber, and on the north prairie hills. After staying here 2 hours we proceeded on down the creek; found the country much the same as that which we had passed through in the forenoon; and having travelled about 20 miles since the morning, encamped[2] for the night. The valley is become more extensive, and our creek has increased to a considerable river. Some rain fell in the afternoon, and our hunters killed two cranes[3] on our way.

1. The party went down the East Fork Bitterroot River to the junction with West Fork Bitterroot River (West Fork Clark's River to the party) and on down the Bitterroot (Clark's) River, Ravalli County, Montana.
2. Southwest of Grantsdale, Ravalli County, on the east side of the Bitterroot.
3. Probably a sandhill crane, *Grus canadensis.*

Sunday 8th.   The morning was wet, and we proceeded on over some beautiful plains. One of our hunters had remained out all night, at noon we halted and they all came in, having killed an elk and a deer. At 2 we proceeded on again, and had a cold, wet and disagreeable afternoon, but our road or way was level along the valley. Having travelled 20 miles, we encamped[1] and our hunters came in, one[2] of whom had killed a deer, and another had caught two mares and a colt, which he brought with him.

1. Near Stevensville, Ravalli County, Montana.
2. Drouillard.

Monday 9th.   The morning was fair, but cool; and we continued our journey down the river. The soil of the valley is poor and gravelly; and the high snow-topped mountains are still in view on our left:[1] Our course generally north a few degrees west. We halted at noon: on our way the hunters had killed 3 wild geese; so we have plenty of provisions at present. At 2 o'clock we again went forward, and crossed over the Flathead river,[2] about 100 yards wide, and which we called Clarke's river; passed through a close timbered bottom of about two miles, and again came into beautiful plains. The timber on this bottom is pitch pine. We travelled 19 miles and encamped on a large creek,[3] which comes in from the south. Our hunters this day killed 3 deer.

1. The Bitterroot Mountains, on the Montana-Idaho border.
2. The Bitterroot River. At this time they called it the Flathead River and, as Gass notes, later renamed it Clark's River.
3. This was the party's Travelers' Rest Creek, now Lolo Creek. The camp, which they called Travelers' Rest, is in the vicinity of Lolo, Missoula County, Montana, on the south side of the creek one or two miles above the Bitterroot River.

Tuesday 10th. We remained here all this day, which was clear and pleasant, to let our horses rest, and to take an observation. At night our hunters came in, and had killed 5 deer. With one of the hunters,[1] 3 of the Flathead Indians[2] came to our camp. They informed us that the rest of their band was over on the Columbia river, about 5 or 6 days' journey distant, withpack-horses; that two of the Snake nation had stolen some of their horses, and that they were in pursuit of them. We gave them some presents, and one stayed to go over the mountains with us; the other two continued their pursuit.

1. Colter
2. They were probably Nez Perces, rather than Flatheads (Salish).

Wednesday 11th. This was a fine morning, and we went out to collect our horses, in order to renew our journey, and found all but one. Capt. Lewis had a meridian altitude that gave 46° 48 28.8 north latitude. In the bottoms here, there are a great quantity of cherries. The mountains are not so high, as at some distance back. At 4 o'clock in the afternoon the horse was found, and we proceeded on up the creek[1] nearly a west course, through small bottoms. We went about 6 miles and encamped;[2] when our hunters came in but had killed nothing. The country is poor and mountainous.

1. They headed west on the Lolo Trail, along Lolo (Travelers' Rest) Creek.
2. About one half mile east of Woodman Creek, Missoula County, Montana.

Thursday 12th. We started early on our journey and had a fine morning. Having travelled 2 miles we reached the mountains which are very steep; but the road over them pretty good, as it is much travelled by the natives, who come across to the Flathead river to gather cherries and berries. Our hunters in a short time killed 4 deer. At noon we halted at a branch of the creek,[1] on the banks of which are a number of strawberry vines, haws, and service berry bushes. At 2 we proceeded on over a large mountain, where there is no water, and we could find no place to encamp until late at night, when we arrived at a small branch, and encamped[2] by it, in a very inconvenient place, having come 23 miles.

1. They traveled up Lolo Creek, passing various branches, and nooned at Grave Creek, where the trail forks, in Missoula County, Montana.
2. About two miles east of Lolo Hot Springs, Missoula County, near U.S. Highway 12.

Friday 13th. A cloudy morning. Capt. Lewis's horse could not be found; but some of the men were left to hunt for him and we proceeded on. When we had gone 2 miles, we came to a most beautiful warm spring,[1] the water of which is considerably above blood-heat; and I could not bear my hand in it without uneasiness. There are so many paths leading to and from this spring, that our guide took a wrong one for a mile or two, and we had bad travelling across till we got into the road again. At noon we halted. Game is scarce; and our hunters killed nothing since yesterday morning; though 4 of the best were constantly out, and every one of them furnished with a good horse. While we remained here, Captain Lewis and the men, who had been left with him, came up; but had not found the horse. At 2 o'clock we proceeded on again over a mountain, and in our way found a deer, which our hunters had killed and hung up. In a short time we met with them, and Capt. Lewis sent two back to look for the horse. We passed over a dividing ridge to the waters of another creek, and after travelling 12 miles we encamped[2] on the creek, up which there are some prairies or plains.

1. Lolo Hot Springs, Missoula County, Montana.
2. They crossed the Montana-Idaho state line into Idaho County, Idaho, east of Lolo Pass, and went down Pack Creek (their Glade Creek) to Packer Meadows, camping at the lower end of the meadows.

Saturday 14th. We set out early in a cloudy morning; passed over a large mountain, crossed Stony creek,[1] about 30 yards wide, and then went over another large mountain, on which I saw service-berry bushes hanging full of fruit; but not yet ripe, owing to the coldness of the climate on these mountains: I also saw a number of other shrubs, which bear fruit, but for which I know no names. There are black elder and bore-tree,[2] pitch and spruce pine all growing together on these mountains. Being here unable to find a place to halt at, where our horses could feed, we went on to the junction of Stony creek, with another large creek, which a short distance down becomes a considerable river, and encamped[3] for the night, as it rained and was disagreeable travelling. The two hunters, that had gone back here joined us with Capt. Lewis's horse, but none of the hunters killed any thing except 2 or 3 pheasants; on which, without a miracle it was impossible to feed 30 hungry men and upwards, besides some Indians. So Capt. Lewis gave out some portable soup,[4] which he had along, to be used in cases of necessity. Some of the men did not relish this soup, and agreed to kill a colt; which they immediately did, and set about roasting it; and which appeared to me to be good eating. This day we travelled 17 miles.

1. Apparently Brushy Creek, Idaho County, Idaho; the captains do not use the name "Stony Creek."

2. The elder is either black elderberry, *Sambucus racemosa* var. *melanocarpa* (Gray) McMinn, or blue elderberry, *S. cerulea* Raf. (formerly *S. glauca* Nutt.), depending on Gass's location; the black elderberry is at higher elevations. Hitchcock et al., *Vascular Plants of the Pacific Northwest*, 4:462–63; Lewis's entries for December 1, 1805, and February 7, 1806. McKeehan may have misread Gass since elder and bore-tree are the same species. Gass's folk name apparently comes from the Native American practice of boring the pith out of elderberry stems and using the hollowed tubes for a variety of purposes. Melvin R. Gilmore, *Uses of Plants by the Indians of the Missouri River Region* (1919. Reprint. Lincoln: University of Nebraska Press, 1977), 63.

3. They reached the Lochsa River and went down it, some two miles below the mouth of Colt Killed Creek (formerly White Sand Creek but now restored to Lewis and Clark's name) and camped near Powell Ranger Station, Idaho County.

4. Lewis purchased this soup in Philadelphia; it may have been kept in the form of dry powder or thick liquid. It was a staple army ration of the time.

Sunday 15th. Having breakfasted on colt, we moved on down the river 3 miles, and again took the mountains.[1] In going up, one of the horses fell, and required 8 or 10 men to assist him in getting up again. We continued our march to 2 o'clock when we halted at a spring and dined on portable soup, and a handful of parched corn. We then proceeded on our journey over the mountain to a high point, where, it being dark, we were obliged to encamp.[2] There was here no water; but a bank of snow answered as a substitute; and we supped upon soup.

1. They went down the Lochsa River, parallel to U.S. Highway 12, and then north along Wendover Ridge back up to the Lolo Trail on the heights.

2. They camped in Idaho County, Idaho, on the Lolo Trail, near Forest Road 500.

Monday 16th. Last night about 12 o'clock it began to snow. We renewed our march early, though the morning was very disagreeable, and proceeded over the most terrible mountains I ever beheld. It continued snowing until 3 o'clock P. M. when we halted, took some more soup, and went on till we came to a small stream where we encamped[1] for the night. Here we killed another colt and supped on it. The snow fell so thick, and the day was so dark, that a person could not see to a distance of 200 yards. In the night and during the day the snow fell about 10 inches deep.

1. Near the rock mounds later called Indian Post Office (which none of the journalists mention), perhaps on Moon Creek, Idaho County, Idaho.

Tuesday 17th. Our horses scattered so much last night, that they were not collected until noon, at which time we began our march again. It was a fine day with warm sunshine, which melted the snow very fast on the south sides of the hills, and made the travelling very fatiguing and uncomfortable. We continued over high desert mountains, where our hunters could find no game, nor signs of any except a bear's tract which they observed to day.— At dark we halted at a spring on the top of a mountain; killed another colt, and encamped[1] there all night.

1. Just east of Indian Grave Peak, Idaho County, Idaho.

Wednesday 18th. This was a clear cold frosty morning. All our horses except one were collected early: Six hunters[1] went on ahead; one man[2] to look for the horse; and all the rest of us proceeded on our journey over the mountains, which are very high and rough. About 12 we passed a part where the snow was off, and no appearance that much had lately fallen. At 3 we came to snow again, and halted to take some soup, which we made with snow water, as no other could be found. Here the man, who had been sent for the horse came up, but had not found him. Except on the sides of hills where it has fallen, the country is closely timbered with pitch and spruce pine, and what some call balsam-fir.[3] We can see no prospect of getting off these desert mountains yet, except the appearance of a deep cove on each side of the ridge we are passing along. We remained here an hour and an half, and then proceeded on down a steep mountain, and encamped[4] after travelling 18 miles. We had great difficulty in getting water, being obliged to go half a mile for it down a very steep precipice.

1. Gass, or McKeehan, omits mentioning that Clark headed this advance party, which included Reubin Field and Shields.
2. Willard.
3. Probably grand fir, *Abies grandis* (Dougl.) Lindl. See Lewis's entry of February 6, 1806.
4. About three miles west of Bald Mountain, Idaho County, Idaho.

Thursday 19th. Our hunters did not join us last night, which was disagreeably cold. About 8 this morning we set out, and proceeded on in our way over the mountains; the sun shining warm and pleasant. We travelled a west course, and about 12 o'clock halted at a spring to take a little more soup. The snow is chiefly gone except on the north points of the high mountains. At 2 P. M. we again went on, and descended a steep mountain into a cove on our left hand, where there is a large creek,[1] which here runs towards the east. The hills on each side, along which the trail or path passes, are very steep. One of our horses fell down the precipice about 100 feet,[2] and was not killed, nor much hurt: the reason was, that there is no bottom below, and the precipice, the only bank, which the creek has; therefore the horse pitched into the water, without meeting with any intervening object, which could materially injure him. We made 17 miles this day and encamped[3] on a small branch of the creek. Having heard nothing from our hunters, we again supped upon some of our portable soup. The men are becoming lean and debilitated, on account of the scarcity and poor quality of the provisions on which we subsist: our horses' feet are also becoming very sore. We have, however, some hopes of getting soon out of this horrible mountainous desert, as we have discovered the appearance of a valley or level part of the country about 40 miles ahead.[4] When this discovery was made there was as much joy and rejoicing among the corps, as happens among passengers at sea, who have experienced a dangerous and protracted voyage, when they first discover land on the long looked for coast.

1. Hungery Creek, Idaho County, Idaho; the name was bestowed by Clark on September 18, "as at that place we had nothing to eate."

2. Frazer's horse, fortunately without Frazer.

3. On Hungery Creek, Idaho County.

4. The open prairies in Lewis and Idaho counties, northwest of Grangeville, including Camas and Nez Perce prairies, observed by Clark on September 18.

Friday 20th. It was late before our horses were collected, but the day was fine; and at 9 o'clock we continued our march. Having proceeded about a mile, we came to a small glade, where our hunters had found a horse, and had killed, dressed and hung him up. Capt. Clarke, who had gone forward with the hunters, left a note informing us that he and they intended to go on to the valley or level country ahead, as there was no chance of killing any game in these desert mountains. We loaded the meat and proceeded along the mountains. At noon we stopped and dined, on our horse flesh: here we discovered that a horse, having Capt. Lewis's clothes and baggage on him, had got into the bushes while we were loading the meat, and was left behind. One of the men[1] therefore was sent back, but returned without finding him. Two other men with a horse were then sent back, and we continued our march along a ridge, where there are rocks, that appear to be well calculated for making millstones; and some beautiful tall cedars[2] among the spruce pine. Night came on before we got off this ridge, and we had much difficulty in finding water.[3] The soil on the western side of the mountains appears much better than on the east; and not so rocky. We can see the valley ahead, but a great way off.

1. Lepage.

2. Presumably western redcedar, *Thuja plicata* Donn., which Lewis notes on this date as "arborvita," an alternate name.

3. They camped on a ridge between Dollar and Sixbit creeks, Idaho County, Idaho.

Saturday 21st. The morning was pleasant; but it was late before we got our horses collected. About 10 o'clock we were ready to start; and passed along the ridge with a great deal of difficulty and fatigue, our march being much impeded by the fallen timber. A great portion of the timber through which we passed along this ridge is dead, and a considerable part fallen; and our horses are weak and much jaded. One of them got into a small swamp, and wet a bale of merchandize. About 4 o'clock in the afternoon we got down the mountain to a creek,[1] which runs nearly southwest. This course we suppose is a very good one for us. We went down this creek about a mile, and encamped[2] on it for the night in a small rich bottom. Here we killed a duck and two or three pheasants; and supped upon them and the last of our horse meat. We also killed a wolf and eat it. The hunters did not join us this evening, nor the two men who went to look for the horse.

1. Lolo Creek, Idaho County, Idaho, which the captains called Collins Creek after John Collins of the party.
2. On Lolo Creek, Clearwater County, Idaho; the creek at this point is the Clearwater-Idaho county line.

Sunday 22nd. This was a fine warm day. About 9 o'clock we continued our route over a ridge about a west course, upon the top of which there is a handsome small prairie; where we met one of our hunters[1] with a supply of roots, berries, and some fish, which he procured from another band of the Flathead nation of Indians.[2] Captain Clarke and the hunters had arrived on the 20th at the encampment or lodges of these Indians which are in a beautiful prairie, about 8 or 9 miles from this place.[3] The roots they use are made into a kind of bread; which is good and nourishing, and tastes like that sometimes made of pumpkins.[4] We remained here about an hour and then proceeded on again, down the ridge along a very rough way: and in the evening arrived in a fine large valley,[5] clear of these dismal and horrible mountains. Here our two men overtook us; who had found the lost horse and clothing, but on their way to us lost both the horses. The Indians belonging to this band, received us kindly, appeared pleased to see us, and gave us such provisions as they had. We were at a loss for an interpreter, none of our interpreters being able to understand them. Captain Clarke met us here: he had been over at the river,[6] and found the distance 18 miles and a good road from this place. He thinks we will be able to take the water again at the place he had been at; and where he left 5 hunters,[7] as there was some game about the river in that quarter.

1. Reubin Field, whom they met at Crane Meadows.
2. The Nez Perces, whom Clark's party had met on September 20.
3. Weippe Prairie, Clearwater County, Idaho.
4. Bread made from the root of camas, *Camassia quamash* (Pursh) Greene.
5. They camped at a Nez Perce village on Jim Ford Creek, on Weippe Prairie, about three miles southeast of Weippe, Clearwater County, Idaho.
6. Clark had been to the Clearwater River, Kooskooskee to the party, at a point about a mile above Orofino, Clearwater County.
7. Including Shields.

Monday 23rd. The morning was warm and pleasant. We stayed here some time to procure provisions from the natives, for which we gave them in exchange a number of small articles. The provisions which we got consisted of roots, bread and fish.— Their bread is made of roots which they call comas, and which resemble onions in shape, but are of a sweet taste. This bread is manufactured by steaming, pounding and baking the roots on a kiln they have for the purpose. About 4 o'clock we renewed our journey, and went 2 miles to another small village, through a beautiful rich plain, in which these roots grow in abundance. We halted at the second village all night[1] and got some more provisions. About dark a shower of rain fell.

1. About a mile southwest of Weippe, Clearwater County, Idaho.

Tuesday 24th. The morning was fine, and about nine o'clock we set forward on our march towards the river, all but one man[1] who had gone back to look for the horses and another that had remained at the first village. The men are generally unwell, owing to the change of diet. The valley is level and lightly timbered with pine and spruce trees. The soil is thin except in some small plains, where it is of the first quality. The adjacent country appears much the same; except that on the river it is broken with hills and some rocks. In the valley there are great quantities of service-berry bushes. In the evening we arrived at the camp of our hunters on a river about 100 yards broad, a branch of the Columbia.[2] The natives say it is two days march to the great river. We encamped[3] on a small island with our hunters who had killed 5 deer, which was a very pleasing circumstance to us; as the Indian provisions did not agree with us. Captain Clarke gave all the sick a dose of Rush's Pills, to see what effect that would have. We found some of the natives here upon the river fishing.

1. Colter, according to Clark.
2. Clearwater River, Clearwater County, Idaho.
3. On China Island, about a mile above Orofino, Clearwater County.

Wednesday 25th. A fine, pleasant, warm morning. The hunters went out early and Captain Clarke rode out to see if there were any trees to be found large enough for canoes. The men in general appear to be getting much better; but Captain Lewis is very sick and taking medicine; and myself and two or three of the men are yet very unwell. The climate here is warm; and the heat to day was as great as we had experienced at any time during the summer. The water also is soft and warm, and perhaps causes our indisposition more than any thing else. In the evening Captain Clarke returned to camp, having discovered a place about 5 or 6 miles down the river, where a large branch[1] comes in on the north side that will furnish timber large enough for our purpose. Our hunters also came in, and had killed nothing but a small panther[2] and a pheasant. The man who had remained at the first village came up.

1. The North Fork Clearwater River, meeting the Clearwater River in Clearwater County, Idaho.
2. Mountain lion, *Felis concolor.*

Thursday 26th. The morning was fine; and at 9 o'clock we left our camp; proceeded down the river about 5 miles to the forks; and pitched our camp in a handsome small bottom opposite the point.[1] A number of the natives came down in small canoes, and encamped close to us, for the purpose of fishing; and while we were encamping we saw a small raft coming down the north fork loaded with fish. There appears to be a kind of sheep in this country, besides the Ibex or mountain sheep, and which have wool on.[2] I saw some of the skins, which the natives had, with wool four inches long, and as fine, white and soft as any I had ever seen. I also saw a buffaloe robe with its wool or fur on as fine and soft as that of beaver. Captain Lewis procured this, which we considered a curiosity, in exchange for another buffaloe robe.

This band of the Flatheads have a great many beads and other articles, which they say they got from white men at the mouth of this river; or where the salt water is.[3] They have a large stock of horses. Their buffaloe robes and other skins they chiefly procure on the Missouri, when they go over to hunt, as there are no buffaloe in this part of the country and a very little other game. The most of the men of this band are at present on a war expedition against some nation to the northwest, that had killed some of their people; as we understood in our imperfect communications with them. We arranged our camp and made preparations for making canoes.

1. At the "Canoe Camp," about five miles west of Orofino, Clearwater County, Idaho, on the south bank of the Clearwater River and opposite the mouth of the North Fork Clearwater, the party's Chopunnish River, from their name for the Nez Perces.

2. The mountain goat, *Oreamnos americanus*.

3. The goods had probably been obtained in trade from white seaborne traders by tribes near the mouth of the Columbia and then worked their way inland through intertribal trade. It is certainly not impossible, however, that some Nez Perces had been down to the mouth of the Columbia.

Friday 27th. A fine warm morning. All the men, who were able were employed in making canoes. About 10 o'clock the man[1] came in who had gone to look for the horses, he had found one of them and killed a deer. I feel much relieved from my indisposition.

In the evening the greater part of the war party came in, and some of the principal men came down to our camp. We could not understand what they had done, as we could only converse by signs. Medals were given by the Commanding Officers to 3 or 4 of them as leading men of their nation; and they remained about our camp. The river below the fork is about 200 yards wide; the water is clear as crystal, from 2 to 5 feet deep, and abounding with salmon of an excellent quality. The bottom of the river is stony and the banks chiefly composed of a round hard species of stone.

1. Colter.

Saturday 28th. We had a pleasant morning and all hands, that were able, employed at the canoes.— Game is very scarce, and our hunters unable to kill any meat. We are therefore obliged to live on fish and roots, that we procure from the natives; and which do not appear a suitable diet for us. Salt also is scarce without which fish is but poor and insipid. Our hunters killed nothing to day.

Sunday 29th. A fine day; all our hunters went out, and all the men able to work, were employed at the Canoes. At noon two of our hunters[1] came in with 3 deer; a very welcome sight to the most of us. Five or six of the men continue unwell.

  1. Drouillard and either Collins or Colter, according to Clark.

Monday 30th. The weather continued pleasant; and our hunters killed a deer.

Tuesday 1st Octr. 1805. This was a fine pleasant warm day. All the men are now able to work; but the greater number are very weak. To save them from hard labour, we have adopted the Indian method of burning out the canoes.[1]

  1. It was necessary to make a large hollow in a log in order to form a dugout canoe. This could be done by using hand tools or by burning the wood and removing the charcoal in pieces.

Wednesday 2nd. Two men[1] were sent to the Indian village to purchase some provisions, as our hunters do not kill enough for us to subsist on. And least the Indian provisions should not agree with us, we killed one of our horses.

On the third, the men were employed as usual; on the morning of the fourth there was a white frost, after it a fine day. In the evening our two men returned, with a good supply of such provisions as the natives have.

  1. Frazer and Goodrich, says Clark.

Saturday 5th. Having got pretty well forward in our canoe making, we collected all our horses and branded them, in order to leave them with the Indians, the old chief[1] having promised that they should be well taken care of. In the evening we got two of our canoes into the water.

During the sixth most of the hands were engaged at the other canoes; and we buried our saddles and some ammunition. The morning of the seventh was pleasant, and we put the last of our canoes into the water; loaded them, and found that they carried all our baggage with convenience. We had four large ones; and one small one, to look ahead. About 3 o'clock in the afternoon we began our voyage down the river, and found the rapids in some places very dangerous. One of our canoes sprung a leak. We therefore halted and mended her, after going twenty miles.[2] The hills come close on the river on both sides; where there are a few pine trees. Back from the river the tops of the hills, to a great distance are prairie land; and the country level.

1. Twisted Hair (Walamottinin); see Clark's entries for September 21, 1805.
2. The camp of October 7, 1805, was on the Clearwater River near Lenore, Nez Perce County, Idaho, opposite Jacks Creek.

Tuesday 8th. At 9 o'clock in a fine morning we continued our voyage down the river: passed three islands and several rapids; and at noon stopped at some Indian lodges, of which there are a great many along the river. At 2 we proceeded on again. In the evening, in passing through a rapid, I had my canoe stove, and she sunk. Fortunately the water was not more than waist-deep, so our lives and baggage were saved, though the latter was wet. We halted and encamped[1] here to repair the canoe, after coming 18 miles. At this place there are some lodges of the natives on both sides of the river; a number of whom keep about us, and we get some fish from them. Two chiefs[2] of the upper village joined us here, and proposed to go with us, until we should meet with white people; which they say will be at no great distance.

1. This camp, where they stayed until October 10, is on the north side of the Clearwater, Nez Perce County, Idaho, below the confluence of the Potlatch and Clearwater rivers, a few miles from Spalding.
2. Twisted Hair and Tetoharsky.

Wednesday 9th.   We stayed here during the whole of this day, which was very pleasant, and repaired our canoe. In the evening we got her completed and all the baggage dry. Here our old Snake guide[1] deserted and took his son with him. I suspect he was afraid of being cast away passing the rapids. At dark one of the squaws who keep about us, took a crazy fit, and cut her arms from the wrists to the shoulders, with a flint; and the natives had great trouble and difficulty in getting her pacified. We have some Frenchmen, who prefer dog-flesh to fish; and they here got two or three dogs from the Indians. All the country around is high prairie, or open plains.

1. Toby.

Thursday 10th.   We had a fine morning; embarked early, and passed over some very bad rapids. In passing over one a canoe sprung a leak, but did not sink; though the greater part of the loading was wet; and we had to halt and dry it. We stopped a short distance above the junction of this with another large river. The natives call this eastern branch Koos-koos-ke, and the western Ki-mo-ee-nem.[1] Yesterday evening I had a fit of the ague, and have been very unwell to day; so much so that I am unable to steer my canoe. In about 2 hours we continued our voyage again; we found the southwest branch very large, and of a goslin-green colour. About a mile below the confluence we halted on the north side and encamped[2] for the night, as the wind blew so hard we could not proceed. We came 20 miles to day.

1. They had arrived at the junction of the Clearwater and Snake rivers, on the Washington-Idaho boundary, between Lewiston, Nez Perce County, Idaho, and Clarkston, Asotin County, Washington. The captains first called the Snake the Kimooenem, then called it Lewis's River, considering it the continuation of the Lemhi and Salmon river, to which they had given this name.
2. In Whitman County, Washington, opposite Clarkston.

Chapter Fifty-Three

Winter on the Coast

October 11, 1805–May 1, 1806

Friday 11th. We set out early in a fine morning; proceeded on about 6 miles, and halted at some lodges of the natives, where we got fish and several dogs. We continued here about an hour and then went on. No accident happened to day though we passed some bad rapids. In the evening we stopped at some Indian camps and remained all night, having come 30 miles.[1] Here we got more fish and dogs. Most of our people having been accustomed to meat, do not relish the fish, but prefer dog meat; which, when well cooked, tastes very well.[2] Here we met an Indian of another nation, who informed us we could get to the falls in 4 days: which I presume are not very high as the salmon come above them in abundance.[3] The country on both sides is high dry prairie plains without a stick of timber. There is no wood of any kind to be seen except a few small willows along the shore; so that it is with difficulty we can get enough to cook with. The hills on the river are not very high, but rocky; the rocks of a dark colour. The bed and shores of the river are very stony; and the stones of a round smooth kind.

1. Below Almota Creek and Lower Granite Dam, in Whitman County, Washington, in the vicinity of Almota, on the Snake River. The camps were those of the Nez Perces and perhaps the Palouses.
2. Just two days earlier Gass was attributing a preference for dog over fish only to the French members of the party.
3. A reference to the Celilo Falls, on the Columbia River between Klickitat County, Washington, and Wasco County, Oregon.

Saturday 12th. We had a fine morning and proceeded on early. Two of the Flathead chiefs remained on board with us, and two of their men went with the stranger[1] in a small canoe, and acted as pilots or guides. We saw some ducks and a few geese, but did not kill any of them. There is no four-footed game of any kind near this part of the river, that we could discover; and we saw no birds of any kind, but a few hawks, eagles and crows. At noon we halted, cooked and eat some fish and then proceeded on. The country and river this day is much the same in appearance as what we passed yesterday. A little before sunset we came to a bad rapid, which we did not wish to pass at night, so we encamped[2] above on the north side, having made 30 miles.

Some of the Flathead nation[3] of Indians live all along the river this far down. There are not more than 4 lodges in a place or village, and these small camps or villages are 8 or 10 miles apart: at each camp there are 5 or 6 small canoes. Their summer lodges are made of willows and flags, and their winter lodges of split pine, almost like rails, which they bring down on rafts to this part of the river where there is no timber.

1. Presumably the Indian of "another nation" mentioned by Gass the previous day. Clark does not note his presence with the party.
2. In the vicinity of Riparia, Whitman County, Washington.
3. Gass uses the term "Flathead" in a very general way, as the captains do, to refer to various peoples west of the Continental Divide. The people along the Snake River in this area were Nez Perces and Palouses.

Sunday 13th. This was a cloudy wet morning, and we did not set out till 11 o'clock: we then proceeded with two canoes at a time over the rapids, which are about 2 miles in length; and in about two hours got all over safe. We then went on again and passed more bad rapids, but got through safe. In the afternoon the weather cleared and we had a fine evening. Having gone 23 miles we encamped[1] on the north side. The country continues much the same, all high dry prairie. One handsome creek[2] comes in on the south side.

1. In Franklin County, Washington, opposite or a little below Ayer, Walla Walla County, on the opposite side of the Snake.
2. Tucannon River, Ki-moo-e-nimm Creek to the party, Columbia County, Washington.

Monday 14th. We embarked early in a fine clear cool morning; passed some rapids; and at 11 came to one very bad, but we got over without injury. We saw some geese and ducks this forenoon and killed some of the ducks. About 1 o'clock a canoe hit a rock, and part of her sunk, and a number of the things floated out. With the assistance of the other canoes all the men got safe to shore; but the baggage was wet, and some articles were lost. We halted[1] on an island to dry the baggage, having come 14 miles.

1. On an island downstream from Burr Canyon, Franklin County, Washington, an area now inundated by Lake Sacajawea.

Tuesday 15th. This day was fine, clear and pleasant; and we continued here until the afternoon to dry our baggage that had been wet yesterday. The natives have great quantities of fish deposited on this island.[1] At 3 o'clock P. M. we got all our effects on board and proceeded on. Passed down a beautiful part of the river; and killed some geese and ducks. This river in general is very handsome, except at the rapids, where it is risking both life and property to pass; and even these rapids, when the bare view or prospect is considered distinct from the advantages of navigation, may add to its beauty, by interposing variety and scenes of romantick grandeur where there is so much uniformity in the appearance of the country. We went 18 miles this evening and halted[2] at an old Indian camp on the north side, where we had great difficulty in procuring wood to cook with, as none at all grows in this part of the country.

1. McKeehan's note: "Immense numbers of salmon must ascend the western rivers every summer from the Pacific, and constitute a chief article in the food of the natives. Mr. Mc-Kenzie informs us that in the river, by which he arrived at the ocean, where it empties itself four or five hundred miles northwest of the mouth of the Columbia, the salmon are so abundant, that the natives have a constant and plentiful supply of that excellent fish. He also on his return states, under the date of the 6th and 7th of August, that the salmon in the waters of the Columbia were driving up the current in such large shoals, that the water seemed to be covered with the fins of them."
2. In Franklin County, Washington, just below Fishhook Rapids.

Wednesday 16th. We had a fine morning and embarked early; proceeded on about 3 miles, when one of our canoes run upon some rocks in a rapid, but by unloading another canoe and sending it to her assistance, we got all safe to land, and then continued our voyage. About 1 o'clock we came to another rapid, where all hands carried a load of the baggage by land about a mile, and then took the canoes over the rapids, two at a time, and in that way we got them all down safe and proceeded on. Having gone 21 miles we arrived at the great Columbia river, which comes in from the northwest.[1] We found here a number of natives, of whose nations we have not yet found out the names.[2] We encamped[3] on the point between the two rivers. The country all round is level, rich and beautiful, but without timber.

1. McKeehan's note: "The size, course and appearance of this great river, seem to confirm beyond a doubt the opinion of Mr. McKenzie, who supposed that the large river, into which the branch he descended on the west side of the Rocky Mountains, having its source in these mountains near that of the Unjigah or Peace river, discharges its waters into the large river in latitude about 54° north, and longitude 122° west from London, or 47° west from Philadelphia, was the Columbia. The information he obtained from the Indians respecting this river before he left the Unjigah was, 'that it was a large river and ran towards the mid-day sun; but did not empty itself into the sea.' This opinion of these natives at a distance, with respect to its not emptying itself into the sea, must have arisen chiefly from what they had heard of its course, which is east of south and nearly parallel to the coast of the Pacific, and of the great distance it continued to run in that direction. The accounts he received after arriving at it, *there* called the *Great river,* or Tacoutche Tesse, also stated that it ran towards the mid-day sun; and that at its mouth, as the natives said they had been informed, white people were building houses. Mr. McKenzie having descended the river some distance, prevailed on a chief to delineate a sketch of the country on a large piece of bark; in which he described the river as running to the east of south, receiving many rivers, and every six or eight leagues, encumbered with falls and rapids, some of them very dangerous and six impracticable. He represented the carrying places as of great length, and passing over hills and mountains. He depicted the lands of three other tribes in succession who spoke different languages. Beyond them he knew nothing of the river or country, only that it was still a long way to the sea; and that, as he had heard, there was a lake before they reached the water, which the natives did not drink. 'The more I heard of the river,' says Mr. McKenzie, 'the more I was convinced it could not empty itself into the ocean to the north of what is called the river of the West, so that with its windings the distance must be very great.' It is not improbable that the distance by water, from the place Mr. McKenzie struck this river, to its mouth (supposing it to be the Columbia, Oregan or Great river of the West) is upwards of 1000 miles, and its whole course from its source 1500. By the lake mentioned by the Indian chief is no doubt meant the bay at the mouth of the Columbia, and wide part of the river where the tide water ascends and renders the whole unfit to drink."

The notion of a Great River of the West as a necessary part of a water route across the continent developed well before the actual discovery of the Columbia in 1792. Before Lewis and Clark only the stretch from the mouth to around Portland, Oregon, was known to Europeans. McKeehan is attempting to connect the information provided by Gass with Mackenzie's explorations in the Canadian Rockies. Within the next few years the explorations of David Thompson and Simon Fraser would greatly clarify the geography of the upper Columbia River.

2. They were Yakima and Wanapam Indians; see Gass's entry of October 18.

3. They had arrived at the junction of the Snake and the Columbia rivers, and camped in the point, in Franklin County, Washington, just southeast of Pasco at the site of Sacajawea State Park.

Thursday 17th. We remained here all day for the purpose of taking an observation. We got a number of dogs from the natives. Salmon[1] are very plenty but poor and dying, and therefore not fit for provisions. In the plains are a great many hares and a number of fowls, between the size of a pheasant and turkey, called heath hens or grous.[2] We killed a great many of these fowls which are very good eating. The small river, which we called Flathead and afterwards Clarke's river, is a branch of the Great Columbia, and running a northwest course, falls into it a considerable distance above this place; we therefore never passed the mouth of that river.[3]

The Columbia here is 860 yards wide, and the Ki-moo-ee-nem (called Lewis's river from its junction with the Koos-koos-ke) 475 yards.[4] They are both very low at this place. Our course since we took water has been a few degrees south of west: here the Columbia turns to the east of south.

1. Either coho salmon, *Oncorhynchus kisutch,* or sockeye salmon, *O. nerka.* They were dying after having laid and fertilized their eggs.

2. Probably sage grouse.

3. The captains' concept of Clark's River is in fact a combination of the Bitterroot, Clark Fork, and Pend Oreille rivers, the last of which does flow into the Columbia well above the Snake. See Lewis's entry of September 10, 1805.

4. Gass agrees with Ordway, and Whitehouse disagrees with Clark. Clark gives distances of 960¾ yards for the Columbia and 575 yards for the Snake.

Friday 18th. This was also a fine day and we remained here till after 12 o'clock. In the forenoon our Commanding Officers were employed in getting specimens of the language of the natives, there being three, or part of three, different nations here.[1] They are almost without clothing, having no covering of any account, except some deer skin robes and a few leggins of the same materials. The women have scarce sufficient to cover their nakedness.— Capt. Lewis had an observation at noon, which gave 46° 15 13.9 north latitude. At one we proceeded on down the Great Columbia, which is a very beautiful river. The course is something to the east of south for about 12 miles and then winds round to almost a west course. We passed some islands and a number of the camps of the natives, which appear to be very shy and distant. We went 21 miles and halted close below an Indian camp;[2] where they have thirty canoes; and a great quantity of dried fish.

1. The Yakimas lived in the immediate vicinity of the Snake-Columbia fork, with the Wanapams nearby. Also nearby were the Walulas (Walla Wallas), Umatillas, and Palouses. All spoke languages of the Shahaptian family.
2. Below the mouth of the Walla Walla River, Walla Walla County, Washington, a little above the Washington-Oregon boundary.

Saturday 19th. The morning was clear and pleasant, with some white frost. A number of the natives came to our camp, and our Commanding Officers presented one[1] of them with a medal and other small articles. At 8 o'clock we proceeded on; passed some islands and bad rapids, but no accident happened. We also passed a great many Indian camps. In the whole country around there are only level plains, except a few hills on some parts of the river. We went 36 miles and halted opposite a large Indian camp;[2] and about thirty-six canoe loads of them came over to see us; some of whom remained all night; but we could not have much conversation with them as we did not understand their language.[3] They are clothed much in the same manner with those at the forks above. The custom prevails among these Indians of burying all the property of the deceased, with the body. Amongst these savages when any of them die, his baskets, bags, clothing, horses and other property are all interred: even his canoe is split into pieces and set up round his grave.

1. Yelleppit, chief of the Walula Indians.
2. Perhaps on Blalock Island, between Irrigon and Boardman, Morrow County, Oregon.
3. Probably Umatilla Indians living in the vicinity of Plymouth, Benton County, Washington, but possibly Cayuses.

Sunday 20th. A fine clear frosty morning. We set out early; passed along a handsome part of the river; saw some pelicans and gulls. And as the shores are lined with dead salmon, there are abundance of crows and ravens.[1] Vast quantities of these fish die at this time of the year. At noon we came to an Indian camp on the point of a large island, where we stopped and got some fish and other provisions. We here saw some articles which shewed that white people had been here or not far distant during the summer. They have a hempen seine and some ash paddles which they did not make themselves. At 1 o'clock we proceeded on again, went 42 miles, and encamped[2] without any of the natives being along, which is unusual on this river. We could not get a single stick of wood to cook with; and had only a few small green willows.

1. Perhaps a subspecies of the common crow, *Corvus brachyrhynchos hesperis.* The raven is *Corvus corax.*

2. Probably in the vicinity of Roosevelt, Klickitat County, Washington.

Monday 21st. We continued our voyage at an early hour, and had a fine morning. At 10, we came to the lodges of some of the natives,[1] and halted with them about 2 hours. Here we got some bread, made of a small white root,[2] which grows in this part of the country. We saw among them some small robes made of the skins of grey squirrels,[3] some racoon skins,[4] and acorns,[5] which are signs of a timbered country not far distant. Having proceeded on again, we passed several more lodges of Indians; and through two very rocky rapid parts of the river with great difficulty. We went 32 miles and encamped at some Indian lodges,[6] where we procured wood from the natives to cook with.

1. Perhaps Methow Indians, living in Klickitat County, Washington, between Roosevelt and Blalock.

2. Probably camas.

3. Perhaps western gray squirrel, *Sciurus griseus.*

4. Raccoon, *Procyon lotor.*

5. Clark reports that they were acorns of the Oregon white oak, *Quercus garryana* Dougl. ex. Hook.

6. In Klickitat County, Washington, in the vicinity of John Day Dam.

Tuesday 22nd. The morning was fine and we went on early, and saw a great number of ducks,[1] geese and gulls. At 10 o'clock we came to a large island, where the river has cut its way through the point of a high hill. Opposite to this island a large river[2] comes in on the south side, called by the natives the Sho-sho-ne or Snake-Indian river; and which has large rapids close to its mouth. This, or the Ki-moo-ee-nem, is the same river, whose head waters we saw at the Snake nation.[3]

The natives are very numerous on the island and all along the river.[4] Their lodges are of bulrushes and flags,[5] made into a kind of mats, and formed into a hut or lodge.

About 3 miles lower down we came to the first falls or great rapids;[6] and had 1300 yards of a portage over bad ground. All our baggage was got over this evening and we encamped with it;[7] but are not certain whether we can take our canoes by water. Our voyage to day, to the head of the rapids or falls was 18 miles.

1. Probably including the mallard, *Anas platyrhynchos,* and canvasback, *Aythya valisineria.*

2. The Deschutes River, on the boundary of Sherman and Wasco counties, Oregon. The captains first called it Clark's River and later Towanahiooks.

3. Evidently the reference to "Snakes" left Gass, or McKeehan, confused. Snake Indians on the Deschutes River would be Paiutes. The Snakes on the Lemhi and Salmon rivers in Idaho, which with the Snake River form the party's Lewis's River, were Shoshones.

4. In this area were the party's Eneeshurs, perhaps the later Tenino Indians, and some Wanapams.

5. Bulrushes may be western bulrush, *Scirpus acutus* Muhl. ex Bigel., or tule, softstem bulrush, *S. validus* Vahl. Flag is probably common cat-tail, *Typha latifolia* L., however, beargrass, *Xerophyllum tenax* (Pursh) Nutt., was often an important component of native mats in the area.

6. Celilo Falls near Wishram, Klickitat County, Washington, and Celilo, Wasco County, Oregon, now inundated by The Dalles Dam.

7. Below the falls near Wishram, Klickitat County, where they remained until October 24.

Wednesday 23rd. A pleasant day. At 9 o'clock in the forenoon all hands, but three left to keep camp, went up and took the canoes over to the south side; as the natives said that was the best side of the river to take them down. Here we had to drag them 450 yards round the first pitch which is 20 feet perpendicular. We then put them into the water and let them down the rest of the way by cords. The whole height of the falls is 37 feet 8 inches, in a distance of 1200 yards. In the evening we got all our canoes safe down to the encampment on the north side. The natives are very numerous about these falls, as it is a great fishing place in the spring of the year. The country on both sides of the river here is high, and the bluffs rocky. Captain Lewis had an observation, which made the latitude of this place 45° 42 57. 3 North. We got several dogs from these Indians, which we find strong wholesome diet. The high water mark below the falls is 48 feet, and above only 10 feet four inches from the surface of the water: so that in high water there is nothing but a rapid, and the salmon can pass up without difficulty. The reason of this rise in the water below the falls is, that for three miles down, the river is so confined by rocks (being not more that 70 yards wide) that it cannot discharge the water, as fast as it comes over the falls, until what is deficient in breadth is made up in depth. About the great pitch the appearance of the place is terrifying, with vast rocks, and the river below the pitch, foaming through different channels.

Thursday 24th. We had a fine morning and proceeded on early; found the water very rapid below the falls; and having gone 4 miles below the narrows, came to other narrows still more confined and the rocks higher.[1] At the head of these narrows we halted about 2 o'clock at a great Indian village, and remained there all night.[2] We got fish and dogs from the natives, and some berries, different from any we got before, some call them cranberries;[3] whether of the real kind or not I am not certain. In our way down to day we saw a great many sea otters[4] swimming in the river, and killed some, but could not get them as they sunk to the bottom. This village has better lodges than any on the river above; one story of which is sunk under ground and lined with flags mats: The upper part about 4 feet above ground is covered over with cedar bark, and they are tolerably comfortable houses.

1. The Short, or Little, Narrows, and the Long Narrows, which they would pass the next day, together constitute The Dalles of the Columbia River, above the town of The Dalles, Wasco County, Oregon. The narrows are now concealed beneath the waters of The Dalles Dam.

2. In Klickitat County, Washington, in the vicinity of Horsethief Lake State Park. The Indians were Wishram-Wasco Chinookans.

3. Probably American cranberrybush, *Viburnum trilobum* Marsh., restricted to the Columbia gorge in this region.

4. Not the sea otter, *Enhydra lutris,* which never leaves salt water, but the harbor seal, *Phoca vitulina richardii.* The captains later became aware of their error in this matter.

Friday 25th.   We found there were bad rapids in the narrows and therefore carried over part of our baggage by land, about three quarters of a mile; and then took the canoes over, one at a time. In going over one of them filled with water, on account of which we were detained three hours. The rapids continued 3 or 4 miles, when the river became more placid. At night we came to a place where there is a considerable quantity of timber on the hills; both oak and pine, and encamped[1] at the mouth of a creek on the south side. The natives about here are, or pretend to be, very uneasy, and say the Indians below will kill us. We purchased from them a quantity of dried pounded fish, which they had prepared in that way for sale. They have six scaffolds of a great size for the purpose of drying their fish on.

1. At the party's "Fort Camp" or "Fort Rock Camp," at the mouth of Mill Creek at the town of The Dalles, Wasco County, Oregon, where they stayed until October 28.

Saturday 26th.   A fine morning. We hauled up all our canoes to dress and repair them, as they had been injured in passing over the portage, round the falls. Some hunters went out and killed 6 deer and some squirrels. In the afternoon about 20 of the natives came to our camp (among whom were the head chiefs of the two villages about the falls) who had been out hunting when we passed down. The Commanding Officers gave medals to the chiefs, and some other small articles; and they appeared satisfied and some remained with us all night.

Sunday 27th.   This was a fine clear morning, but the wind blew very hard up the river, and we remained here all day. This is the first hunting ground we have had for a long time, and some of our men went out. Part of the natives remained with us; but we cannot find out to what nation they belong. We suppose them to be a band of the Flathead nation, as all their heads are compressed into the same form;[1] though they do not speak exactly the same language, but there is no great difference, and this may be a dialect of the same.[2] This singular and deforming operation is performed in infancy in the

162

following manner. A piece of board is placed against the back of the head extending from the shoulders some distance above it; another shorter piece extends from the eye brows to the top of the first, and they are then bound together with thongs or cords made of skins, so as to press back the forehead, make the head rise at the top, and force it out above the ears. In the evening our hunters came in and had killed 4 deer and some squirrels. The wind blew hard all this day.

1. Gass here notices the practice of head deformation common among the peoples of the lower Columbia and the Northwest Coast. See Clark's entries of October 17 and 26.

2. The Dalles area marked the dividing line between the Shahaptian language (upstream) and the Chinookan language (downstream). The Wishrams lived on the north side of the Columbia, and the closely allied Wascos on the south side; both spoke Chinookan languages. It is possible that these people were trying to communicate in Chinook trade jargon. See Clark's entry of this day.

Monday 28th. Just before day light there was a shower of rain; but at sun rise the morning was fine and clear. At 8 o'clock we embarked, went about 4 miles, and halted at a small village of the natives[1] and got some dogs from them. Here we stayed about an hour and proceeded on again for about a mile, when we were compelled to stop on account of the wind, which blew so hard ahead that we were unable to continue our voyage. In the course of the day there were some showers of rain. In the evening one of the men went out and killed a fine deer. We were in good safe harbour and remained there all night,[2] accompanied by the natives.

1. The party's Chiluckittequaws (variously spelled), probably Wishram-Wascos.

2. Clark, unlike Gass, called it "a verry Bad place." It was in Wasco County, Oregon, a few miles below The Dalles, in the vicinity of Crates Point, and above Rowena.

Tuesday 29th. We embarked early in a cloudy morning; passed high hills on both sides of the river, on which there was pine timber; and some birch[1] on the banks of the river. At breakfast time we stopt at a small village of the natives[2] and purchased some more dogs: then proceeded on; passed a number more Indian camps, and a high mountainous country on both sides. In the evening we discovered a high mountain to the south,[3] not more than five miles off, covered with snow. We have here still water; and the breadth of the river is from three quarters to a mile. We went 23 miles and encamped[4] at a small village on the north side.

1. Probably water birch, *Betula occidentalis* Hook.
2. Another village of Chiluckittequaws, Klickitat County, Washington, above Lyle.
3. Mt. Hood, of the Cascade Range in Hood River County, Oregon. The captains called it *Timm*, or Falls Mountain, following the Indians. See Gass's entry of November 3.
4. In Skamania County, Washington, a little above the Little White Salmon River, the captains' Little Lake Creek. The people in the vicinity were White Salmon and Klickitat Indians.

Wednesday 30th.   The morning was cloudy; the river and country we found much the same as yesterday. At noon we stopped to dine and one of the men[1] went out and killed a large buck. A number of fine springs come down the hills on the South side; and we passed a small river on the north.[2] In the evening we came to the head of falls, where there is a large Indian village.[3] On our way down we saw a great many swans,[4] geese and ducks; and a number of sea otter. There are some small bottoms along the river, with cotton wood[5] on them, and on the Banks of the river some white oak, ash and hazlenut.[6] At a distance there are ponds which abound with geese and ducks. It rained hard all day, and we came only 15 miles.

1. Shields.
2. The captains named it Cruzatte's River, after Pierre Cruzatte of the party; it is now Wind River, Skamania County, Washington.
3. They camped here, just above the Cascades of the Columbia River, on an island in Skamania County, nearly opposite Cascade Locks, Hood River County, Oregon. The nearby Indians were Yehuhs, a Chinookan-language people of whom little is known.
4. Probably Lewis and Clark's whistling swan, now the tundra swan, *Cygnus columbianus*.
5. Probably black cottonwood, *Populus trichocarpa* T. & G.
6. Oregon ash, *Fraxinus latifolia* Benth., and hazelnut, *Corylus cornuta* Marsh. var. *californica* (DC.) Sharp.

Thursday 31st.   The morning was cloudy. We unloaded our canoes and took them past the rapids, some part of the way by water, and some over rocks 8 or 10 feet high. It was the most fatiguing business we have been engaged in for a long time, and we got but two over all day, the distance about a mile, and the fall of the water about 25 feet in that distance.

Friday 1st Nov. 1805.   We had a cool frosty morning. We carried down our baggage before breakfast as we could not go into the water, without uneasiness on account of the cold. In the forenoon we took down the other two canoes. A number of the natives with 4 canoes joined us here[1] from above. Their canoes were loaded with pounded salmon, which they were taking down the river to barter for beads and other articles.

1. They camped in Skamania County, Washington, above Bonneville Dam and near the communities of Fort Rains and North Bonneville.

Saturday 2nd.   There is here a small rapid below the falls, where the men had to carry part of the baggage across a portage of two miles and an half, while the rest took down the canoes. At 12 o'clock we proceeded on again; passed a narrow rapid part of the river of about 8 miles, the hills on both sides are very high, and a number of fine springs flowing out of them, some of which fall 200 feet perpendicular. The hills are mostly solid rock. On our way we passed two Indian lodges. At the end of eight miles, the river opens to the breadth of a mile, with a gentle current. We came 23 miles, and encamped[1] at a high peak resembling a tower of the south side. The country here becomes level, and the river broader. One of the Indian canoes remained with us and the other three went on. On our way and at camp we killed 17 geese and brants.[2]

1. In the vicinity of Latourell, within Rooster Rock State Park, Multnomah County, Oregon.
2. *Branta bernicla.*

Sunday 3rd.   The morning was foggy: one of the men[1] went out and killed a fine buck. At 9 we proceeded on, but could not see the country we were passing, on account of the fog, which was very thick till noon when it disappeared, and we had a beautiful day. We at that time came to the mouth of a river[2] on the south side, a quarter of a mile broad, but not more than 6 or 8 inches deep, running over a bar of quicksand. At this place we dined on venison and goose; and from which we can see the high point of a mountain covered with snow, in about a southeast direction from us. Our Commanding Officers are of opinion that it is Mount Hood, discovered by a Lieutenant of Vancoover, who was up this river 75 miles.[3] The river that falls in here has two mouths, through which it drives out a considerable quantity of sand into the Columbia. Opposite the lower mouth there is a handsome island. At 2 o'clock we proceeded on, and passed another island. The country on both sides appears level and closely timbered: on the river the timber is cotton wood, maple[4] and some ash; and back from it mostly spruce pine. We made 13 miles and encamped[5] on a large island, in which is a large pond full of swans, geese and ducks. On our way and here we killed some of each kind. At night, Captain Lewis had a small canoe carried over to the pond in order to hunt by moon light; but the party did not happen to have good luck, having killed only a swan and three ducks.

1. Collins, according to Clark.

2. Sandy River, Multnomah County, Oregon; Quicksand River to the party.

3. Mt. Hood, Hood River County, Oregon, was named for British Admiral Sir Samuel Hood by Lieutenant William Robert Broughton of George Vancouver's seaborne exploring expedition in 1792. They passed his farthest point on the river this day.

4. Probably bigleaf maple, *Acer macrophyllum* Pursh.

5. Either Government or McGuire islands, opposite and above Portland, Multnomah County.

Monday 4th. A fine morning. We embarked early; passed two large is-lands,[1] and a beautiful part of the river. The tide raised the water last night 2 feet. We went about 7 miles and came to a large Indian village,[2] where they informed us that in two days we should come to two ships with white people in them. The Indians here have a great deal of new cloth among them, and other articles which they got from these ships. We got some dogs and roots from the natives. The roots are of a superior quality to any I had before seen: they are called whapto;[3] resemble a potatoe when cooked, and are about as big as a hen egg. Game is more plenty here than up the river, and one of the men killed a deer this morning. At this camp of the natives they have 52 canoes, well calculated for riding waves. We proceeded on, and passed some handsome islands,[4] and down a beautiful part of the river. We also passed a number of Indian lodges; and saw a great many swans, geese, ducks, cranes, and gulls. We went 28 miles and encamped[5] on the north side. In the evening we saw Mount Rainy[6] on the same side. It is a handsome point of a mountain, with little or no timber on it, very high, and a considerable distance off this place.

1. The party's Diamond and Image Canoe islands; the first is apparently later Government and McGuire islands, the second Hayden and Tomahawk islands.

2. Clark calls them Shahalas; they were Watlala Indians, speakers of an Upper Chinookan language. The village, now long destroyed, was within the limits of modern Portland, Multnomah County, Oregon.

3. Wapato, *Sagittaria latifolia* Willd.

4. Including various small islands and the large Sauvie Island, the party's Wappato Island.

5. More correctly on the east side of the Columbia, probably near Salmon Creek, Clark County, Washington.

6. Not Mt. Rainier but Mt. St. Helens, Skamania County, Washington.

Tuesday 5th. We embarked very early. Some rain fell last night about 2 o'clock, and the morning was cloudy. We passed several handsome islands, generally near the shore, on the one side or the other of the river. The county on both sides is somewhat higher than what we passed yesterday, and closely covered with spruce timber. The bottoms are large, covered with cotton wood, maple, and the like kinds of wood. We passed a great many Indian camps, their lodges made chiefly of poles and cedar bark. At noon we stopped about an hour at an island,[1] and some of the men went out and killed nine brants and a swan. Three of the brants[2] were quite white except the points of their wings, which were black. We proceeded on in the afternoon, during which some rain and a little hail fell; went 31 miles and encamped[3] on the north side. Here the tide rises and falls 4 feet.

1. The captains called it E-lal-lar or Deer Island; it is still Deer Island, Columbia County, Oregon.

2. Snow goose, *Chen caerulescens*.

3. Perhaps near Prescott, Columbia County, Oregon.

Wednesday 6th. We set out early in a cloudy morning after a disagreeable night of rain. Saw a number of the natives, going up and down the river in canoes. Also passed some of their lodges. The Indians in this part of the country have but few horses, their intercourse and business being chiefly by water. The high land comes more close on the river in this part. Having gone 29 miles we encamped[1] on the south side.

1. In southwestern Wahkiakum County, Washington (see Clark's entry of this day).

Thursday 7th. We set out again early in a foggy morning; went about 6 miles and came to an Indian camp,[1] where we got some fresh fish and dogs. The dress of the squaws here is different from that of those up the river; it consists of a long fringe made of soft bark, which they tie round the waist, and which comes down almost to their knees;[2] and of a small robe, made out of small skins cut into thongs, and wove somewhat like carpetting. We remained here about 2 hours and then proceeded on. At this place the river is about 3 miles wide, with a number of small islands, and the country broken. In the evening we came to a part of the river, where it is 5 miles broad. We went 34 miles and encamped[3] on the south side at the mouth of a fine spring.

1. A Wahkiakum Indian village in Wahkiakum County, Washington.
2. This same garment also attracted the attention of the captains and prompted Lewis's detailed description of January 19, 1806, apparently copied by Clark under the present date, November 7, 1805, presumably because this was where they first noticed this style.
3. Gass's "south side" is misleading. They camped opposite Pillar Rock, Wahkiakum County, between Brookfield and Dahlia.

Friday 8th. We embarked early. The morning was cloudy, and there was a hard wind from the east. We went about 5 miles and came to a bay[1] 12 or 14 miles wide. We had to coast round it, as the wind raised the waves so high we could go no other way. We halted and dined at a point on the north side of the bay, where a small river comes in.[2] We again proceeded on coasting, till we came to a point of land where the bay becomes much narrower; and the water quite salt. The waves here ran so high we were obliged to lie to, and let the tide leave our canoes on dry ground. This point we called Cape Swell;[3] and the bay above, Shallow Bay, as there is no great depth of water. In crossing the bay when the tide was out, some of our men got sea sick, the swells were so great. In it there are a great many swans, geese, ducks and other water fowls. The whole of this day was wet and disagreeable; and the distance we made in a straight line, was not more than 9 miles; though the distance we coasted was above 20 miles.

    1. Grays Bay, in Pacific and Wahkiakum counties, Washington. The party's name for it was Shallows Bay.
    2. Grays River or Deep River, Wahkiakum County.
    3. They camped here until November 10, either near the Pacific-Wahkiakum county line, or farther west near Frankfurt, Pacific County, and Grays Point.

Saturday 9th.   The morning was windy, rainy and disagreeable, and we were obliged to remain at Cape Swell all day, and unload our canoes to prevent them from sinking; notwithstanding some of them did sink when the tide came in at noon. We had no fresh water, except what rain we caught by putting out our vessels. We remained here all night, and the rain continued.

Sunday 10th.   We had a rainy morning, but the wind was not so high as it had been yesterday; and we set out from Cape Swell, coasted along 8 miles, passed some high cliffs of sandy rocks, and then came to a point; where we found the swells so high, the wind having risen, that we could not proceed; so we had to return back about a mile to get a safe harbour. Here we dined on some pounded salmon, that we had procured from the Indians; and unloaded our canoes. After we had been here about 2 hours, it became more calm, and we loaded the canoes again, but could not get round the point, the swells were still so high; we therefore put too at a branch of fresh water, under high cliffs of rocks and unloaded again.[1] Here we scarcely had room to lie between the rocks and water; but we made shift to do it among some drift wood that had been beat up by the tide. It rained hard all night, and was very disagreeable. While on our way down today, we saw some porpoises,[2] sea otter and a great many sea gulls.[3] The water is become very salt.

    1. They remained here until November 15, on the eastern side of Point Ellice, Pacific County, Washington, east of the Astoria Bridge near Melgar.
    2. Perhaps the harbor porpoise, *Phocoena phocoena.*
    3. Any of the number of species of *Larus.*

Monday 11th.   The morning was wet and the wind still blowing, so that we could not proceed; we therefore built large fires and made our situation as comfortable as possible, but still bad enough, as we have no tents, or covering to defend us, except our blankets and some mats we got from the Indians, which we put on poles to keep off the rain. It continued raining and blowing all day; and at 4 o'clock in the afternoon the tide was so high that we had to leave our lodges, until it got lower in the evening. Some of the men went about 40 perches[1] up the river and caught 15 fine large fish.

1. A perch is a measure of land which varies locally but can be taken as 5½ yards.

Tuesday 12th.   A cloudy wet morning, after a terrible night of rain, hail, thunder and lightening. We thought it best to move our camp, and fixed our canoes and loaded them with stones to keep them down. We went about the eighth of a mile from this place, and fixed ourselves as well as we could, and remained all night. The rain still continued, and the river remained very rough.

Wednesday 13th.   This was another disagreeable rainy day, and we remained at camp, being unable to get away. At 9 o'clock in the forenoon it became a little more calm than usual; and 3 men[1] took a canoe, which we got from the Indians of a kind excellent for riding swells, and set out to go to the point on the sea shore, to ascertain whether there were any white people there, or if they were gone.

1. Colter, Willard, and Shannon, according to Clark. On the Indian canoes, see especially Lewis's entry of February 1, 1806.

Thursday 14th.   We expected last night to have been able to proceed on this morning, but the rain continued, and the river still remained rough; and we are therefore obliged to lie by. About noon one of the 3 men who had gone in the canoe,[1] returned having broke the lock of his gun: but the other two went on by land, as the swells ran so high that they could not possibly get the canoe along. About the same time some Indians in a canoe came up the river, and had stolen a gig from the men; but the one who returned got it from them again when he came up. In the evening Captain Lewis with 4 men[2] started by land to see if any white people were to be found. The rest remained in camp; and the weather continued wet, and the most disagreeable I had ever seen.

1. Colter, reports Clark.
2. Drouillard, Joseph and Reubin Field, and Frazer, says Clark.

Friday 15th. This morning the weather appeared to settle and clear off, but the river remained still rough. So we were obliged to continue here until about 1 o'clock, when the weather became more calm, and we loaded and set out from our disagreeable camp; went about 3 miles, when we came to the mouth of the river, where it empties into a handsome bay.[1] Here we halted on a sand beach, formed a comfortable camp,[2] and remained in full view of the ocean, at this time more raging than pacific. One of the two men who first went out came to us here,[3] the other had joined Captain Lewis's party. Last night the Indians had stolen their arms and accoutrements, but restored them on the arrival of Captain Lewis and his men in the morning.

1. They rounded Point Ellice and entered Baker Bay, Pacific County, Washington, which the captains called Haley's Bay, after a sea captain–trader who used the bay as an anchorage, and whom the Indians had described as their favorite trader. See Clark's entries for November 6, 1805, and January 1, 1806.
2. Southeast of Chinook Point, on the east side of Baker Bay, Pacific County, and west of McGowan. The main party remained here until November 25, with perhaps a short move on November 16 (see Clark's entry for November 16, 1805).
3. Shannon, accompanied by five Indians; Willard had joined Lewis's party.

Sunday 16th. This was a clear morning and the wind pretty high. We could see the waves, like small mountains, rolling out in the ocean, and pretty bad in the bay.[1]

We are now at the end of our voyage, which has been completely accomplished according to the intention of the expedition, the object of which was to discover a passage by the way of the Missouri and Columbia rivers to the Pacific ocean; notwithstanding the difficulties, privations and dangers, which we had to encounter, endure and surmount.

This morning 5 of the men went out to hunt; and about 3 o'clock all came in but one. They had killed 2 deer, 9 brants, 2 geese, 1 crane, and 3 ducks.

The day being clear we got all our baggage dried, and in good order; and quietly rested until Capt. Lewis and his party should return.[2]

1. Here Gass, or rather McKeehan, begins a new chapter, chapter 16, in the middle of the same day's entry, contrary to his usual procedure. The next paragraph is a general statement about the accomplishment of the objective of the expedition, but then the text returns to the daily affairs of November 16.

2. In both his entries for this day Clark seems to say explicitly that the main party moved two miles on this day. Gass, like Ordway and Whitehouse, gives no indication of such a move.

Sunday 17th.   We had a fine pleasant clear morning, and 6 hunters went out. About noon they all came in; but the hunter who remained out last night, did not return. He had killed 2 deer, and the other men brought them in with some brants and a deer they had killed. About the same time Capt. Lewis, and his party returned. They had been round the bay, and seen where white people had been in the course of the summer: but they had all sailed away.[1] Captain Lewis and his party killed a deer and some brants. In the evening the remaining hunter came in and had killed another deer.

There are but few Indians settled down about the seashore;[2] their dress is similar to that of some of those above. The women have a kind of fringe petticoats, made of filaments or tassels of the white cedar bark wrought with a string at the upper part, which tied round the waist. These tassels or fringe are of some use as a covering, while the ladies are standing erect and the weather calm; but in any other position, or when the wind blows, their charms have but a precarious defence.

A number of both sexes keep about our camp; some have robes made of muskrat[3] skins sewed together, and I saw some of loon-skins.[4] Their diet is chiefly fish and roots.

Memorandum[5]

Of the computed distance in miles to the furthest point of discovery on the Pacific Ocean, from the place where the canoes were deposited near the head of the Missouri, which from its mouth is	3096
From the place of deposit to head spring—	24
To first fork of the Sho-sho-ne river—	14

To first large fork down the river—	18
To forks of the road at mouth of Tour creek	14
To fishing creek, after leaving the river—	23
To Flathead, or Clarke's river at Fish camp	41
To the mouth of Travellers-rest creek—	76
To the foot of the great range of mountains, east side	12
To ditto ditto ditto west side	130
To the Flat-head village in a plain—	3
To the Koos-koos-ke river—	18
To the Canoe camp, at the forks—	6
To the Ki-moo-ce-nem—	60
To the Great Columbia, by Lewis's river—	140
To the mouth of the Sho-sho-ne, or Snake river	162
To the Great Falls of Columbia—	6
To the Short Narrows—	3
To the Long ditto—	3
To the mouth of Catarack river, north side	23
To the Grand Shoot, or Rapids—	42
To the Last Rapids, or Strawberry island	6
To the mouth of Quicksand river, south side	26
To Shallow Bay, at salt water—	136
To Blustry Point, on north side—	13
To Point Open-slope, below encampment	3
To Chin-Ook river, at bottom of Haley's Bay	12
To Cape Disappointment, on Western Ocean	13
To Capt. Clarke's tour N. W. along coast	10
	miles 4133

1. Lewis has left no known account of this reconnaissance, but his party clearly reached the Pacific Coast near Cape Disappointment and went up the coast some miles in Pacific County, Washington.

2. The people immediately at the river mouth on the north side were Chinooks, who have given their name to the Chinookan language.

3. Perhaps the robes, noted by the captains, of the skins of the mountain beaver, *Aplodontia rufa,* the captains' sewelel, a rodent but not a beaver. See Clark's entry of November 21, 1805. Otherwise, the muskrat, *Ondatra zibethicus.*

4. Perhaps the pacific loon, *Gavia arctica pacifica,* the western subspecies of the arctic loon, or the common loon, *G. immer.*

5. McKeehan here offers a table of distances similar to, but much briefer than those the captains included at various places in their journals. The points may be identified as follows:

Canoes deposited	Camp Fortunate, Beaverhead County, Montana
Head spring	Head of Trail Creek, Beaverhead County
Shoshone River	Perhaps Lemhi River, Lemhi County, Idaho
First large fork	Perhaps Salmon River, Lemhi County
Tour Creek	Tower Creek, Lemhi County
Fishing Creek	North Fork Salmon River, Lemhi County
Flathead or Clark's River	East Fork Bitterroot River, Ravalli County, Montana
Travellers Rest Creek	Lolo Creek, Missoula County, Montana
Flathead [Nez Perce] village	Weippe Prairie, Clearwater County, Idaho
Kooskooske River	Clearwater River, Clearwater County
Canoe Camp	Near Orofino, Clearwater County
Kimoocenem	Tucannon River, Columbia County, Washington
Columbia	Columbia River
Shoshone or Snake River	Deschutes River
Great Falls of Columbia	Celilo Falls, Klickitat County, Washington-Wasco County, Oregon
Short Narrows	The Dalles of the Columbia, Klickitat County-Wasco County
Long Narrows	The Dalles of the Columbia
Catarack River	Klickitat River, Klickitat County
Grand Shoot or Rapids	Cascades of the Columbia River, Skamania County, Washington-Hood River and Multnomah counties, Oregon
Strawberry Island	Hamilton Island, Skamania County
Quicksand River	Sandy River, Multnomah County
Shallow Bay	Grays Bay, Wahkiakum County, Washington
Blustry Point	Perhaps Point Ellice, Pacific County, Washington
Point Open-slope	Perhaps Chinook Point, Pacific County

Chinook River	Wallacut River, Pacific County
Haley's Bay	Baker Bay, Pacific County
Cape Disappointment	Cape Disappointment, Pacific County

Monday 18th.   The morning was cloudy. Capt. Clarke and 10 men[1] went down to Cape Disappointment, to get a more full view of the ocean; and 3 went out to hunt. In the course of the day we got some dried salmon and roots from the natives. In the evening our hunters came in with a deer, 2 brants, a squirrel, a hawk, and a flounder,[2] which the tide had thrown on a sand-bar. The Indians still remained with us, and Capt. Lewis got a specimen of their language. Those who live about the seashore and on Rogue's-harbour creek,[3] a large creek that comes in on the north side of the bay, call themselves the Chin-ook nation.

1. Charbonneau, Pryor, Ordway, Joseph and Reubin Field, Shannon, Colter, Peter Weiser, Labiche, and York, according to Clark. The captain's second entry for the day adds Bratton.
2. Probably starry flounder, *Platichthys stellatus.*
3. Chinook River or Wallacut River, Pacific County, Washington. The captains seem to refer to the latter as Chinook River, and the present Chinook River as White Brant Creek; this may be Gass's Rogue's-harbour Creek.

Tuesday 19th.   We had a cloudy, rainy morning; but some of the hunters went out. About 1 o'clock, the natives, who had been with us some time, went away; and at 4 another party of the same nation came, and encamped close by us. They consisted of 15 men and one squaw. The dress of the squaw was the same with those of the others. Several of the men have robes made of brant skins: one of them had a hat made of the bark of white cedar and bear-grass, very handsomely wrought and water-proof.— One of our party purchased it for an old razor. Our hunters killed 3 deer to day.

Wednesday 20th.   We had a fine clear morning; the Indians remained at our camp; and Capt. Lewis gave one of them a medal, as he ranked as a chief in the nation. One of the men went out to hunt in the morning, and in a short time killed 2 deer. This day continued clear and pleasant throughout. At 4 o'clock in the afternoon, Capt. Clarke and his party returned to camp,[1] and had killed a deer and some brants. They had been about 10 miles north of the cape, and found the country along the seashore level, with spruce-pine timber, and some prairies and ponds of water. They killed a remarkably large buzzard,[2] of a species different from any I had seen. It was 9 feet across the wings, and 3 feet 10 inches from the bill to the tail. They found some pumice stones, which had been thrown out by the waves, of a quality superior to those on the Missouri; also a number of shells of different kinds.

1. Clark had gone up the coast as far as the vicinity of Long Beach, Pacific County, Washington.

2. California condor, *Gymnogyps californianus*.

Thursday 21st. A cloudy morning. About 8 o'clock, all the natives left us. The wind blew so violent to day, and the waves ran so high, that we could not set out on our return, which it is our intention to do as soon as the weather and water will permit. The season being so far advanced, we wish to establish our winter quarters as soon as possible. One of the natives here had a robe of sea-otter skins, of the finest fur I ever saw; which the Commanding Officers wanted very much, and offered two blankets for it, which the owner refused, and said he would not take five. He wanted beads of a blue colour, of which we had none, but some that were on a belt belonging to our interpreter's squaw; so they gave him the belt for the skins. In the evening more of the natives came to our camp, and the night was very wet and disagreeable.

Friday 22d. This was a rainy and stormy morning; and we were not yet able to set out: the wind blew very hard from the south, and the river was rougher than it has been since we came here. At noon the tide was higher than common, and one of our canoes got among some logs, and was split. The rain and wind continued all day violent.

Saturday 23d. The weather was somewhat cloudy but more calm. Some of the men went out to hunt and some to mend the canoe which had been split in the storm yesterday. The natives still stay with us, and have a few roots and berries to subsist on at present; but I cannot conjecture how they live during the winter. They have no mockasons or leggins of any kind; and scarce any other covering than the small robes, which were mentioned before.

In the afternoon, 10 of the Clat-sop nation[1] that live on the south side of the river, came over to our camp. These are also naked, except the small robes which hardly cover their shoulders. One of these men had the reddest hair I ever saw, and a fair skin, much freckled.[2] In the evening our hunters came in, and had killed 3 deer, 8 brants, and 12 ducks.— In the evening the weather cleared and we had a fine night.

1. The Clatsops were a Chinookan-language people living in villages in Clatsop County, Oregon.
2. Probably the man known as Jack Ramsay; see Clark's entry of December 31, 1805.

Sunday 24th. The morning was fine with some white frost. As this was a fine clear day, it was thought proper to remain here in order to make some observations, which the bad weather had before rendered impossible. The latitude of this bay was found to be 46° 19 11 7 north;[1] and at our camp at the head of the bay the river is 3 miles and 660 yards wide. The natives stayed with us all day. At night, the party were consulted by the Commanding Officers, as to the place most proper for winter quarters; and the most of them were of opinion, that it would be best, in the first place, to go over to the south side of the river, and ascertain whether good hunting ground could be found there.[2] Should that be the case, it would be a more eligible place than higher up the river, on account of getting salt, as that is a very scarce article with us.

1. McKeehan's note: "Geographers have stated that the Columbia enters the ocean in latitude 46° 18' north. The difference is therefore only 1 minute 11 seconds and 7 tenths. The longitude by mistake they have made 236° 34 west; but which is the east longitude, leaving 123° 26 for the west longitude. Mr. M'Kenzie arrived at the ocean in latitude 52° 23 46 or 6° 4 34 north of the mouth of the Columbia; and in longitude 128° 2 or 4° 36 west of the mouth of the Columbia. This will show the general course of the western coast between those places, to which the river and great chain of the Rocky Mountains are nearly parallel."
2. Clark gives each party member's opinion in this "consultation" in his entry for this day.

Monday 25th. The morning was pleasant, though cloudy, with a white frost. We loaded our canoes, and proceeded on: went about 9 miles and made an attempt to cross the river, but failed; we therefore kept up the north side round Shallow-bay, and encamped[1] about four miles above it.

1. Being unable to cross the Columbia, they went around Grays Bay and camped near Pillar Rock, Wahkiakum County, Washington.

Tuesday 26th. The morning of this day was cloudy and wet; but we set out early, west about a mile, and then crossed the river; passing in our way several islands. Immediately after we crossed, we came to a small village of the natives,[1] and procured a few roots, called Wapto, from them, and then proceeded on, coasting down the bay on the south side. The whole of the day was wet and unpleasant, and in the evening, we encamped[2] for the night.

1. The people were Cathlamets, speaking Kathlamet, a Chinookan language, and their village was at Knappa, Clatsop County, Oregon.
2. In Clatsop County, near Svenson.

Wednesday 27th. We set out early in a wet morning; coasted round, and turned a sharp cape[1] about a mile; when we found the swells running so high that we had to halt, unload our canoes, and haul them out on the shore. Here we remained the afternoon, and had a very wet night.[2]

1. The captains called it Point William, probably after Clark; it is now Tongue Point, Clatsop County, Oregon.
2. On the west side of the neck of Tongue Point, Clatsop County, just east of Astoria. Most of the party would remain here under Clark until December 7.

Thursday 28th. We had a wet windy morning; some of the hunters went out, but had no luck. It rained all day; and we had here no fresh water, but what was taken out of the canoes as the rain fell.

Friday 29th. The weather continues cloudy and wet. Capt. Lewis with 4 men[1] started, to go down and examine whether there is good hunting and whether we can winter near the salt water. Some of the hunters went out and in the evening returned without killing any game, which appears scarce. The hunting is also difficult, the country being full of thickets and fallen timber. There were some showers of rain and hail during the day.

1. Lewis says five: Drouillard, Reubin Field, Shannon, Colter, and Labiche.

Saturday 30th. This was a fair day; and some hunters went round the cape and killed two or three ducks. This is all the supply of fresh provisions, that we have had since we have been at this camp. We live almost altogether on pounded salmon. The whole of the day was fair, pleasant and warm for the season.

Sunday 1st Decr. 1805. The whole of this day was cloudy. Some of the hunters went out but had not the fortune to kill any thing, not even a duck.

Monday 2nd. The day was agin cloudy and wet. Some of the hunters[1] went out in the morning; and in the afternoon one[2] of them came in, after killing a fine elk. A party of the men went out to bring in the meat, which is a very seasonable supply, a number complaining of the bad effects of the fish diet. Neither the hunters nor the men, who went for the meat returned. In the evening the weather became clear, and we had a fine night.

1. Joseph Field, Pryor, and Gibson; York and two others went in a canoe looking for "fish and Fowl."
2. Joseph Field.

Tuesday 3rd. The morning was foggy. About 9 o'clock the men came in with the meat of the elk.— They had a disagreeable trip, it being dark before they arrived at the place where the elk had been killed; and the darkness, fallen timber and under-brush prevented their return; so that they had to encamp out all night. Six of the natives came to our camp, the first who have appeared since our arrival, and after staying an hour proceeded down the river. The greater part of the day was fair, but in the evening it clouded over and rained again. At dark our other two hunters came in, and had killed 6 elk some distance from the river.

Wednesday 4th. We had a cloudy rainy morning. The river was so rough, we could not set with the canoes and six or seven men[1] were sent to dress the elk that had been killed, and take care of the meat. The rain continued all day.

1. Six men under Pryor.

Thursday 5th. Again we had a wet stormy day, so that the men were unable to proceed with the canoes. About 11 o'clock Capt. Lewis and three of his party came back to camp; the other two were left to take care of some meat they had killed. They have found a place about 15 miles from this camp, up a small river[1] which puts into a large bay on the south side of the Columbia, that will answer very well for winter quarters, as game is very plenty, which is the main object with us; and we intend to move there as soon as circumstances will admit. There is more wet weather on this coast, than I ever knew in any other place; during a month, we have had three fair days; and there is no prospect of a change.

1. The site of Fort Clatsop on Lewis and Clark River, Clatsop County, Oregon, called Netul River by the party; see Gass's entry for December 7.

Friday 6th. We had another wet morning, and were not able to set out. At noon it rained very hard, and the tide flowed so high, that in some part of our camp the water was a foot deep: we had therefore to remove to higher ground. In the afternoon it still continued to rain hard.

Saturday 7th. About 12 last night the rain ceased and we had a fine clear morning. We put our canoes into the water, loaded them, and started for our intended wintering place. We coasted down the south side about a mile, and then met with the six men, who had gone for meat.[1] They had brought four of the skins but no meat, the distance being great and the weather very bad. The swells being too high here to land we went two miles further and took the men in. We then proceeded round the bay[2] until we came to the mouth of a river[3] about 100 yards broad, which we went up about 2 miles to the place fixed upon for winter quarters,[4] unloaded our canoes, and carried our baggage about 200 yards to a spring, where we encamped.

1. York, one of this group, was left behind, which delayed the party.
2. Youngs Bay, Clatsop County, Oregon, which the party called Meriwether's Bay, in honor of Lewis.
3. Lewis and Clark River, Clatsop County.
4. Fort Clatsop on the Lewis and Clark River, Clatsop County, southwest of Astoria. There the party remained until March 23, 1806.

Sunday 8th. We had a fine fair morning, with some white frost. Capt. Clarke with 5 men[1] set out to go to the ocean, and myself with 11 more to bring in the meat, which the two men left by Captain Lewis, were taking care of. We went up the small river[2] in our canoes about two miles, then up a branch[3] of it on the west side two miles, then by land about two miles more, where we found the men and the meat, of which we all carried two large loads to our canoes, and proceeded down to camp. In the evening it began to rain again. The country towards the south is mountainous at some distance off; and there is some snow on the mountains. Near our camp, the country is closely timbered with spruce-pine, the soil rich, but not deep; and there are numerous springs of running water.

1. Including Drouillard and Shannon, according to Clark's entry of December 9.
2. Presumably Lewis and Clark River.
3. Perhaps Johnson Slough, Clatsop County, Oregon, the captains' Kil la malk-ka Creek.

Monday 9th. The morning was cloudy and wet. A sergeant[1] and 8 men were sent to bring in the remainder of the meat we left yesterday; some were employed in making our camp comfortable, and others in clearing a place for huts and a small fort. In the evening some of the natives came to our camp, the first we have seen for some days. It continued cloudy and wet all day.

1. Ordway, according to himself.

Tuesday 10th. We had another wet cloudy morning; and all hands were employed at work notwithstanding the rain. About 2 o'clock Capt. Clarke and 3 of his party returned to camp; the other two remained out to hunt.[1] They found the ocean to be about 7 miles from our camp; for 4 miles the land high and closely timbered: the remainder prairie cut with some streams of water. They killed an elk and saw about fifty in one gang. They also saw three lodges of Indians on the seashore. The natives which were at our camp, went away this morning after receiving some presents. In the evening we laid the foundation of our huts.

1. Drouillard and Shannon, according to Clark's entry of December 9.

Wednesday 11th.   This day was so cloudy and wet; but we continued at our hut-building.

Thursday 12th.   This morning was cloudy without rain. In the forenoon we finished 3 rooms of our cabins, all but the covering; which I expect will be a difficult part of the business, as we have not yet found any timber which splits well; two men went out to make some boards, if possible, for our roofs. About 3 o'clock in the afternoon a number of the natives from the seashore came to our camp,[1] and remained all night. Some rain fell in the evening.

1. Including Coboway, a Clatsop leader, according to Clark.

Friday 13th.   We had a cloudy, but fine morning; and all hands were engaged at work. The party of Indians who came yesterday went away, and another party came about the middle of the day. Two hunters came in, and had killed 18 elk, not more than 4 miles distant. The day continued cloudy and some rain fell in the evening.

Saturday 14th.   The two hunters that had killed the elk, went back with two other men to take care of the meat. In the course of the day a good deal of rain fell; the weather here still continues warm, and there has been no freezing, except a little white frost. In the afternoon, the savages all went away. We completed the building of our huts, 7 in number, all but the covering, which I now find will not be so difficult as I expected; as we have found a kind of timber in plenty, which splits freely, and makes the finest puncheons I have ever seen.[1] They can be split 10 feet long and two broad, not more than an inch and an half thick.

1. Opinions differ on this tree, but it is most likely grand fir; see Clark's entry for December 13, and Lewis's description of February 6, 1806.

Sunday 15th. The morning was cloudy. Captain Clarke with 16 of the party[1] started to bring in the meat the 4 men were taking care of; myself and 2 others were employed in fixing and finishing the quarters of the Commanding Officers, and 2 more preparing puncheons for covering the huts. Some light showers fell during the day; and at night 3 Indians came to our camp, and brought us two large salmon.

1. Including Ordway, Colter, Collins, Whitehouse, and McNeal, according to Clark.

Monday 16th. This was a wet morning with high wind. About 8 Capt. Clarke and 15 men came in loaded with meat; they left a canoe with 7 men to bring in the remainder. They had a very bad night, as the weather was stormy and a great deal of rain fell. Notwithstanding this, a serjeant and four men,[1] who had got lost, lay out all night without fire. As soon as they arrived all hands were set to carrying up the meat, and putting it in a house we had prepared for the purpose. The whole of the day was stormy and wet.[2]

1. The men noted on December 15.
2. Clark declared it, "Certainly one of the worst days that ever was!"

Tuesday 17th. This was another cloudy day, with some light showers of rain and hail. About 11 o'clock the 7 men came with the canoe and the remainder of the meat. We still continued working at our huts.

Wednesday 18th. Snow fell last night about an inch deep, and the morning was stormy. In the middle of the day the weather became clear, and we had a fine afternoon.

Thursday 19th. This was a fine clear cool morning, and we expected to have some fair pleasant weather, but at noon it became cloudy again and began to rain.

Friday 20th. The morning was cloudy and wet.— We collected all the puncheons or slabs we had made, and some which we got from some Indian huts up the bay, but found we had not enough to cover all our huts. About 10 o'clock the weather became clear; but before night it rained as fast as before. From this day to the 25th we had occasionally rain and high winds, but the weather still continued warm. On the evening of the 24th we got all our huts covered and daubed.

Wednesday 25th.   Was another cloudy wet day.— This morning we left our camp and moved into our huts. At daybreak all the men paraded and fired a round of small arms, wishing the Commanding Officers a merry Christmas. In the course of the day Capt. Lewis and Capt. Clarke collected what tobacco remained, and divided it amongst those who used tobacco, as Christmas-gift; to the others they gave handkerchiefs in lieu of it. We had no spirituous liquors to elevate our spirits this Christmas; but of this we had but little need, as we were all in very good health. Our living is not very good; meat is in plenty, but of an ordinary quality, as the elk are poor in this part of the country. We have no kind of provisions but meat, and we are without salt to season that.

The 26th, 27th and 28th, were cloudy with rain. We found our huts smoked; there being no chimneys in them except in the officers' rooms. The men were therefore employed, except some hunters who went out, in making chimnies to the huts. In the evening of the 27th we were informed that a large fish, answering to the description of a whale, was driven upon shore. In the forenoon of the 28th six men[1] started for the sea shore to make salt, as we have none in the fort. Two hunters returned, having killed a deer, and three went out to hunt.[2]

1. Clark names only five: Joseph Field, Bratton, Gibson, Willard, and Weiser.
2. Clark gives the names of the hunters: Drouillard, Shannon, Labiche, Reubin Field, and Collins.

Sunday 29th.   This was a cloudy morning; but a fair day succeeded; and three more hunters went out. In the afternoon several of the Chin-ook nation came to our fort with Wapto roots and dried salmon to trade. We purchased some from them and found the supply seasonable as our meat on land is somewhat spoiled. The men about the fort are engaged in finishing our small fortification.

Monday 30th. Heavy showers of rain fell last night, but the morning was fair, and we had some sunshine, which happens very seldom; light showers of rain fell during the day. About 2 o'clock the three hunters[1] that first went out came in; and had killed four elk. Seven men went out immediately and brought them into the fort safe, which was a pleasing sight, the meat we had on hand being spoiled. This evening we completely finished our fortification.

1. Including Drouillard.

Tuesday 31st. Another cloudy morning. Some more of the natives[1] came to trade with Wapto roots and salmon: the first party had gone off in the morning.—

1. Clark identified them as Wahkiakums and Skillutes. The latter were probably Watlalas, an Upper Chinookan-language people living near the Cascades of the Columbia.

Wednesday 1st Jan. 1806. The year commenced with a wet day; but the weather still continues warm; and the ticks,[1] flies[2] and other insects are in abundance, which appears to us very extraordinary at this season of the year, in a latitude so far north. Two hunters went out this morning. We gave our Fortification the name of Fort Clatsop. In the evening our two hunters, that went out this morning, returned and had killed two large elk about three miles from the Fort.

1. Perhaps the Rocky Mountain woodtick, *Dermacentor andersoni,* or the unnamed tick, *Ixodes pacificus.*
2. Perhaps including crane flies, family Tipulidae.

Thursday 2nd. This also was a cloudy wet day. Fourteen men went out in the morning and brought the meat of the elk into the Fort.

Friday 3rd. The weather is still cloudy and wet. I set out this morning with one of the men[1] to go to the salt-works, to see what progress those engaged in that business had made; and why some of them had not returned, as they had been expected for some time. We proceeded along a dividing ridge,[2] expecting to pass the heads of some creeks, which intervened. We travelled all day and could see no game; and the rain still continued. In the evening we arrived at a place where two of the men had killed an elk some time ago.[3] Here we struck up a fire, supped upon the marrow-bones and remained all night.

1. Shannon, according to Clark.

2. Gass's account of his journey to the saltworks is not altogether clear, no directions or names being given, but the dividing ridge must be the high ground between Lewis and Clark River and the coast, Clatsop County, Oregon. Various small streams run from the ridge toward the river, and it was the heads of these he hoped to clear, apparently without success. He was going generally south, and west toward the coast.

3. Somewhere along the ridge in Clatsop County, probably north of Cullaby Creek.

Saturday 4th. The morning was wet; but we proceeded on, and passed the head of a creek[1] which we supposed was the last in our rout to the salt works. Immediately after passing the creek, the man with me killed an elk; when we halted and took breakfast off it, and then went on. We got into low ground, passed through a marsh about ½ a mile in breadth, where the water was knee-deep; then got into a beautiful prairie,[2] about 5 miles wide, and which runs along the sea shore about 30 miles from Point Adams[3] on the south side of Hayley's Bay,[4] in nearly a southwest course and ends at a high point of a mountain, called Clarke's View[5] on the sea shore. Through this plain or prairie runs another creek,[6] or small river which we could not pass without some craft: so we encamped on the creek and supped on the elk's tongue, which we had brought with us.

1. Probably the head of Cullaby Creek, Clatsop County, Oregon.

2. The coastal plain in Clatsop County, north of Gearhart, in the vicinity of Sunset Beach.

3. Point Adams is the headland at the southern side of the mouth of the Columbia, Clatsop County. It was named for then Vice President John Adams in 1792 by Robert Gray.

4. Baker Bay, on the north side of the Columbia estuary, Pacific County, Washington, opposite Point Adams.

5. Tillamook Head, Clatsop County. It became Clark's Point of View to the party after Clark climbed it on January 7.

6. Probably Thompson Creek, which meets the Pacific in Clatsop County, just north of Seaside.

Sunday 5th. This was a very wet day. We killed a squirrel and eat it; made a raft to cross the creek; but when it was tried we found it would carry only one person at a time; the man with me was therefore sent over first, who thought he could shove the raft across again; but when he attempted, it only went half-way: so that there was one of us on each side and the raft in the middle. I, however notwithstanding the cold, stript and swam to the raft, brought it over and then crossed on it in safety; when we pursued our journey, and in a short time came to some Indian camps[1] on the sea shore. The rain and wind continued so violent that we agreed to stay at these camps all night.

1. Clatsop winter dwellings at Seaside, Clatsop County, Oregon.

Monday 6th. We had a fair morning and the weather cleared up, after two months of rain, except 4 days. We therefore set out from these lodges; passed the mouth of a considerable river;[1] went about two miles up the shore, and found our salt makers at work.[2] Two of their detachment had set out for the fort on the 4th and the man that had come with me and two more went to hunt.[3]

1. Necanicum River flowing into the Pacific in Clatsop County, Oregon, at Seaside. Clark calls it both Colimex River and Clatsop River in entries for January 7.
2. The saltmaking camp was in the southern part of Seaside, Clatsop County.
3. Shannon, who had come with Gass, went out with Joseph Field and Gibson, according to Clark's entry of January 7.

Tuesday 7th. Another fine day. About noon Captain Clarke with 14 men[1] came to the salt-makers camp, in their way to the place where the large fish had been driven on shore, some distance beyond this camp.[2] The Indians about our fort had procured a considerable quantity of the meat, which we found very good. The 8th was a fine day and I remained at camp. The 9th was also fair and pleasant; and about noon Captain Clarke and his party returned here; the distance being about 17 miles. They found the skeleton of the whale which measured 105 feet in length and the head 12. The natives had taken all the meat off its bones, by scalding and other means, for the purpose of trade. The Indians, who live up there are of another nation, and call themselves the Callemex nation.[3] They are a ferocious nation: one of them was going to kill one of our men,[4] for his blanket; but was prevented by a squaw of the Chinook nation, who lives among them, and who raised an alarm. There is a small river[5] comes into the sea at that place. Captain Clarke and his party remained at the camp all night, during which some rain fell.

1. Clark's party apparently included Pryor, Cruzatte or Weiser (probably the former), Frazer, Colter, Werner, Lepage, Reubin Field, Potts, McNeal, Labiche, Windsor, Shields, Charbonneau, Sacagawea, and Jean Baptiste Charbonneau. See Clark's entries for January 6.

2. It was probably a blue whale, *Balaenoptera musculus,* at Cannon Beach, Clatsop County, Oregon. See Clark's entries of January 6–10, 1806.

3. The Tillamooks, speaking a language of the Salishan family, lived along the Oregon coast south of the Clatsops.

4. McNeal; see Clark's account of January 9.

5. Ecola Creek, Clatsop County, given that name by Clark from the Lower Chinookan term for "whale."

Friday 10th. The morning was fine and Captain Clarke and his party started, and I remained at this camp, to wait the return of the man who had come with me and who was out hunting.[1] The 11th was also pleasant, and I proceeded with a party[2] for the fort; where about nine o'clock we arrived the next day. Two hunters had gone out from the fort in the morning, and killed seven elk about two miles from it.

1. Shannon.

2. Evidently including Shannon, Frazer, and Gibson. See Clark's entry for this date.

Monday 13th. The weather changed and we had a cloudy wet day; and all the hands, who could spared, were engaged in bringing the meat of the elk, killed yesterday to camp.

Tuesday 14th. The morning was pleasant; and two men were sent to the salt works to assist in making salt. The rest of our people were employed in drying and taking care of the meat; and in dressing elk skins for mokasins, which is a laborious business, but we have no alternative in this part of the country.[1]

1. Gass means that the Indians of this region did not make moccasins, forcing the party to make their own.

The 15th and 16th were both wet throughout, and the men employed as on the 14th. In the morning of the 17th there were some clouds; but about 10 o'clock they disapeared and we had a fine day.— About the same time 8 of the natives of the Clatsop nation[1] came to our fort, and stayed till the evening. A hunter[2] went out in the morning and killed a deer.

1. Including Chief Coboway.
2. Colter.

Saturday 18th. Last night was very dark; and early in it rain came on and continued all night. This day is also wet. Some of the natives visited us and went away in the evening.

Sunday 19th. Four hunters[1] went out this morning, which was fair with flying clouds; but in the evening it began to rain again. We had another visit from some of the natives.

1. According to Lewis, the hunters were Collins, Willard, Labiche, and Shannon. "Collins" may be an error for Colter; see Lewis's entry.

Monday 20th. It rained hard all day. Some of the natives again came to see us, whom we suffered, contrary to our usual practice, to remain in the fort all night; the evening was so wet and stormy. It also rained on the 21st and 22nd. Our hunters[1] killed three elk. On my way with a party to bring in the meat of these, I saw some amazingly large trees of the fir kind;[2] they are from 12 to 15 feet in diameter.

1. Shannon and Labiche, according to Lewis and Ordway.
2. Perhaps Sitka spruce, *Picea sitchensis* (Bong.) Carr, which Lewis describes as a fir on February 4, 1806.

Thursday 23rd. We had a fine clear cool morning, and two men[1] were sent to the salt works. The day continued pleasant until about four o'clock in the afternoon, when the weather became cloudy, and it began to rain.

1. Howard and Werner, say Lewis and Clark.

Friday 24th. At daylight some snow fell, and there were several snow showers during the day. In the afternoon two of the hunters[1] and some of the natives came to the fort in an Indian canoe with the meat of two deer and an elk they had killed. The Indians were barefooted notwithstanding the snow on the ground; and the evening was so bad we permitted them to stay in the fort all night.

1. Drouillard and Lepage, according to the captains.

Saturday 25th. The morning was cloudy and some showers of snow fell in the course of the day; and in the night it fell to the depth of 8 inches. On the 26th there were some light showers during the day; but in the evening the weather cleared up, and it began to freeze hard. This is the first freezing weather of any consequence we have had during the winter.

Monday 27th. This was a clear cold frosty morning, and the snow about 9 inches deep. Where the sun shone on it during the day, a considerable quantity of it melted; but these places were few, as the whole face of the country near this is closely covered with fir timber. In the afternoon a hunter[1] came in and informed us that the party he had been with had killed ten elk.

1. Shannon, according to Lewis, Clark, and Ordway.

Tuesday 28th. A clear cold morning, and the weather continued cold all day. About half of our men[1] were employed in bringing home meat; and it was found a very cold uncomfortable business. The two men[2] who lately went to the salt works returned with a small supply.

1. Fourteen persons, including Whitehouse and apparently Ordway.
2. Howard and Werner, who left on January 23.

Wednesday 29th. We had a cold clear morning; and the day continued clear throughout. On the 30th the weather was cloudy; and not so cold as the day before; and some snow fell.

Friday 31st. This was a clear cold morning.— Seven of us went up the small river in a canoe to hunt; but after we had gone a mile, we were stopped by the ice and had to return to the fort. One of the men[1] at the salt works had been out hunting, and killed an elk; and called at the fort for men to assist him in taking the meat to their camp.

1. Joseph Field, who had been hunting with Gibson and Willard, according to the captains.

Saturday 1st Feb. 1806. We had a fine clear cold morning. A number of the men[1] went out to bring meat to the fort, and to take some to the salt-works.[2]

1. Gass with a party of five men, according to Lewis.
2. Joseph Field and the party he had come for the previous day.

Sunday 2nd. The morning was pleasant and the weather more moderate. About the middle of the day it began to thaw and in the evening to rain. Some of our men were engaged to day bringing in more meat.

Monday 3rd. Some light showers of rain fell in the course of last night; and this day is still somewhat wet and cloudy. One of our hunters[1] came in, who had killed seven elk, and returned with a party and a canoe to bring in the meat. We are fortunate in getting as much meat as we can eat; but we have no other kind of provisions.

1. Drouillard and Lepage both returned, according to Lewis and Clark.

Tuesday 4th. This was a fine clear morning. Last night the men, who had gone to carry the meat to the salt works returned, and brought us a bushel of salt. This day continued throughout clear and pleasant; and the 5th was a clear cool day. One of our hunters[1] came in, who had killed 6 elk.

1. Reubin Field, say Lewis and Clark.

Thursday 6th. We had a cool fair morning. Ten of us[1] started with a canoe to bring in the meat of the elk, killed yesterday; and had to encamp out all night, but, with the assistance of the elk skins and our blankets, we lodged pretty comfortable, though the snow as 4 or 5 inches deep.

1. Including Ordway, Gass, Reubin Field, and Weiser; see Lewis for February 6 and 7.

Friday 7th. The morning was fair, and all hands engaged in bringing in the meat; we got some to the fort; but myself and part of the men[1] had again to encamp out. It rained hard and we had a disagreeable night.

1. According to Lewis, Ordway and Weiser returned while Gass and the rest of the detachment stayed out.

Saturday 8th. About noon there were showers of rain and hail. Some of the hunters[1] killed 4 more elk and we got all the meat safe to camp in the evening.

1. Shannon and Labiche, according to Lewis.

Sunday 9th. We had a fine morning; but in the course of the day we had sometimes sunshine, and sometimes showers of rain. One of our hunters[1] caught a beaver.

1. Drouillard, according to Lewis.

Monday 10th. A light snow fell last night, and the morning was pleasant. In the afternoon two men came from the salt works,[1] with information that two others were sick and a third had cut his knee so badly he could scarcely walk.

1. The captains say that Willard came from the saltworks, with an injured knee, and reported that Gibson and Bratton were seriously ill.

Tuesday 11th. This was a fine morning. A sergeant and six men[1] were sent to bring the sick men to the fort. At the same time myself and two men[2] went out to hunt, and remained out to the 17th during which time there was a great deal of heavy rain, and the weather changeable and disagreeable.— While we were out we killed 8 elk. During one of the most disagreeable nights, myself and another lay out in our shirts and overalls,[3] with only one elk-skin to defend us from a violent night's rain. We had started a gang of elk, and in order to be light in the pursuit left our clothes where the first was killed, and could not get back before dark. Our shirts and overalls being all of leather made it the more disagreeable.

1. Pryor and four men went to the saltworks to carry Gibson back; Colter and Weiser went along to continue the salt-boiling with Joseph Field.
2. Reubin Field and John B. Thompson.
3. Heavy trousers worn for protection over regular clothes.

Monday 17th. The day was stormy; we set out for the fort, and arrived there in the afternoon. We found the sick men[1] at the fort, and still very bad. One of the men[2] brought word from the salt works, that they had made about four bushels of salt; and the Commanding Officers thought that would be sufficient to serve the party, until we should arrive at the Missouri where there is some deposited.

1. Gibson and Bratton.
2. Joseph Field, relate the captains.

Tuesday 18th. The morning of this day was cloudy. A sergeant[1] and six men set out to go to the salt works, to bring the salt and kettles to the fort. At the same time I started with ten more to bring in meat; but the weather was so stormy, we could not get round the bay, and we all returned to the fort.

1. Ordway, who like Gass, found the waves so high that he could not enter the Skipanon River on the first leg of his trip, and so returned to the fort.

Wednesday 19th— We were employed in bringing in meat, and the sergeant and seven men[1] again set out for the salt works by land, to bring the salt and kettles to the fort. The day was very wet and stormy.

1. Ordway again, but with six men (including Whitehouse), according to Ordway and Whitehouse.

Thursday 20th. This was a cloudy morning. A number of the Chinook Indians[1] came to the fort with hats to trade. They are made of the cedar bark and silk grass, look handsome and keep out the rain. But little rain fell to day, and in the evening, we turned out the natives as usual, and they all went home.

1. Including Chief Tahcum; see the captains' entries.

Friday 21st. About 1 o'clock, our salt makers came home,[1] with the salt and baggage. They had a very unpleasant day, as it rained hard during the whole of it.

1. Led by Ordway and now closing the saltmaking camp at Seaside, Clatsop County, Oregon.

Saturday 22nd. This was a fine clear day; and some of the natives again visited us, and brought some hats, which we purchased at a moderate price. The 23rd was also clear and pleasant; but the morning of the 24th was cloudy, and at 10 o'clock it began to rain hard. About noon a number of the natives[1] came to the fort to trade. The rain continued with high stormy wind; and we suffered the Indians to remain in the fort all night.

1. Coboway was among them.

Tuesday 25th. The rain continued and the weather was stormy. About 10 o'clock the natives went away, though it continued to rain very fast. They brought us yesterday a number of small fish,[1] of a very excellent kind, resembling a herring, and about half the size.

1. The eulachon, or candle fish, *Thaleichthys pacificus;* the captains called it an anchovy.

Wednesday 26th. We had a fair morning; some of the hunters went out, as our store of provisions was getting small, and three men[1] went in search of these small fish, which we had found very good eating.— The 27th was a cloudy wet day. Three of our hunters came in, and had killed an elk.[2]

1. Drouillard, Cruzatte, and Weiser; see the captains' entries.
2. The captains say Reubin Field and Collins returned, the latter having killed the elk.

Friday 28th.   This was a foggy morning, and the forenoon cloudy. A sergeant[1] and six men went out to bring in the meat, and returned about noon. The greater part of this day was fair and pleasant; and in the evening three hunters[2] came in, and had killed five elk.

1. Since neither Gass nor Ordway indicates being in charge, it must have been Pryor.
2. Shields, Joseph Field, and Shannon, according to the captains.

Saturday 1st March, 1806.   We had a cloudy wet morning. I set out with 8 men and 4 hunters to bring the meat of the elk that had been killed, which was at a greater distance from the fort than any we had yet brought in. There is a large river that flows into the southeast part of Hayley's Bay;[1] upon which, about 20 miles from its mouth, our hunters discovered falls,[2] which had about 60 feet of a perpendicular pitch.

1. Youngs River, the party's Kilhow-a-nah-kle River, which actually flows into Youngs Bay, their Meriwether's Bay, Clatsop County, Oregon. Gass obviously considered Baker (Haley's) Bay to extend across the Columbia from the north side.
2. Youngs River Falls, about seventy-five feet high, Clatsop County, about ten miles south of Astoria. See Clark's entry for March 5.

Sunday 2d—   This day was also wet. The fishing party[1] returned at night, and brought with them some thousands of the same kind of small fish we got from the natives a few days ago, and also some sturgeon.[2]

The Indian name of the river we were up yesterday is Kil-hou-a-nak-kle, and that of the small river which passes the fort, Ne-tul.[3]

1. Drouillard, Cruzatte, and Weiser.
2. This could be green sturgeon, *Acipenser medirostris*, or white sturgeon, *A. transmontanus.* See Clark for November 19, 1805, and Lewis for February 24, 1806.
3. The "Kil-hou-a-nak-kle" is Youngs River, and the Netul is Lewis and Clark River, both in Clatsop County, Oregon. The terms are both Chinookan, *giɫawanaxɫ* and *níɫuɫ.*

Monday 3d— It rained all this day and the following. Our sick men are getting better, but slowly, as they have little or no suitable nourishment.

Wednesday 5th— About twelve o'clock last night, the rain ceased, and we had a fine morning. A number of the natives[1] visited us, and at night our hunters returned, but had killed nothing.

1. Clatsops, according to the captains.

Thursday 6th— Our stock of provisions being nearly exhuasted, six men[1] were sent out in different directions to hunt, and three more were sent to endeavour to procure some fish, as the natives take a great number of the small fish about 20 miles distant from the fort by water. Some men were also employed in repairing the canoes, that we may be able to set out on our return immediately, should our hunters be unsuccessful. The elk, almost the only game in this part of the country, are chiefly gone to the mountains. This day continued fair throughout.

1. Including Drouillard, Collins, and Labiche, according to the captains' entries of March 7.

Friday 7th. This was a wet morning, and some showers fell occasionally during the day. Among our other difficulties we now experience the want of tobacco and out of 33 persons composing our party, there are but 7 who do not make use of it; we use crab-tree[1] bark as a substitute. In the evening one of our hunters[2] came in and had killed an elk a considerable distance off.

1. Presumably Oregon crabapple, *Malus diversifolia* (Bong.) Roem.
2. Drouillard and Labiche both returned, according to the captains.

Saturday 8th. Some snow fell last night, and the morning was stormy and disagreeable. About 9 o'clock another of our hunters[1] came in, who had killed 2 elk; and after some time the remaining three,[2] having killed but one deer, and lost their canoe.

1. Collins.
2. Shields, Reubin Field, and Frazer.

Sunday 9th.   This morning 10 men[1] went out to hunt. There were some light showers of snow this forenoon, but during the greater part of it, the sun shone clear and warm. In the afternoon some of the natives came to visit us, and brought some of the small fish, which they call Ulken.[2] Two hunters[3] came in in the evening, but had not killed any thing. The men[4] sent to fish are still absent, owing perhaps to the high swells in the bay. The Indians remained in the fort all night.

1. Ordway says that the ten went out under his leadership to bring in the meat of elk already killed.
2. The captains wrote it "ol-then," a Chinookan term, *ú-ɬxan,* for dried eulachon; see Lewis's entry of March 25.
3. Drouillard and Joseph Field, say the captains.
4. Under Pryor.

On the 10th, we had changeable weather, with snow showers. At noon two more hunters[1] went out.

1. Two parties, according to the captains, along the Lewis and Clark River, and another, consisting of Drouillard, Reubin Field, and Frazer, to go beyond Youngs River. See the captains' entries for March 10 and 11.

Tuesday 11th.   The weather was nearly the same as yesterday. Three men[1] went across the bay in a canoe to hunt. Two hunters came in but had killed nothing. At noon, our fishermen[2] returned, with some ulken and sturgeon. The morning of the 12th was pleasant; but towards the evening the day became cloudy. Another hunter went out.

1. According to the captains, Drouillard, Joseph Field, and Frazer went across Youngs Bay to hunt east of Youngs River.
2. Led by Pryor.

Thursday 13th.   The morning was fine, and two more hunters went out early. about ten, the hunters who had gone across the bay returned, and had killed 2 elk and 2 deer.

I this day took an account of the number of pairs of mockasons each man in the party had; and found the whole to be 338 pair. This stock was not provided without great labour, as the most of them are made of the skins of elk. Each man has also a sufficient quantity of patch-leather. Some of the men went out to look for the lost canoe, and killed two elk.[1]

1. The party was led by Pryor; Collins killed the elk. See the captains' entries for the date.

Friday 14th. We had a fine morning; and four hunters set out early. I went with a party and brought in the meat of the 2 elk which were killed last evening. Two hunters,[1] who had gone out yesterday morning returned very much fatigued, and had killed nothing but a goose and a raven which they ate last night. While out to day I saw a number of musquitoes flying about. I also saw a great quanity of sheep-sorrel[2] growing in the woods of a very large size.

1. Reubin Field and Thompson, who, according to the captains on March 13, left on the twelfth, not the thirteenth as Gass indicates.
2. Gass was acquainted with the introduced European species, garden sorrel, *Rumex acetosa* L. Here he may be seeing either western dock, *R. occidentalis* Wats., or seaside dock, *R. maritimus* L. Hitchcock et al., *Vascular Plants of the Pacific Northwest,* 2:169, 171, 173, 175, 177.

Saturday 15th. There was a fine plesant morning. About noon our hunters came in and had killed four elk.[1] A number of the natives came to the fort today.[2]

1. All killed, according to the captains, by Labiche.
2. From the captains' account these included the Chinook chief Delashelwilt, "the old baud his wife," and six women whom the captains urged their men to stay away from. A Clatsop named Catel and his family also came to visit.

Sunday 16th. Last night it became cloudy and began to rain; and the rain has continued all day.— The Indians stayed about the fort the whole of this day. Yesterday while I was absent getting our meat home, one of the hunters killed two vultures,[1] the largest fowls I had ever seen. I never saw any such as these except on the Columbia river and the seacoast.

1. Presumably California condors, but it is curious that the captains say nothing about these specimens on this date.

On the 17th it rained occasionally during the whole of the day. We got a canoe from the natives, for which we gave an officier's uniform coat.[1]

1. Drouillard purchased it from Cathlamet Indians with Lewis's coat.

Tuesday 18th. The weather was much like that of yesterday, and some hail fell in the course of the day. Some of the men are repairing the small canoes, and making preparations to return up the river, as soon as the weather will permit. One of the hunters[1] killed an elk.

1. Joseph Field, say the captains. Gass, or McKeehan, does not choose to mention, as Ordway and Whitehouse do, that on this date the captains sent a party to steal a canoe from the Clatsops, since the captains could not afford to buy another at the asking price. They justified the action because some elk were stolen from them earlier. See Lewis's and Clark's entries of March 17.

The morning of the 19th was stormy, some hard showers of hail fell and it continued cloudy through the day.

Thursday 20th. The whole of this day was wet and disagreeable. We intended to have set out today on our return, but the weather was too bad. I made a calculation of the number of elk and deer killed by the party from the 1st of Dec. 1805 to the 20th March 1806, which gave 131 elk, and 20 deer. There were a few smaller quadrupeds killed, such as otter and beaver, and one raccoon. The meat of some of the elk was not brought to the fort.

Friday 21st. We had a cloudy wet morning. Two of the hunters[1] went out this morning; and about 10 o'clock we were visited by some of the Clatsop Indians. These, and the Chin-ook, Cath-la-mas, Cal-a-mex,[2] and Chiltz[3] nations, who inhabit the seacoast, all dress in the same manner. The men are wholly naked, except a small robe; the women have only the addition of the short petticoat. Their language also is nearly the same; and they all observe the same ceremony of depositing with the remains of the dead all their property, or placing it at their graves. I believe I saw as many as an hundred canoes at one burying-place of the Chin-ooks, on the north side of the Columbia, at its entrance into Hailey's Bay: and there are a great many at the burying-place of every village. These Indians on the coast have no horses, and very little property of any kind, except their canoes. The women are much inclined to venery, and like those on the Missouri are sold to prostitution at an easy rate. An old Chin-ook squaw[4] frequently visited our quarters, with nine girls which she kept as prostitutes. To the honour of the Flatheads,[5] who live on the west side of the Rocky Mountains, and extend some distance down the Columbia, we must mention them as an exception; as they do not exhibit those loose feelings of carnal desire, nor appear addicted to the common customs of prostitution: and they are the only nation on the whole route where any thing like chastity is regarded. In the evening our two hunters[6] returned, but had killed nothing.

1. Shields and Collins, say the captains.
2. Tillamook Indians.
3. The Salish-speaking Lower Chehalis, living on the Washington coast in Grays Harbor and Pacific counties, from Grays Harbor south to Willapa Bay.
4. The wife of Delashelwilt; see the captains' entries for March 15. Gass, like other whites, could only see the custom he was describing as commercial prostitution, without realizing it might serve a social and even a spiritual purpose for the Indians. See Clark's entries of October 12, 1804, and January 5, 1805. In this instance, to be sure, the commercial element may have been more prominent.
5. Probably referring to the Nez Perces and to other Shahaptian-language people on the Snake and Columbia rivers encountered by the party on their westward journey. McKeehan's reflections echo those attached to Gass's entry of April 5, 1805.
6. Shields and Collins, as the captains note.

Saturday 22nd. We had a cloudy wet morning. Three hunters[1] were sent on ahead to remain at some good hunting ground until we should all come up; and six others to hunt near the fort. In the evening all these came in except one,[2] without any success.

1. Drouillard and the Field brothers, the captains say.
2. Colter.

Sunday 23d. There was a cloudy wet morning.— The hunter[1] who remained out last night, came in early, and had killed an elk. We were employed this forenoon in dividing and packing up our loading; and distributing it among the canoes, which were five in number, three large and two small. At noon, we put it on board; and at 1 o'clock, left fort Clatsop. The afternoon was fair. We proceeded round Point William,[2] went about 19 miles, and encamped[3] at the mouth of a creek, where we found the three hunters[4] that had been sent on a-head, and who had killed two elk about a mile and an half distant.

1. Colter.
2. Tongue Point, Clatsop County, Oregon.
3. John Day River, Clatsop County.
4. Drouillard and the Field brothers.

Monday 24th. After a bad night's rest, on account of the rain 15 men[1] went out and brought the meat of the two elk to our camp. The morning was fair and after breakfast they all embarked, except the men belonging to my canoe which the tide had left aground. The hunters went on in the small canoe ahead, and I had to wait for the rising of the tide. In about two hours I was able to follow the other canoes, and proceeded on about 12 miles, to a village of the Cath-la-mas[2] where the rest of the party had halted. When I arrived we all proceeded on again, and in the evening encamped[3] at an old village, which had been vacated.

1. Led by Ordway, as he notes.
2. On Cathlamet Bay, in the vicinity of Knappa, Clatsop County, Oregon; the people were Cathlamets.
3. Northeast of Brownsmead, Clatsop County, on Aldrich Point opposite the downstream end of Tenasillahe Island.

Tuesday 25th. We set out after breakfast and had a fair morning; proceeded on to 12 o'clock, when we again halted, the wind and tide being both against us. When the tide began to rise we went on again, saw some of the natives[1] in canoes descending the river, and in the afternoon passed an Indian lodge,[2] where one of the men purchased an otter skin.— At this time the wind rose and blew very hard accompanied with rain; notwithstanding we proceeded on till night, when we came to the mouth of a small creek,[3] which formed a good harbour for our canoes. Here we found several of the natives[4] encamped and catching sturgeon, of which they had taken 14 large ones.

1. Clatsops, say the captains.
2. A Cathlamet lodge on Puget Island, Wahkiakum County, Washington.
3. In Columbia County, Oregon, below one of the mouths of the Clatskanie River, opposite Cape Horn on the Washington shore; see the captains' entries for the day.
4. Cathlamets.

Wednesday 26th.   After a disagreeable night's rain, and wind, we continued our voyage. As we passed along, I saw a great many flowers full blown of different colours; and grass and other herbage growing fast: I saw nettles[1] two feet high of this spring's growth.[2]

1. Stinging nettle, *Urtica dioica* L. ssp. *gracilis* (Ait.) Seland.
2. They camped on one of the small islands, including Walker and Dibblee islands, below Longview, Cowlitz County, Washington, in Columbia County, Oregon.

Thursday 27th.   There was a cloudy wet morning. We embarked early and went about 6 miles, when we came to a small Indian village,[1] where the natives received us very kindly. They belong to the Chil-ook nation,[2] and differ something in their language from the Chin-ooks. We got some Wapto roots and fish from them and then proceeded on, though it rained very hard. Two small canoes went on ahead to Deer island,[3] in order to kill some game by the time we should come up. We passed several Indian lodges where the natives[4] were fishing for sturgeon, and got a large one out of a small canoe; a number of which followed us with 2 Indians in each of them. At night we encamped[5] where we had plenty of good wood, oak and ash.[6]

1. A "Skillute" village near Rainier, Columbia County, Oregon. See the captains' entries for March 25 and 27, 1806.
2. That is, they spoke a Lower Chinookan dialect.
3. Still Deer Island, Columbia County, Oregon.
4. More "Skillutes"; see above.
5. In the vicinity of Goble, Columbia County, Washington, with the Kalama River on the opposite side in Cowlitz County, Washington.
6. The oak is probably Oregon white oak and the ash may be Oregon ash.

Friday 28th.   The morning was cloudy. We set out early, and at 10 o'clock came to Deer island; where those who had gone ahead in the small canoes had encamped, and all gone out to hunt except one. In a short time a hunter returned with a large deer, and we concluded to stay here all day[1] and repair two of our canoes, that leaked. It rained at intervals during the day. Our hunters came in and had killed 7 deer in all. Some of the men went to bring in the meat, and others went out and killed some geese and ducks. At the last village we passed I took notice of a difference in the dress of the females, from that of those below, about the coast and Hailey's Bay. Instead of the short petticoat, they have a piece of thin dressed skin tied tight round their loins, with a narrow slip coming up between their thighs. On this island there are a greater number of snakes,[2] than I had ever seen in any other place; they appeared almost as numerous as the blades of grass; and are a species of Garter snake. When our men went for the deer, they found that the fowls had devoured four of the carcases entirely, except the bones. So they brought in the other two; and we finished our canoes and put them in the water. The Columbia river is now very high, which makes it more difficult to ascend.

1. Near the upper end of Deer Island.
2. Lewis described the Pacific red-sided garter snake, *Thamnophis sirtalis concinnus*, a new subspecies, on this day.

Saturday 29th. The morning was pleasant with some white frost and we proceeded on early; passed some old Indian lodges, and in the afternoon came to a large village,[1] where we were received with great kindness, and got fish and wapto roots to eat. Here we bought some dogs and waptos, and then went on again, about a mile and encamped.[2] One of the sick men is quite recovered and the other two are getting better.[3]

1. Nahpooitle, a village of the Cathlapotle, an Upper Chinookan-language people, Clark County, Washington, just above the mouth of Lewis River and behind Bachelor Island.
2. Behind Bachelor Island, Clark County, near Ridgefield.
3. Clark notes that Willard was well and Bratton stronger.

Sunday 30th. The morning was fair with some dew. We set out early accompanied by several of the natives in canoes. The river is very high, overflowing all its banks. We passed some villages of the natives on Wapto island,[1] which is about 20 miles long and one broad, but did not halt at any of them. The natives of this country ought to have the credit of making the finest canoes, perhaps in the world, both as to service and beauty; and are no less expert in working them when made.[2] We had a beautiful day throughout, and in the evening encamped[3] on a handsome prairie in sight of a large pond on the north side of the river.

1. Sauvie Island, Multnomah County, Oregon. Various Upper Chinookan-language people lived on and around the island, including the Katlaminimin.

2. McKeehan's note: "I had imagined that the Canadians, who accompanied me were the most expert canoe-men in the world, but they were very inferior to these people [the natives near the coast] as they themselves acknowledged, in conducting those vessels." McKeehan again cites Mackenzie to corroborate Gass and he inserted the bracketed material in his edition. Lewis described the local canoes at length on February 1, 1806.

3. At Vancouver, Clark County, Washington.

Monday 31st. This was a beautiful clear morning, and we proceeded on early. One of the men went along shore, and in a short time killed a deer: the deer are very plentiful on this part of the river.— We proceeded on, and passed a large village which was full of people as we went down, but is now all deserted except one lodge.[1] In the evening, we came to a small prairie, opposite the mouth of Quicksand river, where we encamped.[2]

1. The captains called the people Shahalas; they were probably Watlalas. The village was within Portland, Multnomah County, Oregon, probably on the site of the airport.

2. In Clark County, Washington, above the entrance of Washougal River (the party's Seal River), near Washougal. Quicksand River is present Sandy River, Multnomah County.

Tuesday 1st April, 1806. We had a cloudy morning; and we agreed to stay here all day, for the purpose of hunting. So 9 hunters[1] set out early; 3 of whom[2] went up Quicksand river, and killed a deer; the other six killed 4 elk and a deer. In the evening nine of us went to bring in the meat of the elk; but it being late we were obliged to encamp out all night.

1. Gibson was one of the hunters.

2. It is not entirely clear if Gass is referring to Pryor's exploring party which was sent up Sandy River, or to a party of three hunters sent to the area above Sandy River.

Wednesday 2nd. We returned in the morning to camp; and it was agreed to stay here some time longer to hunt and dry meat. Therefore 3 parties[1] went out to hunt. Myself and 4 men[2] went below the mouth of Sandy river, and killed an elk, some deer and a black bear.

1. Included in one party were Drouillard and the Field brothers.
2. Among those with Gass were Windsor and Collins. They remained in the area below Sandy River, Multnomah County, Oregon, until April 4, when they returned to the main party's camp.

Thursday 3rd. We went out and killed some deer; and then to bring in the meat of the bear and dry that of the elk; but it rained so hard we could not dry the meat; and therefore brought in the carcase of the bear. On our way, we saw 3 small cubs in a den, but the old bear was not with them. In the evening we returned to our camp, and remained there all night.

Friday 4th. After a cloudy morning, we turned out and killed a deer and some geese, and then went to the camp.[1] A party that went out on the upper side of Sandy river, killed 4 elk, and some of the men were out drying the meat.

While I was out hunting, Captain Clarke got information that a large river[2] came in on the south side of the Columbia, about 40 miles below this place, opposite a large island,[3] which had concealed it from our view; and went down with six men[4] to view it. He found it to be a very large river, 500 yards wide, with several nations of Indians[5] living on it; and its source supposed to be near the head waters of some of the rivers, which fall into the gulph of California.[6] On their return, they bought some dogs at an Indian village; and last night arrived at camp. Four men[7] were sent on ahead this forenoon in a canoe to hunt; and I went out with two more[8] to the den where we saw the cubs, to watch for the old bear; we stayed there until dark and then encamped about a quarter of a mile off,[9] and went back early in the morning; but the old one was not returned: so we took the cubs and returned to camp.

1. They returned to the main party's camp in Clark County, Washington, above the Washougal River.
2. The Willamette River, which enters the Columbia at Portland, Multnomah County, Oregon. The captains called it the Multnomah, and assumed that it drained a large area in the interior of the continent.

3. Their Diamond Island, now divided into Government and McGuire islands.

4. Clark set out on April 2 with a party including Thompson, Potts, Cruzatte, Weiser, Howard, Whitehouse, and York.

5. Those Clark actually met were apparently Watlalas. See his entry for April 3 for information on other tribes.

6. The captains, like other geographers of the time, assumed that all of the region west of the Continental Divide drained into the Pacific through some stream, and that the major western rivers had their sources in the same general area. Therefore they assumed that the Willamette originated somewhere near the sources of the Colorado River. They had no way of knowing of the existence of the Great Basin, which has no exterior drainage, and which lies between the Colorado and the rivers of the Northwest.

7. Gibson, Shannon, Howard, and Weiser.

8. Collins and Windsor.

9. In Multnomah County, below Sandy River.

Saturday 5th. The weather was plesant. There is a beautiful prairie and a number of ponds below the mouth of Sandy river; and about two miles from the Columbia the soil is rich with white cedar timber,[1] which is very much stripped of its bark, the natives making use of it both for food and clothing.[2] A number of the Indians visit us daily; and the females in general have that leather covering round their loins, which is somewhat in the form of a truss.

1. Gass here refers probably to western redcedar, which the captains' usually called white cedar, but McKeehan's note, next, relates perhaps to western hemlock, *Tsuga heterophylla* (Raf.) Sarg.

2. McKeehan's note: "Mr. M'Kenzie also mentions that the western Indians make use of the inner tegument of the bark of trees for food; and that it is generally considered by the more interior Indians as a delicacy, rather than an article of common food: that on this and herbs they are used to sustain themselves on their journies. He likewise states that of the inner rind of the hemlock, taken off early in the spring they make a kind of cakes, which they eat with salmon oil, and of which they appear very fond."

Sunday 6th. We had a fine morning, with some fog; about 10 o'clock we set out; passed a beautiful pairie on the north side, which we could not see for the fog as we went down; proceeded on about 9 miles and came to our hunters' camp.[1] they had killed 5 elk; so we halted, sent out for the meat and began to dry it. We are now at the head of the Columbia valley; which is a fine valley about 70 miles long, abounding with roots of different kinds, which the natives use for food, especially the Wapto roots which they gather out of the ponds. The timber is mostly of the fir[2] kind, with some cherry,[3] dog-wood,[4] soft maple[5] and ash;[6] and a variety of shrubs which bear fruit of a fine flavour, that the natives make use of for food.

1. Where they remained until April 9. The question of the location of this camp is rather involved; see Lewis's entry for the date. Apparently it was in Multnomah County, Oregon, above Latourell Falls and Rooster Rock State Park, in an area known as Sheppards Dell.

2. Most likely Douglas fir, *Pseudotsuga menziesii* (Mirb.) Franco.

3. Perhaps bitter cherry, *Prunus emarginata* Dougl., or choke cherry. See Lewis's entry of April 12, 1806.

4. Nuttall's dogwood, *Cornus nuttallii* Aud. ex T. & G.

5. Perhaps bigleaf maple, usually called broad leaf ash by the captains. Other possibilities are vine maple, *Acer circinatum* Pursh, and Rocky Mountain maple, *A. glabrum* Torr.

6. Most probably Oregon ash.

Monday 7th. This was a plesant day, but cloudy. Three hunters[1] went on ahead again and the rest of the party remained drying meat to subsit on while we passed the Columbia plains, as there is no game in that part of the country, according to the accounts given by the natives, who are daily coming down; and say that those remaining in the plains are in a starving condition, and will continue so until the salmon begin to run, which is very soon expected. We continued here all day; and one of our hunters killed a beautiful small bird of the quail kind.[2]

1. Drouillard and the Field brothers again.

2. Lewis says on this date that this happened "last evening," and that Reubin Field was the hunter. The bird is the mountain quail, *Oreortyx pictus,* a new species. See Clark's entry for April 6 and Lewis's for April 7.

Tuesday 8th. This was a fine morning, but the wind blew so hard from the north-east, that it was impossible to go on; and about 8 o'clock the swells ran so high, that we had to unload our canoes, and haul some of them out of the water to prevent their being injured. Some of the men are complaining of rheumatick pains; which are to be expected from the wet and cold we suffered last winter, during which from the 4th of November 1805 to the 25th of March 1806, there were not more than twelve days in which it did not rain, and of these but six were clear. Two hunters,[1] who had gone out in the morning, returned, but had killed nothing, except a beautiful small duck.[2]

1. Clark identifies four hunters who came in this day: Collins, Shannon, Colter, and Drouillard, who killed the duck.

2. Clark says this was a "summer duck," the men's term for the wood duck, *Aix sponsa*.

Wednesday 9th.   The morning was plesant; we therefore loaded our canoes and proceeded on till 11 o'clock when we stopped at a large Indian village on the north side;[1] but a number of the huts were unoccupied. They are of the Al-e-is nation. At the time we halted 3 canoe-loads of them were setting out for the falls to fish. We took breakfast here and bought 5 dogs from them. The women all wear the small leather bandage, but are quite naked otherwise, except what is covered by the small robe they wear round their shoulders. In the afternoon the weather became cloudy and some rain fell. In the evening we came to a large rapid at the lower end of Strawberry island;[2] where there are a number of the natives about settling on the north side.[3] Here we crossed over, after buying two dogs from them, and encamped[4] behind the island. Some rain continued falling.

1. A Watlala village in Skamania County, Washington, a little below Beacon Rock.
2. Hamilton Island, Skamania County.
3. Designated by the captains as Clahclellahs, a branch of the Watlalas.
4. In Skamania County, in the eastern part of North Bonneville.

Thursday 10th.   A party of men went out to collect pitch to repair one of our canoes, which was split; and the rest went round the point of the island, and took the canoes over the rapid, one at a time, with the assistance of a line. When we got over the rapids we crossed to another village of the natives of the north side,[1] where I saw the skin of a wild sheep,[2] which had fine beautiful wool on it. Here we took breakfast and waited the arrival of the other canoe, which in about an hour came up; and the men[3] when out for pitch killed three deer. We proceeded on, and the water was so rapid that we had to tow the canoes up by the line almost all the way to the landing at the lower end of the portage, a distance of about six miles. In passing a bad place the tow-line of the small canoe, which the hunters had on ahead, broke; but fortunately there was nothing in her, as the three hunters were on shore dragging her up, and had taken out all the loading.[4] As she passed by us Capt. Lewis got some of the natives to bring her to shore. In the evening, we got to the end of the portage, which is about two miles. We took our baggage to the top of the hill[5] and remained with it all night; during which, some showers of rain fell.

1. Another "Clahclellah" (Watlala) village, Skamania County, Washington, at or near North Bonneville.

2. The captains purchased this skin of the mountain goat, the only specimen they obtained.

3. Including Pryor and Gibson, who had waited for Collins, who was hunting; they were collecting pitch to repair cracks in the canoes while they waited.

4. Lewis says the canoe had "a tin vessel and tomahawk in her."

5. A site to the east of North Bonneville, Skamania County.

Friday 11th. We had a cloudy morning. All our men, who were able set out to take the canoes through the grand shoot.[1] About 1 o'clock we got two over; and then proceeded to take two more, which we succeeded in after great toil and danger; and 3 hunters[2] went on ahead in the least.[3]

1. The Cascades of the Columbia River.

2. Once again, Drouillard and the Field brothers.

3. Presumably meaning the smallest canoe.

Saturday 12th. This morning was wet. We all set out to take the other canoe over; but after we had fastened the rope to her she swung out into the current, which was so strong, that it pulled the rope out of the men's hands and went down the river.— We then went to carry our baggage across the portage, which was a very fatiguing business; but about sunset, we got all over. It rained at intervals all day; and upon the very high mountains on the south side of the river,[1] snow fell and continued on the trees and rocks during the whole of the day. We had a number of the natives about us in the day time; but they left us at night. We encamped,[2] all excessively fatigued, at the upper end of the portage.

1. Part of the Cascade Range.

2. Evidently at the camp of October 30–31, 1805, Skamania County, Washington, on a small island just above the narrows.

Sunday 13th. There was a cloudy morning. Having divided the load of the lost canoe among the 4 that were left, we renewed our voyage and passed a large deserted village on the north side.[1] Captain Lewis with the two small canoes, crossed to the south side,[2] where there is a large village inhabited, to endeavour to purchase a small canoe or two, as we were very much crowded in the four we had. Capt. Clarke with the two large canoes continued on along the northern shore, till we passed Crusatte's river,[3] when the wind rose so high we could not go on, so we halted and waited for Capt. Lewis. Two hunters went out about 3 hours, but killed nothing.[4] By this time the wind fell and we went on 3 miles to a better harbour, where we halted on the north side of the river.[5] Capt. Clarke and 3 men went out to hunt; and Capt. Lewis having come up and crossed over to us, we fixed our camp for the night. He got 2 canoes and 3 dogs from the inhabitants of the large village.— They are of the Wey-eh-hoo nation and have twelve lodges here. At dark Capt. Clarke and party returned, and had killed two deer.

1. A "Yehuh" village in Skamania County, Washington; see Clark's entry for October 30, 1805.

2. In Hood River County, Oregon.

3. Wind River, Skamania County.

4. Clark says that Shields and Colter went out, and that Shields shot two deer but could not get them.

5. In Skamania County, south of Dog Mountain, apparently between Collins Creek and Dog Creek.

Monday 14th. The morning was fine with some fog. Abut 9 o'clock our 3 hunters,[1] who had gone ahead and proceeded up Crusatte's river some distance returned, having killed 4 deer. At 10 o'clock we continued our voyage, and at 1 came to a new settlement of the natives on the north side,[2] where we saw some horses, the first we have seen since October last. These horses appeared in good case. The wind blew hard from the southwest and the weather was clear and cool, but there has been no frost lately, except on the tops of the high hills. We stayed here three hours, and then proceeded on; passed several Indian camps, and halted at a small creek on the north side,[3] where there are a number of Indian lodges.

1. The captains say Pryor returned with the three hunters (Drouillard and the Field brothers).

2. The White Salmon people, speaking an Upper Chinookan dialect and living in Klickitat County, Washington.

3. Major Creek, Klickitat County, above and opposite Mosier, Wasco County, Oregon.

Tuesday 15th. The morning was fair. The Commanding Officers attempted to purchase some horses, but could not agree with the Indians on the price; so we proceeded on about four miles to another village, at the mouth of Catarack river.[1] Here we got some Shap-e-leel,[2] a kind of bread the natives make of roots, and bake in the sun; and which is strong and palatable. Here another trial was made to get some horses, but without success; and we again proceeded on; passed a place where there was a village in good order last fall when we went down; but has been lately torn down, and again erected at a short distance from the old ground where it formerly stood.[3] The reason of this removal I cannot conjecture, unless to avoid the fleas,[4] which are more numerous in this country than any insects I ever saw.[5] About three o'clock in the afternoon, we came to Rock Camp,[6] where we stayed two days as we went down. Some hunters[7] went out in the evening, and killed a deer.

1. Klickitat River, Klickitat County, Washington. The people were Smackshops, an Upper Chinookan-language people.

2. Otherwise "chapellel," and other spellings to the party, it is cous, *Lomatium cous* (Wats.) Coult. & Rose.

3. According to the captains there were two villages of "Chilluckittequaws" in this area in Klickitat County. They were apparently Wishram-Wasco Indians.

4. Proably human body lice, *Pediculus humani*. See Clark's entry for October 26, 1805.

5. McKeehan's note: "'We had however the curiosity to visit the houses (of a deserted village) which were erected upon posts; and we suffered very severely from the indulgence of it; for the floors were covered with fleas, and we were immediately in the same condition, for which we had no remedy but to take to the water. There was not a spot round the houses, free from grass, that was not alive, as it were, with this vermin.' *M'Kenzie*."

6. The "Fort Rock" camp of October 25–28, 1805, on the downriver journey, just below Mill Creek at The Dalles, Wasco County, Oregon. This time they would remain until April 18.

7. One of them was Drouillard, as the captains indicate.

Wednesday 16th. This was a plesant day. As we did not expect to be able to navigate the Columbia river much farther, Captain Clarke, with some of the men[1] and some goods went over the river to endeavour to procure some horses. I was out hunting this morning, and killed a rattlesnake among the rocks. Some hunters that went out in the morning returned in the evening and had killed two deer, some ducks and four squirrels,[2] three of a beautiful speckled kind, and as large as a common grey squirrel, but the tail not so bushy.

1. With Clark were Drouillard, Charbonneau, Sacagawea, Cruzatte, Goodrich, Frazer, Willard, McNeal, Weiser, and perhaps Werner. They went across the Columbia to Klickitat County, Washington, and camped in the vicinity of Dallesport.

2. Perhaps the California ground squirrel, *Spermophilus beecheyi;* see Lewis's entry for this date. Joseph Field brought the animals in.

Thursday 17th. This was a fine morning. Some hunters[1] went out and we remained at this camp all day; in the evening our hunters came in and had killed a deer. We made 12 packsaddles. Captain Clarke still remains over the river.

1. Joseph Field and Shields were apparently among the hunters, as indicated by Lewis.

Friday 18th. We had fine weather, and all set out from this place, and proceeded on with great difficulty and danger to the foot of the long narrows;[1] and expect to be able to take the canoes no further.— Here we met one of the men[2] from Captain Clarke, with 4 horses. In coming up, one of our small canoes got split so that we were obliged to carry the load two miles by land to this place.[3] Wood here is very scarce, as the Columbia plains have commenced. Several of the men[4] went up to the village with their buffaloe robes, to dispose of them for horses. Could we get about 12 horses we would be able to go by land.

1. Part of The Dalles of the Columbia River.
2. Clark says he sent Charbonneau and Frazer with these horses.
3. In Klickitat County, Washington, perhaps at today's Spearfish Lake.
4. Ordway and three men, according to Clark.

Saturday 19th. The morning was cloudy and all hands were engaged in carrying the baggage and canoes over the portage, which is two miles in length. Five more horses were got in the course of the day. Some light showers of rain fell in the afternoon, and about 4 o'clock, we got all our baggage and canoes across except the two large ones, of which we made firewood. At the same time Captain Clarke and four men[1] went on ahead to the village at the great falls[2] to endeavour to get some more horses, by the time we arrive there, a distance of about 8 miles from this village.[3] In the evening the weather cleared up and we had a fine night.

1. Pryor, Shannon, Cruzatte, and Labiche, notes Clark.
2. Celilo Falls; Clark's party went to the vicinity of Wishram, Klickitat County, Washington, to a village of "Eneshurs," actually Shahaptian-language Teninos.
3. The main party's camp was above the Long Narrows of The Dalles in Klickitat County, near Horsethief Lake State Park and the camp of October 24, 1805. They now remained there until April 21.

Sunday 20th.   This was a pleasant morning with some white frost. We got two more horses and lost one; remained here all day and had a great deal of trouble with our horses, as they are all studs, and break almost every rope we can raise. We had to tie them up at night, and one broke away notwithstanding all our care and attention. We have also much trouble with the Indians as they are disposed to steal whenever they have an opportunity. With all our care they stole 4 or 5 tomahawks.

Monday 21st.   This was another pleasant morning with some white frost. We found the horse, which had broke away last night, and made preparations for setting out from this place. While we were making preparations to start, an Indian stole some iron articles from among the men's hands; which so irritated Captain Lewis, that he struck him; which was the first act of the kind, that had happened during the expedition.[1] The Indians however did not resent it, otherwise it is probable we would have had a skirmish with them. This morning we disposed of two canoes and used another for firewood. At 10 o'clock we set out from the first narrows, with nine of our own and one we borrowed,[2] and two canoes all loaded heavy. I went with three other men in the canoes, and had some difficulty in passing the short narrows. About 3 in the afternoon we arrived at the great falls of Columbia, where we met with Captain Clarke and the men that were with him. Here we got another horse; carried our canoes and baggage round the falls and halted for dinner. We also got some dogs here, and shapaleel, which we subsist on chiefly at present. We halted here two hours and then proceeded on again. The party that went by land had to leave the river, and take out to the hill a part of the way. I crossed with my canoe to the south side, where there is the best water, and passed a large rock island,[3] opposite to which the Sho-sho-ne river[4] flows in from the south. We went on till dark, and then run our small canoe among some willows, and laid down to sleep.[5] We did not make any fire for fear the savages, who are very numerous along this part of the river, might come and rob us.

1. Lewis says the Indian stole the iron socket off a canoe pole and admits giving him "several severe blows."
2. Horses.
3. Miller Island.
4. The Deschutes River, Wasco County, Oregon. Gass's name refers to the "Snake" (Paiute) Indians living on the river, whom he supposes to be the same as the Shoshones (Snakes) the party encountered in Idaho.
5. Somewhere above Deschutes River, on the Oregon side of the Columbia.

Tuesday 22nd. This was a pleasant morning and high wind. We proceeded on about 3 miles, when the wind became so violent, that we could not proceed any further, and halted an unloaded our canoes. Having remained here two hours, the other canoe came up, and we proceeded on though the wind was high and river rough. At sunset I crossed over, where the party going by the land came in sight, and halted at a small village on the north side;[1] but the other canoe[2] kept on along the southern shore. In the course of this day two more horses were procured, and at this small village we got some more dogs and shapaleel.

1. A Tenino Indian village in Klickitat County, Washington, in the vicinity of John Day Dam, where they camped for the night.
2. In it were Colter and Potts; Reubin Field was in the same canoe with Gass. See journal entries of the captains and of Ordway for this day.

Wednesday 23rd. We had a cloudy morning. I went also by water to day, and we had very laborious work in getting along. In the evening we met the party at a large village of the Wal-la-waltz nation,[1] on the north side of the river; where the other canoe had also arrived. Here we halted, unloaded the canoes and encamped. A horse had got away last night and could not be found.

1. A "Wah-how-pum" village at the mouth of Rock Creek, Klickitat County, Washington. These Shahaptian-language people are now generally classified as Teninos, with others in the vicinity. The party camped here, somewhat above the mouth of John Day River, their River Lapage, after party member Jean Baptiste Lepage, opposite.

Thursday 24th. The weather was pleasant. We lost another horse last night, and were detained here this morning, looking for him. We got six horses at this place, three of which were borrowed from an Indian[1] who was going with his family along with us. We sold our two small canoes; and at noon an Indian who had gone to look for the lost horse returned with him. At 2 o'clock we all started by land on the north side of the river, accompanied by several of the natives with their families and horses. We entered the low country, the great and beautiful plains of Columbia, and proceeded on till evening when we encamped at two mat-lodges of the natives,[2] and got two dogs and some shapaleel. The natives who were travelling in our party encamped with us.

1. A "Chopunnish" (probably Nez Perce), according to the captains.
2. On the identification of these people, see Lewis's entry for this date. The camp was in Klickitat County, Washington, roughly opposite Blalock, Gilliam County, Oregon.

Friday 25th. The morning was pleasant, and we set out early. At 10 o'clock we met a great many of the natives on horseback, who turned back with us. At noon, we came to a very large band of the Wal-a-waltz nation,[1] the most numerous we had seen on the Columbia; I suppose it consisted of 500 persons, men, women, and children; and all of them tolerably well clothed children with robes of the skins of the deer, the ibex or big-horned animal and buffaloe. They have a great many horses, and lately came to the river to fish for salmon. We halted here two hours and then went on. The men in general complain of their feet being sore; and the officers have to go on foot to permit some of them to ride. We went 13 miles and encamped at a small grove of willows.[2] There being no other wood for a considerable distance.

1. Note that Gass used the same term for the people met on April 23, perhaps because they were both speakers of Shahaptian language. The captains call them "Pish-quit-pahs." For the question of their identity, see Lewis's entry. They live near the Klickitat-Benton county line, Washington, near Crow Butte State Park.

2. For the problems of locating this camp, see Lewis's entry for the day. It may have been in Klickitat County, near Alderdale, or in Benton County, at Glade Creek.

Saturday 26th. Last night Capt. Lewis and Capt. Clarke got each a horse, and we set out early, had a fine morning, and proceeded on very well, most of the men having their knapsacks carried on the horses. At noon we halted and took a little of our dried meat, which is the only food we have. At 2 o'clock we continued our journey, and the officers were obliged to go on foot again, to let some of the men ride whose feet were very sore. The country is level and has a most beautiful appearance. On the plains there is a species of clover,[1] as large as any I have seen, and has a large red handsome blossom. The leaves are not quite so large as those of the red clover cultivated in the Atlantic States, but has seven and eight leaves on a branch. We were overtaken and passed by a great number of the natives, with large droves of horses, that look well and are in good order. We travelled about 25 miles and encamped[2] at a small grove of willows.

1. Large-head clover, *Trifolium macrocephalum* (Pursh) Poiret. This species was collected by Lewis on April 17. The red clover used for comparison is *T. pratense* L., an introduced European species.

2. In Benton County, Washington, below or near Plymouth, roughly opposite the mouth of the Umatilla River. The captains note that it was seven miles above the camp of October 19, 1805. See their entries for this date.

Sunday 27th. The morning was cloudy with some light showers of rain; and about 9 o'clock we proceeded on through the plains, accompanied by a great many of the natives. Some light showers of rain fell at intervals during the day; and after halting about 2 hours we continued our journey to sunset, when we came to a large village of mat-lodges, belonging to a band of the Wal-la-wal-las, who have encamped here on the north side of the river.[1] Here we remained all night, and the natives were good enough to supply us with some faggots of brush, they had gathered in the plains from the sage bushes,[2] which grow in great abundance on some part of these plains and are very large.

1. A Walula (Walla Walla) village in Benton County, Washington, below and opposite the mouth of the Walla Walla River, south of Yellepit way station and perhaps now under Lake Walula. The party remained with them until April 29, at their insistence.
2. Big sagebrush.

Monday 28th. The morning was pleasant, and we spent it with the Indians, and got dogs, fish, shap-a-leel and roots from them. At 10 o'clock we began to take our horses over the river at this place, as we can lessen our journey considerably by crossing: We borrowed canoes from the natives, and swam the horses alongside, and at 2 o'clock in the afternoon had them all landed safe, after a good deal of trouble. From this place we can discover a range of mountains,[1] covered with snow, in a southeast direction and about fifty miles distant. In the evening the weather was cloudy, and it thundered and threatened rain, a few drops of which fell. We remained here all night, and about dark above a hundred of the natives[2] came down from the forks to see us. They joined with those at this place and performed a great dance. We were a very interesting sight to the surrounding crowd, as nine-tenths of them had never before seen a white man.

1. The Blue Mountains of northeast Oregon and southeast Washington.
2. Designated by the captains as Chymnapos, or Chimnapums, these people were Yakimas, living at the mouth of the Yakima River and the junction of the Columbia and the Snake.

Tuesday 29th. The natives remained about our camp all night; and we bought some dogs and a horse from them. The day was fair, and we got all our baggage transported to the south side of the river.[1] Here are a great many of the natives encamped on a large creek,[2] which comes in from the south, and those on the north side are moving over as fast as they can. We encamped on the creek, and got three horses, some dogs, shap-a-leel, some roots called com-mas[3] and other small roots, which were good to eat and nourishing.

1. Really from the west to the east side of the Columbia, which is flowing southerly at this point. They landed in Walla Walla County, Washington, above the mouth of the Walla Walla River.

2. The Walla Walla River. The people were Walulas.

3. Camas, which the captains called "quawmash," a staple in the diet of the people of the interior Northwest.

Wednesday 30th. This was a cloudy morning, and we stayed here till about 11 o'clock to collect our horses, got two more; and have now altogether twenty-three horses. We then set out from Wal-la-wal-la river and nation; proceeded on about fourteen miles through an extensive plain, when we struck a branch of the Wal-lo-wal-la river, and halted for the night.[1] We saw no animals or birds of any kind, except two pheasants,[2] one of which Capt. Clarke killed. The whole of this plain is of a sandy surface and affords but thin grass, with some branches of shrubs which resemble sage or hyssop.[3] On the south side of this branch the soil is of earth and rich, covered with grass,[4] and very handsome. We are still accompanied by several of the natives.

1. On Touchet River, Walla Walla County, Washington, some ten miles south of Eureka.

2. Probably some species of grouse, which they commonly called pheasants.

3. Besides big sagebrush, characteristic shrubs of the Columbia Basin include rubber rabbitbrush *Chrysothamnus nauseosus* (Pall.) Britt. var. *albicaulis* (Nutt.) Rydb., and twisted leaf rabbitbrush, *C. viscidiflorus* (Hook.) Nutt.

4. The grass is probably Sandberg bluegrass, *Poa secunda* Presl.

Thursday 1st May, 1806. Some rain fell during the night, and the morning continues cloudy. We set out early and travelled up the branch, which is a fine stream about twenty yards wide, with some cottonwood, birch and willows on its banks. One of four hunters,[1] who went forward very early this morning, returned at noon with a beaver he had killed; other game is scarce. We then halted to dine, where the road forks, one going up the branch an east course, and the other north towards the large river.[2] Here our Indians differed in opinion with respect to the best road to be taken. The man with the family and gang of horses said he would go across to the Great river to-morrow; but we followed the opinion of the young man our guide, and proceeded on up the creek.[3] We travelled about twenty-five miles, and encamped[4] without any of the natives, except our guide, who generally keeps with the hunters, one of whom[5] killed a deer this evening. The higher we go up the creek the cotton-wood[6] is more large and plenty; and the plains beautiful.

1. Drouillard, according to the captains.
2. The branch is Touchet River; the large river is the Snake.
3. They went up Touchet River, Walla Walla County, Washington.
4. In the vicinity of Waitsburg, in eastern Walla Walla County.
5. Labiche, according to the captains.
6. Black cottonwood.

Chapter Fifty-Four

Homeward Bound

May 2–September 23, 1806

Friday 2nd. A fine morning. Last night about 9 o'clock, three of the Wal-la-wal-las came up with us, and brought a steel trap that had been left at our camp on the north side of the Columbia, opposite the mouth of Wal-la-wal-la river; perhaps one of the greatest instances of honesty ever known among Indians.[1] Some hunters went on ahead, and having collected our horses, we found one missing; some of the men went to look for him, and brought him back.[2] We then continued our journey up this branch;[3] and saw to our right a range of high hills[4] covered with timber and snow, not more than ten miles distant. We went fifteen miles and encamped[5] on the north fork, the creek having forked about two miles below our encampment. The south fork is the largest, and from its course is supposed to issue from those snow-topped hills on our right. In the evening our hunters joined us, and had killed only one beaver and an otter. The three Indians remained with us all day; and at night we set three steel traps, there being a great many beaver signs on this branch.

1. Gass's expression is very similar to that used by the captains about the same incident; see their entries for May 1.
2. Joseph Field and one of the Walulas just mentioned; see the captains' entries for the day.
3. Touchet River, passing from Walla Walla County into Columbia County, Washington.
4. The Blue Mountains.
5. On Patit Creek, Columbia County, several miles south of Marengo.

Saturday 3rd. We had a wet uncomfortable morning, and when the horses were collected one was found missing, and one of our hunters went back after him, while the rest of us continued our journey. This morning our guide and the three other Indians went on ahead. We continued our route about 10 miles, when we struck a creek,[1] having left the other entirely to our right; and halted. Our hunter came up with the horse. The wind was very high this forenoon, and rather cold for the season; with some rain. We continued about two hours and eat the last of our dried meat; and are altogether without other provisions, as our stock of dogs is exhausted, and we can kill no game in these plains. In the evening we met a chief[2] and nine of his men, who appeared glad to see us. We encamped[3] on a small branch or spring, as it was too far to go over the hills. The Indians say we can get over to-morrow by noon. The wind continued to blow hard and some snow showers fell in the afternoon.

1. The stream they named Kimooenem Creek, from a Nez Perce word, is now Tucannon River, reached near the Columbia-Garfield county line in Washington. It flows into the Snake.

2. The Nez Perce chief they called We-ark-koomt, more correctly Apash Wyakaikt. See the captains' entries of this date.

3. On Pataha Creek, Garfield County, near a bend in the creek east of Pataha City near U.S. Highway 12.

Sunday 4th.   We had a severe frost last night; and the morning was cold and clear. We were early on our march over a handsome plain; and came to another creek,[1] which we kept down until we came to Lewis's river,[2] some distance below the forks of Koos-koos-ke;[3] where we halted at an Indian lodge, and could get nothing to eat, except some bread made of a kind of roots I was unacquainted with. We had, however, a dog, which we bought from the Indians, who met us last night; but this was a scanty allowance for thirty odd hungry men. We remained here about two hours, got a dog, and proceeded up the south side of Lewis's river, about three miles, when we met with one of our old chiefs,[4] who had come down with us last fall; and who advised us to cross the river, as the best road is on the north side. We therefore were occupied in crossing, during the remainder of the day, as we could raise but four small canoes from the natives at this place. We, however, by dark got all safe over, and encamped[5] on the north side, accompanied by a great many of the natives, who appear a friendly and well disposed people.

1. Alpowa Creek, Garfield County, Washington; they may first have struck an upper branch.

2. Alpowa Creek reaches the Snake (Lewis's) River in Asotin County, Washington. The point is near former Silcott, site of the Nez Perce village visited on October 11, 1805.

3. The Koos-koos-ke is the Clearwater River; Gass evidently means the point where it joins the Snake on the Idaho-Washington border.

4. Tetoharsky, the Nez Perce chief who, with Twisted Hair, accompanied them down the Clearwater, Snake, and Columbia rivers some distance on the westbound journey.

5. They crossed the Snake above Silcott into Whitman County, Washington, continued up on the north side, and camped some three miles below Clarkston.

Monday 5th. We had a fine morning, and proceeded on early, accompanied by our old chief and a number of the natives. About 10 o'clock we passed the forks,[1] and kept along the north side of Koos-koos-ke; at noon we halted at three lodges of Indians,[2] where we got three dogs and some roots.— We also got one of our horses, which we had left here last fall in the care of the old chief who is now with us; and says that the Snake guide,[3] who deserted us last fall, stole and took two of our horses with him. We remained here about an hour, and then continued our journey; came to a large lodge of the natives, at the mouth of a creek, where we encamped.[4] This lodge is built much after the form of the Virginia fodder houses; is about fifty yards long, and contains twenty families. We here could get no provisions but shap-a-leel and roots.

1. The confluence of the Clearwater (Koos-koos-ke) River with the Snake at Lewiston, Nez Perce County, Idaho; they continued up the Clearwater.

2. A Nez Perce village in Nez Perce County, opposite the mouth of Lapwai Creek.

3. Toby, the Shoshone who guided them across the mountains; see Lewis's entry of August 20, 1805.

4. This camp was in the vicinity of Arrow, Nez Perce County, just below the confluence of Potlatch River (their Colter's Creek, after John Colter of the party) and Clearwater River.

Tuesday 6th. There was a cloudy wet morning; and we stayed in our camp. Capt. Lewis and Capt. Clarke acted as physicians to the sick of the village or lodge, for which they gave us a small horse, that we killed and eat, as we had no other meat of any kind. We continued here until about 3 o'clock, when we started and went on about nine miles, and encamped[1] close to a lodge of the natives.

1. On the Clearwater River, Nez Perce County, Idaho, but there is considerable disagreement about a more precise location. The site was perhaps at the mouth of Pine Creek, or near Cherrylane, some two miles below Pine Creek. See Lewis's entry for this day.

Wednesday 7th.   This was a fine morning, and we continued here till after breakfast, when we proceeded on about four miles to another Indian lodge, at the mouth of a small creek,[1] where we had to cross the river again, in order to get to a better road. At this lodge the natives found two cannisters of ammunition, which we had buried last fall on our way down, and which they took care of and returned to us safe. All the Indians from the Rocky mountains to the falls of Columbia, are an honest, ingenuous and well disposed people; but from the falls to the sea-coast, and along it, they are a rascally, thieving set. We were here detained about three hours in crossing, as we had but one canoe to transport ourselves and baggage. We then proceeded over a large hill, and struck a small creek,[2] about five miles below the place, where we made our canoes in October last. Here we encamped[3] for the night, accompanied by two Indians, one of whom can speak the Sho-sho-ne or Snake language. We shall therefore be able to hold some conversation with the natives in this part of the country, as our squaw is of the Snake nation.

1. There is a question about the location of this crossing, for it depends on the site of the camp of May 6 (see that entry). They may have crossed the Clearwater, Nez Perce County, Idaho, at Bedrock Creek or at Fir Bluff. See Lewis's entry of this day.
2. Big Canyon Creek, Nez Perce County.
3. Probably south of Peck, on the east side of Big Canyon Creek, Nez Perce County.

Thursday 8th.   The morning of this day was pleasant; and we remained here some time, to endeavour to kill some deer; and the hunters[1] were sent out.— Here some of the natives came to our camp, and informed us, that we could not cross the mountains for a moon and a half; as the snow was too deep, and no grass for our horses to subsist on. We have the mountains in view from this place, all covered white with snow. At noon our hunters came in, and had killed four deer and some pheasants. About 3 o'clock we continued our journey; passed over a very high hill, and encamped[2] on a small run; where we met our other old chief,[3] who had gone down the river with us last fall. He told us that his men had found our saddles, where we had hid them, and that he had them safe. He also gave us an account of thirty-six of our horses, and where they were.[4]

1. According to the captains the hunters included Shields, Drouillard, Cruzatte, and Collins.

2. In Clearwater County, Idaho, west or southwest of Orofino, on one of the small streams flowing south into Little Canyon Creek.

3. Twisted Hair; see Clark's entry of September 21, 1805.

4. Things did not go nearly as smoothly as Gass implies here; see the captains' entries for this date.

Friday 9th. There was a cloudy morning; and some hunters[1] went out, and we proceeded on for about six miles, when we came to the old chief's lodge,[2] where his family is encamped to gather roots. We are now got into a part of the country where timber is plenty, chiefly pitch pine.[3]

Between the great falls of the Columbia and this place, we saw more horses, than I ever before saw in the same space of country. They are not of the largest size of horses, but very good and active.[4] At noon two of the Indians went to look for our horses, and the old chief with one of our men who knew where some powder and ball was buried, went to bring our packsaddles. In the evening they returned with 21 horses, and about as many packsaddles. Our horses are generally in good order. Our hunters also returned but had killed nothing.

1. As usual, Drouillard was one.

2. The party camped here for the night. The site was in Clearwater County, Idaho, southwest of Orofino. It may have been on Wheeler Draw, but see the captains' entries.

3. Probably lodgepole pine; see Gass's entry for September 4, 1805.

4. The Nez Perces and other tribes of the Northwest Plateau became famous for their breeding of the Appaloosa horse.

Saturday 10th. At dark last night the weather became cloudy and it rained about an hour, when the rain turned to snow, and it continued snowing all night. In the morning the weather became clear. Where we are lying in the plains the snow is about five inches deep; and amidst snow and frost we have nothing whatever to eat. Without breakfast we started to go to a village of the natives, who live on a branch of the river, about a south course from this place. We travelled through the snow about 12 miles, and then went down a long steep descent to the branch where the village is situated. When we were about half way down the hill there was not a particle of snow nor the least appearance of it. It was about 3 o'clock when we arrived at the village,[1] and the Commanding Officers held a conversation with the natives, who informed them that they had not more provisions and roots, than they wanted for themselves. They, however, divided their stock with us; and told us what they had given was all they could spare; but drove up some horses and told us to shoot one, which we did. They then offered another, but that was reserved for another time, and we dressed the one we had killed; and in our situation find it very good eating. We remained here all night. One of the hunters who had gone on before the party did not join us yet.[2]

1. In Lewis County, Idaho, southwest of Kamiah, on Lawyer Creek, which they called Com-mearp Creek, from its Nez Perce name. They remained here until May 13.

2. Apparently Drouillard, who came in the next day.

Sunday 11th. This was a fine clear morning; and we lay here all day. The natives treat us very well; the officers practise as physicians among their sick, and they gave them a very handsome mare and colt. About 12 o'clock our hunter[1] came in and brought two deer with him. We now find a great many more men among the Indians than when we went down last fall; and several chiefs, which had them been out at war. In the evening the natives brought in six more of our horses.

1. Drouillard.

Monday 12th. We had another fine morning and remained here also to-day. The natives in the course of the day gave us four horses, one of which we killed to eat. We also got bread made of roots, which the natives call Co-was,[1] and sweet roots which they call Com-mas.[2] In the afternoon they brought three more of our old stock of horses.[3]

1. Cous.

2. Camas.

3. Acknowledging that there is little information about the country west of the Rockies,

McKeehan then expounds on the subject. Note that he uses the term "our country" for the region west of the Continental Divide, which was not part of the Louisiana Purchase. Before Lewis and Clark, Europeans knew virtually nothing of what lay inland from the Pacific coastal ranges, except for what Mackenzie had learned by reaching the Pacific in British Columbia. There is indeed a "large tract of open country" in the area McKeehan describes, including the Great Columbian Plain, the Snake River Plains, and the Great Basin. McKeehan inserted the bracketed material.

McKeehan's note: "The information yet acquired, furnishing but few certain data, on which a correct general view of the country west of the Rocky Mountains could be founded, especially on the south side of the Kooskooske, Lewis's river, and the Columbia after its confluence with that river, it would only be attempting imposture to pretend to be able to give it. A few observations, however, may be of some use to such readers, as have paid but little attention to the Geography of our country, and prompt to further inquiry.

"Between the Rocky Mountains, which running a northwest course, are said to enter the North Sea [Arctic Ocean] in latitude 70° north, and longitude 135° west from London or 60° west from Philadelphia (about 11° west of the mouth of the Columbia) and another range of high mountains, running nearly in the same direction along the coast of the Pacific, there is a large tract of open country extending along the above rivers and towards the north, in breadth from east to west 350 to 400 miles; but which, by Mr. M'Kenzie's account, appears to be contracted in the latitude of his route near the 53rd degree to the breadth of about 200 miles, where the country is rough and covered with timber. Mr. M'Kenzie represents some part of these mountains to be of an amazing height, with their snow-clad summits lost in the clouds, Describing the situation of his party 'sitting round a blazing fire' the first evening of the day, which they had begun to ascend these mountains on their return, and which was that of the 25th of July; he observes 'even at this place, which is only, as it were, the first step towards gaining the summit of the mountains, the climate was very sensibly changed. The air that fanned the village which we left at noon, was mild and cheering: the grass was verdant, and the wild fruits ripe around it. But here the snow was not yet dissolved, the ground was still bound by the frost, the herbage had scarce begun to spring, and the crowberry bushes were just beginning to blossom.' This range of lofty mountains prevents the Tacoutche or Columbia river from finding a direct course to the ocean, and forces it in direction somewhat east of south, until it arrives near the 45th degree of latitude, when it turns to the west, and at length finds its way to the Ocean through the Columbia valley.

"From the information gained by the late expedition, by M'Kenzie's voyage, the discoveries of Captain Cooke and others, it appears there are great quantities of timber, chiefly of the pine or fir kind, between the shore of the Pacific and the chain of mountains which run near it; but between there and the Rocky Mountains, especially south of M'Kenzie's route, a great part is open prairie or plains almost totally without timber. Mr M'Kinzie says of the information of the chief, who delineated for him a sketch of the river and country on a piece of bark, 'As far as his knowledge of the river extended, the country on either side was level, in many places without wood, and abounding in red deer, and some of the fallow kind.'

"According to the verbal relation of Mr. Gass, the land on the Columbia is generally of a better quality than on the Missouri; and where a greater number of roots grow, such as the natives subsist on. The Missouri in its general course is deeper, more crooked and rapid than the Columbia; but the latter has more rapids or cataracts; and its water is clear."

Tuesday 13th. We had a fine morning with white frost. Having collected our horses, we found we had 60 and all pretty good except 4, which were studs and had sore backs. At noon we proceeded down the branch,[1] which has a good deal of cotton wood, willow, and cherry tree[2] on its banks; and is a bold rapid stream, about 15 yards wide. We kept down the branch about four miles; and then came to the river[3] where it passes through a beautiful plain.— Here we halted to wait for a canoe, which we expected that some of the natives would bring up the river, to assist us in crossing; when we intended to encamp until the snow shall have sufficiently melted to admit of our crossing the mountains. At dark the canoe came, but it being too late to cross we encamped[4] on the south side.

1. Down the north bank of Lawyer Creek, Lewis County, Idaho.
2. Any of several varieties of cherry, *Prunus* sp.
3. The Clearwater River, their Kooskooske.
4. Near the Kamiah railroad depot, Lewis County.

Wednesday 14th. The morning was pleasant with some white frost. Three hunters[1] went over very early to the north side of the river. All the rest of the men were employed in collecting our horses and taking over the baggage. About noon we got all the horses and baggage over safe; and met with one of our hunters,[2] who had killed two bears, some distance off. So two men[3] were dispatched with him to bring in the meat; and we set about forming a camp[4] at the remains of an ancient village on the north side of the Kooskoos-ke river. We were accompanied by a number of the natives, one of whom gave us a horse; and three more of our old stock were brought in by them. In the afternoon we had an operation performed on seven of our horses, to render them more peaceable; which was done by one of the natives upon all but one.[5] In the evening the men came in with the meat of the two bears; and also our other hunters who had killed three more, all of the grizly kind. We gave some of the meat to the natives at our camp, who cooked it in their own way; which was done in the following manner. They first collected some stones and heated them, upon which they placed a part of the meat, and upon the meat some small brush, and so alternately meat and brush, until all the meat was on; when the whole was covered with brush and lastly with earth; so that the heap or mass had something of the appearance of a small coalpit on fire. An hour and an half was necessary to cook it in this way. The natives remained at our camp all night.

1. Collins, Labiche, and Shannon, according to Clark.
2. Collins.
3. Clark says they were Joseph Field and Weiser.
4. Later historians, following Elliott Coues, have called this campsite, where the party remained until June 10, Camp Chopunnish, after the party's name for the Nez Perces. It is in Idaho County, Idaho, near the eastern boundary of the Nez Perce Reservation, on the east bank of the Clearwater River, about one and one-half miles northwest of the U.S. Highway 12 bridge over the Clearwater at Kamiah, and about two miles below the mouth of Lawyer Creek. See Lewis's description on this date.
5. See Lewis's account of this date of the Nez Perce method of castrating their horses.

Thursday 15th. This was a fine morning, and some hunters went out early. The rest of the party were engaged in making places of shelter, to defend them from the stormy weather. Some had small sails[1] to cover their little hovels, and others had to make frames and cover them with grass. Around our camp the plains have the appearance of a meadow before it is mowed, and affords abundance of food for our horses. Here we expect to remain a month before we can cross the mountains. The natives staid all day at our camp; and one[2] of them had round his neck a scalp of an Indian, with six thumbs and four fingers of other Indians he had killed in battle, of the Sho-sho-ne, or Snake nation. The nation here, the Cho-co-nish,[3] is very numerous, as well as the other. These nations have been long at war and destroyed a great many of each other in a few years past.

From the Mandan nation to the Pacific Ocean, the arms of the Indians are generally bows and arrows, and the war-mallet.[4] The war-mallet is a club, with a large head of wood or stone; those of stone are generally covered with leather, and fastened to the end of the club with thongs, or straps of leather, and the sinews of animals.[5]

In the afternoon two of our hunters[6] came in and had killed nothing but some grous; four more[7] continued out.

1. Presumably pieces of canvas, but perhaps Gass means blankets or hides serving the same purpose. The "hovels" were probably some version of an Indian brush shelter.

2. Perhaps Hohots Ilppilp, whom the captains mention on May 13 as wearing a "tippet" decorated in this fashion. See Lewis's entry of May 10.

3. Gass's version of "Chopunnish," the captains' name for the Nez Perces.

4. The stone-headed war club which Lewis on August 19 and 23, 1805, calls a poggamoggan, from the Chippewa name. As McKeehan's note suggests, its use was even more widespread than Gass indicates.

5. McKeehan's note: "The publisher has seen one of these stone heads, lately found at *Hatfield,* the farm of Mr David Davis, three miles from Pittsburgh on the Allegheny river. It is of a hard species of stone and weighs seven ounces. It is nearly spherical with a groove cut round to hold, as is supposed, the strap by which it is fastened to the club. Mr Gass says it is exactly like those he had seen to the westward. There is perhaps nothing which in form it so much resembles as a common round pincushion. In close combat the war-mallet, when skilfully wielded, must be a destructive and deadly weapon."

6. The captains say Shields, Reubin Field, and Willard came in.

7. Labiche, Shannon, Drouillard, and Cruzatte, according to the captains.

Friday 16th. The morning was cloudy and some rain fell; but in about two hours it cleared away and we had a fine day. An Indian performed the quieting operation on two more of our horses. In the evening two of our hunters[1] came in, and brought with them two deer and some ducks. Two of the hunters[2] still remained out. The natives all left our camp this evening.

1. Drouillard and Cruzatte returned together, and later Shannon and Labiche.
2. Pryor and Collins stayed out, according to the captains.

Thursday [Saturday] *17th.* We had a cloudy wet morning and some light rain all day. Our other two hunters[1] came in, and had killed two large bears. They said it snowed on the hills, when it rained at our camp in the valley.

1. Pryor and Collins.

Sunday 18th. The morning was cloudy, but without rain; and ten[1] of the party turned out to hunt.— None of the natives visited us yesterday, or to day; until about 2 o'clock in the afternoon, when five came that had not I seen before. They remained about an hour and had some eye-water[2] put into their eyes, which were sore; after which they went away, and an old man and his wife came for some medicine, as the old woman was sick. In the evening four hunters[3] came in and had killed nothing but some grous.

1. The captains say twelve; they included the Field brothers, Drouillard, Lepage, Shannon, Collins, Labiche, Cruzatte, Shields, and Gibson. Potts and Whitehouse went with Collins to pick up a bear he had shot earlier; they probably account for the numerical discrepancy.

2. Ingredients of the eye-water included zinc sulphate and lead acetate. See Lewis's entry of April 28, 1806.

3. Joseph and Reubin Field, Drouillard, and Lepage.

Monday 19th.   We had a cloudy wet morning. The old Indian and his wife staid all night and got more medicine. A party of the men[1] went to some Indian lodges about four miles up the river to buy roots; and in the afternoon returned with a good many of them. Several of the natives came to our camp with the men, and in the evening all went away. We got another of our old stock of horses; and have now all we left except three; two of which the old Snake guide[2] took with him. At dark two of our hunters[3] came in but had not killed any thing. The day was fair during the whole of the afternoon.

1. As indicated by the captains, they were Charbonneau, Thompson, Potts, Hugh Hall, and Weiser.

2. Toby.

3. Shields and Gibson.

Tuesday 20th.   We again had a very wet morning. Two more of our hunters[1] came in, but had killed nothing. It continued raining till about noon, when we had fair weather with some sunshine. The hunters said it also snowed on the hills today, where they were hunting, while it rained at our camp. About 2 o'clock in the afternoon, another hunter[2] came in and brought a deer that he had killed. In the afternoon four of our hunters[3] again went out. In the evening there were some light showers.

1. Shannon and Colter, say the captains.

2. Labiche.

3. According to the captains, Drouillard and the Field brothers set out in the morning, and Labiche and Lepage in the afternoon.

Wednesday 21st. There was a cloudy morning. Two more hunters[1] went out; and some men[2] set about making a canoe to fish in, when the salmon come up, as we do not expect to leave this place before the middle of June. To day we made a small lodge of poles and covered it with grass, for Captain Lewis and Captain Clarke, as their tent is not sufficient to defend them from the rain. At 10 o'clock the weather became clear, and in the evening, was cold.

1. Shields and Gibson, say the captains.
2. Five men, say Lewis and Clark.

Thursday 22d. We had a fine clear morning with some white frost. At three o'clock, five of our hunters[1] came in with five deer; previous to which we had killed a fine colt. In the afternoon we saw a great number of the natives on horseback pursuing a deer on the opposite side of the river. They drove it so hard that it was obliged to take the water, when some of our men[2] went down the bank and shot it, and the natives got on a raft and caught it. These Indians are the most active horsemen I ever saw: they will gallop their horses over precipices, that I should not think of riding over at all.

The frames of their saddles are made of wood nicely jointed, and then covered with raw skins, which when they become dry, bind every part tight, and keep the joints in their places. The saddles rise very high before and behind, in the manner of the saddles of the Spaniards, from whom they no doubt received the form; and also obtained their breed of horses.[3] When the Indians are going to mount they throw their buffaloe robes over the saddles and ride on them, as the saddles would otherwise be too hard.

1. According to the captains, Drouillard, the Field brothers, Gibson, and Shields.
2. "Capt. C. Myself & three of our men," says Lewis.
3. Gass is undoubtedly correct, although the idea and form of the saddle must have passed through several tribes before reaching the Nez Perces. The Spanish settlements of New Mexico were the origin point for the horses, and many of the horse-using methods, of the Western tribes.

Friday 23d. We again had a fine morning.— One of our sergeants[1] shot a deer at a lick close to our camp, and wounded it very bad, but it got to the river and swam over. Two young Indians who had been at our camp all night, then mounted their horses, swam over and drove it back; and we killed it and gave them half of it. The river is about two hundred yards wide and cold and rapid. In the afternoon, all the hunters came in but had killed nothing more.[2]

1. Pryor, say Lewis, Clark, and Ordway.

2. Shannon, Colter, Labiche, Cruzatte, Collins, and Lepage. The captains say they had killed "a few pheasants of the dark brown kind," probably blue grouse.

Saturday 24th. This was another fine morning, and two hunters[1] went out. One of the men[2] that were sick, still keeps unwell, with a bad pain in his back; and is in a helpless state. Yesterday we gave him an Indian sweat and he is some better to day.

1. Clark mentions several men as being sent out: Drouillard, Cruzatte, Collins, and the Field brothers.

2. Bratton, who had been ill since the stay at Fort Clatsop. For details of his illness and treatment, see the captains' entries of this date.

Sunday 25th. There was a cloudy morning, and some light showers of rain fell. Five more hunters[1] went out to day. In the evening yesterday two of the natives brought an Indian[2] to our camp, who had lost the use of his limbs, to see if the officers could cure him, and to day we gave him a sweat.— Our interpreter's child[3] has been very sick, but he is getting better. In the afternoon the two hunters[4] who went out yesterday returned; but had not killed any thing. The weather became clear and we had a fine evening, and three more hunters[5] went out.

1. Lewis and Clark say they were Drouillard, Labiche, Cruzatte, and the Field brothers.

2. This man may have suffered from hysterical paralysis; see the captains' entries of May 11, 25, and 27.

3. Jean Baptiste Charbonneau, then about fifteen months old; see Lewis's and Clark's entries of May 22.

4. Shields and Gibson. Ordway agrees that they had killed nothing, while the captains note that they had killed a sandhill crane.

5. Possibly Collins, Shannon, and Colter, mentioned by the captains as leaving the next day.

Monday 26th. This day was fine and pleasant, and we finished our canoe and put her into the water.— In the afternoon two hunters[1] came in, but had not killed any thing: they had procured some roots at a village about fourteen miles up the river. Our stock of provisions is exhausted, and we have nothing to eat but some roots, which we get from the natives at a very dear rate.

1. The Field brothers; Lewis and Clark note that they were accompanied by Hohots Ilp-pilp and other Nez Perces.

Tuesday 27th. The morning was fair and pleasant, and several of our men[1] went to the villages around us to procure roots. These roots are a good diet, but in general we do not relish them so well as meat. We therefore killed another horse to-day, which one of the natives gave us sometime ago for that purpose. He was so wild and vicious that we could not manage him, or do any thing with him.

Our sick man[2] is getting somewhat better, and the interpreter's child[3] is recovering fast. The Indian, that we have under cure, had another sweat to day; and our horses, that have had the quieting operation performed on them are all mending. In the afternoon some rain fell, and three of our hunters[4] came in, and brought with them five deer, they had killed: three men[5] also came in from the villages and brought a good supply of roots; six yet remained out.

1. Including Pryor, Charbonneau, and York, say the captains. Ordway also set out with Frazer and Weiser to the Snake River for salmon.
2. Bratton.
3. Jean Baptiste Charbonneau; see the captains' entries.
4. Drouillard, Cruzatte, and Labiche.
5. Pryor, Gibson, and Shields.

Wednesday 28th. There was a cloudy foggy morning. Some hunters[1] went out this morning, and in the afternoon three of them[2] came in with eight deer; at the same time three more of our men[3] returned from the villages.

1. According to Lewis and Clark, the Field brothers.
2. Collins, Shannon, and Colter.
3. Charbonneau, York, and Lepage.

Thursday 29th. The morning was cloudy and wet, and the river is rising very fast; which gives us hopes that the snow is leaving the mountains. At 10 o'clock the river ceased rising and the weather became clear.

Friday 30th. The morning was fine, with a little fog. Two of our men[1] in a canoe attempting to swim their horses over the river, struck the canoe against a tree, and she immediately sunk; but they got on shore, with the loss of three blankets, a blanket-coat, and some articles of merchandize they had with them to exchange for roots. The loss of these blankets is the greatest which hath happened to any individuals since we began our voyage, as there are only three men in the party, who have more than a blanket a piece. The river is so high that the trees stand some distance in the water. In the afternoon one of our hunters[2] came in, who with another had killed three deer, which one of them stayed to take care of as their horses had left them.

1. Shannon and Collins, but Potts seems to have been with them at the time of the accident.
2. Joseph Field came in, while his brother Reubin stayed with the deer.

Saturday 31st. We had a fine clear morning with a heavy dew. The hunters[1] went out with two horses for the vension; and two men[2] went over the river to the villages. About noon a deer was seen swimming the river and some of our men killed it. Our canoe still lies under water at the opposite shore, but we have a small Indian canoe, that serves to cross in. In the afternoon the two men came from the village with some of the natives, and one of our old stock of horses, which is the last, except the two which they assure us the old Snake guide took. In the evening the weather became cloudy, and we had some rain with sharp thunder and lightning. The two hunters came in with the venison.

1. Apparently Joseph and Reubin Field, although Reubin was supposed to have stayed out the previous night. They were also the two hunters who returned at the end of this entry.
2. Goodrich and Willard.

Sunday 1st June, 1806. We had a fine morning after some light showers of rain during the night.— Since last evening the river rose eighteen inches.

Two hunters[1] went out this morning, and some of the natives came to see us. The sick Indian is getting much better. The officers got some bear-skins from the Indians, that are almost as white as a blanket.[2] They say, that the bears from which they get these skins are a harmless kind, and not so bold and ferocious as the grizly and brown bear.

1. Colter and Willard, say the captains.
2. Lewis and Clark discuss the characteristics of the bears and bearskins at some length on May 31. Gass seems to have become confused, however; the white skins are from grizzly bears, while the relatively gentle bears are the "cinnamon" bears, a reddish-brown color phase of the black bear.

Monday 2nd.   The morning was cloudy, and six of the men[1] went out to hunt. About noon three men,[2] who had gone over to Lewis's river, about two and half days' journey distant, to get some fish, returned with a few very good salmon, and some roots which they bought at the different villages of the natives, which they passed. One of these men got two Spanish dollars from an Indian for an old razor.—[3] They said they got the dollars from about a Snake Indian's neck, they had killed some time ago. There are several dollars among these people which they get in some way. We suppose the Snake Indians, some of whom do not live very far from New Mexico, got them from the Spaniards in that quarter.[4] The Snake Indians also get horses from the Spaniards.— The men had a very disagreeable trip as the roads were mountainous and slippery. They saw a number of deer, and of the ibex or big-horn.

1. Shields, Collins, the Field brothers, and Shannon went out, according to the captains; no sixth man is mentioned.
2. Ordway with Frazer and Weiser had gone to the Snake River for salmon. For a detailed account of their journey, see Ordway's entries of May 28–June 2, 1806, where the question of their route is examined in the notes.
3. Frazer; see Ordway's entry of May 29.
4. An example of how European goods penetrated to people who had never seen whites. The Spanish coins may have passed through several hands. See James P. Ronda, "Frazer's Razor: The Ethnohistory of a Common Object," *We Proceeded On* 7 (August 1981): 12–13.

Tuesday 3rd.   This was a cloudy morning with a few drops of rain; and there were some light showers during the forenoon at intervals. The river rises in the night, and falls in the day time; which is occasioned by the snow melting by the heat of the sun on the mountains, which are too distant for the snow water to reach this place until after night. In the evening three hunters[1] came in with the meat of five deer and a small bear. Several of the natives continued at our camp.

1. Colter, Joseph Field, and Willard, according to the captains.

Wednesday 4th.   It rained slowly almost all last night, and for some time this morning. The river fell considerably yesterday, and in the night rose only an inch and a half. At noon one of our hunters[1] came in with two deer he had killed. The afternoon was clear and pleasant.

1. Shields, the captains say.

Thursday 5th.   There was a fine plesant morning with heavy dew. In the afternoon four hunters[1] came in with the meat of five more deer, and a bear. An Indian[2] came with them, who had been part of the way over the mountains; but found the road too bad and the snow too deep to cross; so we are obliged to remain where we are sometime longer.

1. Reubin Field, Shannon, Labiche, and Collins, according to Clark.
2. The captains do not mention this man, although his information must have been unwelcome.

Friday 6th.   The morning was pleasant, and Capt. Clarke and five of the party[1] went over the river to buy some roots at the villages, and in the evening returned with a good supply, accompanied by some of the natives.

1. Identified only as "Drewyer & three other men" by Clark.

Saturday 7th.   We had a cloudy morning with a few drops of rain. I went over with five of our party[1] to the village, on the other side of the river; and while we were going some snow fell. The greater part of the natives were out hunting. In the evening we all returned to camp, except two, who remained at the village. Some of the natives again came to visit us, one of whom[2] gave a horse to one of our men,[3] who is very fond of conversing with them and of learning their language.

1. The captains give only four names: Charbonneau, McNeal, Whitehouse, and Goodrich.
2. Hohots Ilppilp.
3. Frazer. The captains note that Frazer had given the chief a pair of "Canadian shoes," but say nothing of his camaraderie with the Nez Perces.

Sunday 8th.   There was a pleasant morning; and our two men[1] came over from the village, and a hunter,[2] who had been out, returned without killing any thing. Several of the natives still stay about our camp,[3] and are of opinion we cannot cross the mountains for some time yet. We, however, mean to remove a short distance to where the hunting is better.

1. Whitehouse and Goodrich; see the captains and Ordway for June 7.
2. Drouillard, say the captains.
3. Some of them ran foot races with members of the party, the captains relate.

Monday 9th.   This was a fine plesant day. We caught all our horses and hoopled[1] them, so that wc might get them easily to-morrow. We also exchanged some mares with young colts, and some of the horses who had not got quite well, for others more capable of bearing the fatigue of crossing the mountains.

1. Hobbled.

Tuesday 10th.   We collected all our horses, but one, and set out accompanied by several of the natives, travelled about twelve miles and arrived at what we call the Com-mas flat,[1] where we first met the natives after crossing the Rocky mountains last fall. Here we encamped[2] and some hunters[3] went out. The com-mas grows in great abundance on this plain; and at this time looks beautiful, being in full bloom with flowers of a pale blue colour.— At night our hunters came in and had killed one deer.

1. Weippe Prairie, Clearwater County, Idaho, where they first met the Nez Perces on September 20, 1805.
2. Near the western bank of Jim Ford Creek, about two miles southeast of Weippe, Clearwater County.

3. Collins is the only one named, by the captains and Ordway; he killed the one deer mentioned later.

Wednesday 11th.   We had a fine morning with some white frost. Several of the men [1] turned out to hunt; and returned at noon, having killed a bear and two deer. In this plain there are the most strawberry [2] vines I ever saw, and now all in blossom. This plain contains about two thousand acres, and is surrounded with beautiful pine timber of different kinds. The soil is very good; the underwood among the timber chiefly service-berry and gooseberry bushes. In the evening several of the men started, with an intention of encamping out to hunt; and one [3] went back to our late camp [4] to look for the horse, which had been left behind. The natives all left us and we remained in quietness by ourselves.

1. The captains name Labiche, Shannon, and Gibson.
2. Either wild strawberry or woodland strawberry.
3. Whitehouse, whose horse was the one lost, as Lewis and Clark say.
4. Camp Chopunnish.

Thursday 12th.   We had a fine lovely morning with a heavy dew. I went out with some of the party to hunt; about 8 o'clock the musquitoes became very troublesome; and at 10 we all came in without any success. About the same time the man who had gone back for the horse returned with him. About an hour after four hunters, who had been out during the night came in; three of them had been without success, but the other [1] brought in two deer. There are a good many deer here, and some bears, but they are very wild, as they are much pursued by the natives. There is no game of any other kind, except squirrels and some other small animals. The squirrels [2] are about the size of our common grey squirrels, and very handsome. They are of a brown grey colour, beautifully speckled with small brown spots, and burrow in the ground. We killed several of them since we came to this camp. The magpie is also plenty here, and woodpeckers [3] of a different kind from any I had before seen. They are about the size of a common red-headed woodpecker; but are all black except the belly and neck, where the ends of the feathers are tipped with a deep red, but this tipping extends to so short a distance on the feathers, that at a distance the bird looks wholly black. In the afternoon one of the natives came to our camp, and one of the two hunters that were out, returned but had killed nothing. In the evening some hunters went out with intention to stay all night. The Indian who came to our camp said he had a notion to cross the mountains with us.

1. Shields, according to Lewis and Clark.
2. Columbian ground squirrel, *Spermophilus columbianus*; see Lewis's entry for June 10.
3. Lewis's woodpecker, *Melanerpes lewis,* a Lewis discovery and named for him. It is compared to the red-headed woodpecker *M. erythrocephalus.*

Friday 13th. There was a fine morning, and a hunter or two went out. The Indian exchanged horses with one of our men, whose horse had not recovered, and was unable to cross the mountains; and then went home to the village. At noon two of our men[1] took their loads and went on ahead about eight miles to a small prairie to hunt until we should come up. During the afternoon the men[2] who went out yesterday to hunt, returned with eight deer. In the evening the weather became cloudy. The musquitoes are very troublesome.

1. Reubin Field and Willard, according to Lewis and Clark.
2. Ordway mentions Gibson, Shields, Shannon, Collins, Joseph Field, Drouillard, Labiche, and Colter.

Saturday 14th. We had a cloudy morning. Some hunters[1] again went out; at 10 o'clock, one[2] came in with a deer; and in the evening the rest of them, but they had not killed any thing.

1. The captains mention Colter and Drouillard.
2. Colter.

Sunday 15th. This was a cloudy wet morning with some thunder. We left Com-mas flat to attempt to cross the mountains; and had sixty-six horses, all very good. We ascended a high mount with a good deal of difficulty, as the path was very slippery, but got over safe to a small prairie, where the two men[1] who had gone on ahead had killed two deer and hung them up. We took the meat, proceeded down the hill and found the hunters who had killed another deer. We halted at a creek and took dinner; then proceeded over a very difficult road on account of the fallen timber. We had rain at intervals during the forenoon, but the afternoon was clear. We encamped[2] in a small glade, where there was plenty of grass for the horses.

1. Reubin Field and Willard; see June 13.
2. On Eldorado Creek, near the mouth of Lunch Creek, Idaho County, Idaho.

Monday 16th. We had a pleasant morning, and renewed our journey; went up a handsome creek about three miles, and then took to the hills which are very rough, with a great many banks of snow, some of them four or five feet deep. These banks are so closely packed and condensed, that they carry our horses, and are all in a thawing state. We halted for dinner at a handsome stream where there was some grass for our horses; and in about two hours proceeded on again, and had some rain. In the afternoon we found the snow banks more numerous, extensive and deep: in some of them the snow as much as eight feet deep. In the evening we came to Hungry creek (where Capt. Clarke killed a horse last fall and left it for the party) and encamped,[1] that our horses might get some grass as we do not expect they will get any soon again; and there is not much here.

1. Apparently on a branch of Fish Creek, Idaho County, Idaho, although Lewis also identifies the main stream as Hungery Creek.

Tuesday 17th. There was a cloudy morning, but without rain. We early continued our march; took down Hungry creek about six miles, and then took up a large mountain. When we got about half way up the mountain, the ground was entirely covered with snow, three feet deep; and as we ascended, it still became deeper, until we arrived at the top, where it was twelve or fifteen feet deep; but it in general carried our horses. Here there was not the appearance of a green shrub, or any thing for our horses to subsist on; and we know it cannot be better for four days march even could we find the road or course, which appears almost impossible, without a guide perfectly acquainted with the mountains. We therefore halted to determine what was best to be done, as it appeared not only imprudent but highly dangerous to proceed without a guide of any kind. After remaining about two hours, we concluded it would be most adviseable to go back to some place where there was food for our horses. We therefore hung up our loading on poles,[1] tied to and extended between trees, covered it all safe with deer skins, and turned back melancholy and disappointed. At this time it began to rain; and we proceeded down to Hungry creek again; went up it about two miles, and encamped[2] for the night where our horses could get something to eat. The grass and plants here are just putting out, and the shrubs budding. It rained hard during the afternoon.

1. They left the baggage at Willow Ridge, just west of Sherman Saddle, Idaho County, Idaho.
2. On the south side of Hungery Creek, Idaho County.

Wednesday 18th.   The morning was cloudy and several showers of rain fell during the day. We started about 8 o'clock, and found the road very slippery and bad. Two men[1] went on ahead to the village to enquire for a guide, and two more[2] remained to look for two horses that could not be found. We proceeded on with four men in front to cut some bushes out of the path; but did not go far till one of the men[3] cut himself very badly with a large knife; when we had to halt and bind up his wound. We again went forward, and in crossing the creek the horse of one of our men[4] fell with him, threw him off, hurt his leg, and lost his blanket. We halted for dinner at the same place were we dined on the 16th and had a gust of rain, hail, thunder and lightening, which lasted an hour, when the weather cleared and we had a fine afternoon. We continued our march till we came to a small glade on the branch of a creek, where we encamped,[5] and some hunters went out in the evening; we had left two[6] men to hunt at the place where we dined. We found the musquitoes very troublesome on the creek, notwithstanding the snow is at so short a distance up the mountains. At night our hunters came to camp, having killed nothing; but saw some large fish[7] in the creek, which they supposed were salmon.

1. Drouillard and Shannon, as noted by the captains and Ordway.
2. Shields and Lepage, the captains say.
3. Potts; see Lewis's entry for the treatment.
4. Colter.

5. On Eldorado Creek, at the mouth of Dollar Creek, Idaho County, Idaho.
6. The Field brothers, noted by Lewis, Clark, and Ordway.
7. Steelhead trout, *Oncorhynchus mykiss*; see the captains' entries, and Ordway.

Thursday 19th.   This was a fine morning; some hunters[1] went out and we agreed to stay here all day that our horses might rest and feed. At 10 o'clock our hunters came in and had killed a deer. Two men[2] are trying to take some of the fish with a gig. At noon the two men[3] who had been left at Hungry creek to look for the horses came up, but had not found them: and with them the two hunters,[4] who were left at the place we dined yesterday, and had killed two deer. In the evening one of the large fish was caught, which we found to be a salmon-trout.[5]

1. Collins, Labiche, and Cruzatte, notes Clark.
2. Gibson and Colter, Clark says.
3. Shields and Lepage; see June 18.
4. The Field brothers; see June 18.
5. Steelhead trout.

Friday 20th.   There was a fine morning; we caught six of the salmon-trout; and some hunters went out. About 9 o'clock one[1] of them returned, and had killed a brown bear. The musquitoes and gnats are very troublesome. In the evening the other hunters[2] came in and had killed only one deer.

1. Reubin Field, noted by the captains and Ordway.
2. Labiche and Cruzatte.

Saturday 21st.   We had again a fine morning; and we collected our horses in order to return to the Com-mas flat. We proceeded on to a creek, where we met two young Indians, who said they were come to go over the mountains with us. We halted here for dinner; after which, all our party proceeded on to Com-mas flat, except myself and two men[1] who remained here to hunt.[2] We wish to kill as much meat as will serve the party, until we get back where our loading was left, as we have plenty of roots there to serve us over the mountains. One of our best horses got snagged to-day, and was left here. The two Indians remained with us, and in the evening one of the men killed a deer.

1. The Field brothers, say Lewis, Clark, and Ordway.

2. Gass's hunting party remained at Crane Meadows, Clearwater County, Idaho. The rest of the party returned to Weippe Prairie.

Sunday 22nd. We had a pleasant day. The two hunters went out early and the Indians remained with me at the camp. At noon the hunters came in, but had killed nothing but one small pheasant.[1] In the evening they made another excursion, but were unsuccessful.

1. Again, some type of grouse.

Monday 23rd. We had again a fine morning; and the men went out to hunt. While they were out the two Indians went on. About 11 o'clock the hunters came in without having killed any thing; and at noon two men [1] came to our camp with orders for four of us to follow the Indians, if they were gone, until we should overtake them, and get them to halt if possible, till the party should come up; but if not, to follow them on and blaze the way after them; as the man [2] who had gone to enquire for a guide had not returned, and it was not known whether he would get one or not. The men said they had had good luck at the Com-mas flat, having killed ten deer and three bears. I immediately started with three of the men after the Indians, leaving one to take care of the camp, and the lame horse and some more that were there. We proceeded on till we came to the creek [3] where we had stayed the 19th and 20th, and overtook the Indians encamped there, and encamped with them.

They had caught two salmon-trout since they came to this camp; and shortly after we came one of our men killed a duck; and we remained together during the night.

1. Frazer and Weiser, as noted by the captains.

2. The captains had sent Drouillard and Shannon to the Nez Perces on June 18 to obtain guides; they returned to the camp at Weippe Prairie later this day with three young men who agreed to assist them.

3. Eldorado Creek, Idaho County, Idaho, where the party camped from June 18 to 21.

Tuesday 24th. There was a cloudy morning. We gave each of the Indians a pair of mockasons, and they agreed to stay to day and wait for the party.—

One of our hunters went out, but had no success. The day keeps cloudy, and the musquitoes are very troublesome. There is also a small black fly[1] in this country, that so torments our horses, that they can get no rest, but when we make small fires to keep them off. At noon two hunters[2] went on ahead to a small creek, to endeavour to kill some provision, as we cannot kill any here; and unless the party come up to night, I intend to go on with the Indians to-morrow morning. In the evening the party arrived with three more Indians, and we all encamped together for the night.

1. Probably the black fly, *Simulium vittatum.*
2. The Field brothers; see the captains' entries for June 25.

Wednesday 25th.   There was a light shower of rain this morning. We proceeded forward early; and two men[1] and an Indian were sent ahead to look for the horses we left behind when we were here before. At noon we halted at the creek where the two men[2] were hunting, but they had killed nothing. We here took dinner, and proceeded on to Hungry creek, where we met the men[3] with the horses, and encamped[4] for the night. A considerable quantity of rain had fallen during the afternoon.

1. Drouillard and Shields were sent ahead to Hungery Creek, as indicated by Lewis and Clark.
2. The Field brothers, as the captains and Ordway note.
3. Drouillard and Shields
4. Probably at or near the main party's camp of September 19, 1805, on an unnamed creek running into Hungery Creek, Idaho County, Idaho.

Thursday 26th.   We had a foggy morning; proceeded on early; and found the banks of snow much decreased: at noon we arrived at the place where we had left our baggage and stores.[1] The snow here had sunk twenty inches. We took some dinner, but there was nothing for our horses to eat. We measured the depth of the snow here and found it ten feet ten inches. We proceeded over some very steep tops of the mountains and deep snow; but the snow was not so deep in the drafts between them; and fortunately, we got in the evening to the side of a hill where the snow was gone; and there was very good grass for our horses. So we encamped[2] there all night. Some heavy showers of rain had fallen in the afternoon.

1. The cache on Willow Ridge, Idaho County, Idaho.
2. On Bald Mountain, Idaho County.

Friday 27th. We had a cloudy morning and at 8 o'clock we renewed our march, proceeding over some of the steepest mountains I ever passed. The snow is so deep that we cannot wind along the sides of these steps, but must slide straight down. The horses generally do not sink more than three inches in the snow; but sometimes they break through to their bellies. We kept on without halting to about 5 o'clock in the evening, when we stopped at the side of a hill where the snow was off, and where there was a little grass; and we here encamped[1] for the night. The day was plesant throughout; but it appeared to me somewhat extraordinary, to be travelling over snow six or eight feet deep in the latter end of June. The most of us, however, had saved our socks as we expected to find snow on these mountains.

1. On Spring Hill, or Spring Mountain, a little south of the Clearwater-Idaho county line, Idaho.

Saturday 28th. The morning was pleasant, we set out early, and passed the place where we had encamped on the 15th Sept. last when the snow fell on us. After passing this place about a mile, we took a left-hand path,[1] and travelled along high ridges till noon, when we came to a good place of grass; where we halted and remained[2] all the afternoon to let our horses feed, as they had but little grass last night. Some hunters went out, as we saw some elk signs here, and our meat is exhausted. We still have a good stock of roots, which we pound and make thick soup of, that eats very well. In the evening our hunters came in but had not killed any thing. On the south side of this ridge there is summer with grass and other herbage in aboundance; and on the north side, winter with snow six or eight feet deep.

1. They followed the Lolo Trail along the ridge in Idaho County, Idaho, instead of retracing their westward route, which would have taken them down into the valley of the Lochsa River.
2. Here they camped for the night, near Powell Junction on Forest Road 500, Idaho County, also near Papoose Saddle and a few miles north of Powell Ranger Station.

Sunday 29th. There was a foggy morning. We went out early, proceeded over some bad hills, and came to the old path;[1] at which time there was a shower of rain, with hail, thunder and lightening, that lasted about an hour. At 10 o'clock we left the snow, and in the evening we arrived at the warm spring;[2] where we encamped for the night, and most of us bathed in its water. One of our hunters killed a deer where we dined at the glades or plains on Glade creek;[3] and where there is good grass, and com-mas also grows. Two other hunters went on ahead and killed another deer on the way.

1. Their westbound route, which they now rejoined, having avoided the portion that went down into the Lochsa River valley.

2. Lolo Hot Springs, in Missoula County, Montana.

3. Packer Meadows on Pack (Glade) Creek, Idaho County, Idaho.

Monday 30th. We continued our march early and had a fine morning. When we were ready to set out, we saw a deer coming to a lick at the hot spring, and one of our hunters[1] shot it. Two hunters[2] went on ahead. At noon another went out a short time, and killed a fine deer. We halted for dinner at the same place, where we dined on the 12 of Sept. 1805,[3] as we passed over to the Western ocean. After dinner we proceeded on, and on our way found three deer that one of the hunters[4] had killed and left for us. In the evening we arrived at Travellers'-rest creek,[5] where the party rested two days last fall, and where it empties into Flathead (called Clarke's) river, a beautiful river about one hundred yards wide at this place; but there is no fish of any consequence in it; and according to the Indian account, there are falls on it, between this place and its mouth, where it empties into the Columbia, six or seven hundred feet high;[6] and which probably prevent the fish from coming up. Here we encamped and meet with the hunters.

1. Reubin Field, says Ordway.

2. Drouillard and Joseph Field, say the captains.

3. On Grave Creek, Missoula County, Montana.

4. Apparently Drouillard, from Lewis and Clark's entries; Shields also killed two deer.

5. The camp they called Travelers' Rest is on the south side of Lolo Creek, about two miles up the creek from Bitterroot (Flathead or Clark's) River, Missoula County, Montana. They would remain there until July 3.

6. The captains gave the name Clark's River to a combination of the Bitterroot, Clark Fork, and Pend Oreille rivers, the last of which finally flows into the Columbia. The falls referred to may be Thompson Falls, on the Clark Fork, Sanders County, Montana.

Tuesday 1st July, 1806.   We had a fine morning, and remained here to rest ourselves and horses after the severe fatigue of coming over the mountains, and some hunters went out. The Indians still continue with us. Here the party is to be separated; some of us are to go straight across to the falls of the Missouri and some to the head waters of Jefferson river, where we left the canoes.[1] At the falls, we expect to be subdivided, as Capt. Lewis, myself and four or five men, intend to go up Maria's river, as far as the 50th degree of latitude; and a party to remain at the falls to prepare harness and other things necessary for hauling our canoes and baggage over the portage.— Perhaps Capt. Clarke, who goes up the river here, may also take a party and go down the Riviere Jaune, or Yellow-stone river. In the afternoon our hunters came in, and had killed twelve deer, most of them in good order.

1. For a more detailed account of Lewis and Clark's plans, see their entries for this date.

Wednesday 2nd.   We continued here during this day, which was fine and pleasant, fixing our loading and making other arrangements for our separation. One of the hunters[1] went out and killed two deer.— The musquitoes are very troublesome at this place.

1. Ordway reports Collins as having killed one deer.

Thursday 3rd.   We had again a fine morning; collected our horses and set out. Captain Lewis and his party[1] went down Clarke's river, and Captain Clarke with the rest of the party went up it. All the natives accompanied Captain Lewis. We proceeded on down Clarke's river about 12 miles, when we came to the forks;[2] and made three rafts to carry ourselves and baggage over. The river here is about 150 yards wide, and very beautiful. We had to make three trips with our rafts, and in the evening got all over safe; when we moved on up the north branch, which is our way over to the falls of the Missouri, and, after travelling a mile and a half encamped[3] for the night. Two hunters went out and killed three deer. The musketoes are worse here than I have known them at any place, since we left the old Maha village on the Missouri.[4] This north branch of the river is called by the natives Isquet-co-qual-la,[5] which means the road to the buffaloe.[6]

1. Besides Gass, Lewis's party included Drouillard, the Field brothers, Werner, Frazer, Thompson, McNeal, and Goodrich.

2. Lewis's party went down the west side of the Bitterroot River to its junction with the Clark Fork, and crossed the latter some two miles below the forks in Missoula County, Montana.

3. They went up Clark Fork and camped on Grant Creek near its junction with the river, northwest of Missoula in Missoula County.

4. The deserted Omaha village near Homer, Dakota County, Nebraska, visited by some of the party on August 13, 1804.

5. Gass's version of the Nez Perce name for the Clark Fork, which Lewis gives as Cokalarishkit (variously spelled); it is *qoq̇á' lx̣'iskit,* "bison trail."

6. McKeehan's note: "The rout taken by Captain Lewis and his party is the direct rout to the falls of the Missouri, mentioned in Captain Clarke's letter; that taken by Captain Clarke and his party leads to the head waters of the main branch of the Missouri, which they ascended in their outward bound voyage, and which is a considerable distance south of the direct course from the falls to the crossing place of the great chain of Rocky Mountains." McKeehan refers again to Clark's letter to his brother in September 1806, the first published report of the expedition.

Friday 4th. We had a beautiful morning and waited here for some time, in order to have a morning hunt, as our guides intend to return,[1] and we wish to give them a plentiful supply of provisions to carry them back over the mountains. While our hunters[2] went out a young Indian came to our camp, who had crossed the mountains after us. At 10 o'clock our hunters came in, but had not killed any thing. We were, however, able to furnish them with two deer and a half, from those that were killed yesterday. We then gave them some presents, and took a friendly leave of them: and it is but justice to say, that the whole nation to which they belong, are the most friendly, honest and ingenuous people that we have seen in the course of our voyage and travels. After taking our farewell of these good hearted, hospitable and obliging sons of the west, we proceeded on up Isquet-co-qual-la through a handsome prairie of about 10 miles, after which the hills come close on the river, on both sides, and we had a rough road to pass.[3] Having made 18 miles we encamped[4] for the night; where the country is very mountainous on both sides of the river, which runs nearly east and west, and is a deep rapid stream about 80 yards wide.

1. Their Nez Perce guides were going to visit the Flatheads and then return home.

2. Drouillard and the Field brothers, as Lewis says.

3. They went up Clark Fork River in Missoula County, Montana, through the northern

part of present Missoula, to where the Blackfoot River enters the Clark Fork, then up Black-foot River going northeasterly.

4. In Missoula County, on the north side of Blackfoot River, some eight miles up from the Clark Fork.

Saturday 5th. We had another beautiful morning, set out early and proceeded on the same course as yesterday through a rough country, with a number of branches or small streams flowing from the hills. We killed one deer, and about 11 o'clock came to a valley three quarters of a mile wide,[1] all plains, where we halted to dine and to let our horses feed. The hills upon each side are handsomely covered with timber of the fir kind. While we rested here one of hunters killed a cabre or antelope. At 1 o'clock we proceeded on again up the valley. When we had gone about nine miles we came to and crossed a river,[2] about 35 yards wide, which flows in with a rapid current from some snow topped mountains on the north,[3] where the valley is two or three miles wide. Having gone about four miles further we came to the head of the valley, where the hills came close upon the river for two miles. After we had passed these narrows we came to another large and beautiful valley four or five miles wide, and all plains, except some timber on the river banks. In the evening we encamped[4] on the bank of a handsome creek which comes in from the north, bold stream of 15 yards wide.

1. Ninemile Prairie, along the Blackfoot River in Missoula County, Montana.
2. Clearwater River, which flows into Blackfoot River in Missoula County; Lewis called it Werner's Creek, after William Werner of the party.
3. Clearwater River is formed by streams rising in the Mission Range and the Swan Range.
4. On the west side of Monture Creek, just above its entrance into Blackfoot River, Powell County, Montana.

Sunday 6th. We had a fine clear morning with some white frost, and renewed our journey early; saw a great many serviceberries, not yet ripe, and some flax which grows on these plains. Having gone about seven miles we passed a north branch of the Co-qual-la-isquet,[1] which is 40 yards wide and was mid-rib deep to our horses, with a rapid current. About seven miles up the valley we passed a beautiful small lake;[2] where the river and road leave the valley, and bears towards the northeast between two hills not very large. We kept up the river, through a small brushy valley about the eighth of a mile wide, for a mile and half, and then halted for dinner. Here our two hunters came to us, and had killed a deer. We kept two men out every day hunting. In this small valley there is a considerable quantity of cotton wood timber; and the musketoes are very troublesome. At 1 o'clock we proceeded on, passed a number of handsome streams which fall into the river, and a number of old Indian lodges. As we advance the valley becomes more extensive, and is all plain. At night we encamped[3] on a beautiful creek, having travelled twenty five miles. Our hunters killed four deer to day.

1. North Fork Blackfoot River, meeting Blackfoot River in Powell County, Montana, south of Ovando. Note that Gass's version of the Nez Perce name used on July 3 is now more like Lewis's.

2. Of the several lakes in Powell County east of the North Fork Blackfoot River, it was perhaps Kleinschmidt Lake.

3. For the problems surrounding the location of this campsite see Lewis's entry of this date. It was in Lewis and Clark County, Montana, perhaps at the junction of Poorman Creek and Blackfoot River, or the junction of Landers Fork and Blackfoot River.

Monday 7th. We had a wet night, and a cloudy morning. Continued our journey early along the valley, which is very beautiful, with a great deal of clover in its plains. Having gone about five miles, we crossed the main branch of the river,[1] which comes in from the north; and up which the road goes about five miles further and then takes over a hill towards the east.[2] On the top of this hill there are two beautiful ponds,[3] of about three acres in size. We passed over the ridge and struck a small stream,[4] which we at first thought was of the head waters of the Missouri, but found it was not. Here we halted for dinner, and after staying three hours, we proceeded on four miles up the branch, when we came to the dividing ridge between the waters of the Missouri and Columbia; passed over the ridge and came to a fine spring the waters of which run into the Missouri.[5] We then kept down this stream or branch about a mile; then turned a north course along the side of the dividing ridge for eight miles, passing a number of small streams or branches, and at 9 o'clock at night encamped[6] after coming thirty two miles.

1. Landers Fork Blackfoot River, Lewis and Clark County, Montana, which they crossed and went up on the east side.

2. The trail went northeasterly toward Silver King Mountain and Lewis and Clark Pass.

3. One of them may be present Krohn Lake, Lewis and Clark County.

4. Alice Creek, Lewis and Clark County. It was not one of the "headwaters" of the Missouri because they had not yet crossed the Continental Divide; Alice Creek flows into Landers Fork. Lewis considered it the right branch of Blackfoot River.

5. Lewis's party crossed the Continental Divide at Lewis and Clark Pass, Lewis and Clark County, about seventeen miles northeast of Lincoln. See Lewis's entry. The stream that runs to the Missouri is probably Green Creek.

6. About three miles east of Table Mountain, Lewis and Clark County.

Tuesday 8th.   The morning was pleasant with some white frost. We started early and proceeded on nearly north; saw several deer, cabre and wolves in the plains, and after going three miles and a half passed Torrent creek,[1] a large creek that runs into Medicine river. Shortly after we passed this creek we went off the path or trail, travelled straight across the plains, and in about fifteen miles struck Medicine river,[2] close above the forks where we halted for dinner; and one of our hunters killed a deer and a cabre. In the afternoon we proceeded down Medicine river nine miles; and, having come, in the whole to day twenty eight miles encamped[3] for the night; and found the musketoes very troublesome.

1. In fact, this was Dearborn River, Lewis and Clark County, Montana, although they did not recognize it at first, thinking it a tributary of Sun River, their Medicine River.

2. They traveled a little east of north until they struck Elk Creek, a branch of Sun River.

3. On an island in Sun River, between Lewis and Clark and Cascade counties, Montana, just north of Montana Highway 21.

Wednesday 9th.   A cloudy morning. We set out early to go down the river; but had not proceeded far before it began to rain, and we halted at some old Indian lodges, where we took shelter. In an hours time the rain slackened, and we proceeded on; but had not gone far before it began to rain again, and the weather was very cold for the season. At noon we came up with our hunters, who had killed a large buffaloe; so we halted, and some of us went and dressed it, and brought in the best of the meat which was very good. We encamped[1] here and lay by during the afternoon as the rain continued during the whole of it.

1. On the south side of Sun River, near the mouth of Simms Creek, Cascade County, Montana, a little over one mile northwest of Simms.

Thursday 10th. At dark last evening the weather cleared up, and was cold all night. This morning was clear and cold, and all the mountains in sight were covered with snow, which fell yesterday and last night. At 8 o'clock we started down the river, and in the course of the day our hunters[1] killed five deer, two elk and a bear. The road was very muddy after the rain. The country on both sides is composed of beautiful plains; the river about 80 yards wide and tolerably straight, with some cotton wood timber on its banks; and plenty of game of different kinds ranging through the plains. Having made 24 miles we encamped[2] for the night.[3]

1. Lewis says that he and Frazer killed the elk.

2. On the south side of Sun River, Cascade County, Montana, some four or five miles northwest of the city of Great Falls. Gass makes no mention of an incident in which he and Thompson were chased by a grizzly bear this day, as narrated by Lewis.

3. McKeehan's note: "It will not be a subject of surprise that snow should fall here in the middle of summer, when the elevation of this part of the country, which divides the eastern from the western waters, is taken into view. Every person will be able to comprehend, that no small degree of elevation, above its mouth, will be sufficient to give so rapid a course to the Missouri for upwards of 3000 miles, even supposing there were no great falls or cataracts."

Friday 11th. This was a fine morning, and we set out early to cross the point,[1] and having gone eight miles, came to the Missouri at the Bear islands, nearly opposite our old encampment.[2] Here our hunters, in a short time, killed five buffaloe; and we saved the best of the meat; and of the skins made two canoes[3] to transport ourselves and baggage across the river. The buffaloe are in large droves about this place.

1. Apparently the point referred to is the area between the Sun River and the Missouri, southwest of Great Falls, Cascade County, Montana.

2. They camped here on the west bank of the Missouri, Cascade County, opposite the White Bear Islands and a little below the mouth of Sand Coulee Creek on the other side.

3. Mandan bullboats.

Saturday 12th. Again a fine morning. We went out to collect our horses and found that ten of them were missing. I then set out to look for them, went seven miles up Medicine river, where I found three of them and returned to camp. Two more[1] went to hunt for them, and the rest of us crossed the river in our new craft,[2] which we find answer the purpose very well. At night one of the men[3] returned without finding the lost horses.

1. Joseph Field and Drouillard, says Lewis.
2. They camped on the east bank of the Missouri, Cascade County, Montana, somewhat below the old White Bear Islands camp and south of the city of Great Falls.
3. Joseph Field, Lewis says.

Sunday 13th. The morning was pleasant, and we moved about a mile up to our old encampment;[1] opened a deposit[2] we had made here, and found some things spoiled; and the other man[3] that went to look for the horses not being returned we remained here all day airing and sunning the baggage and stores. The musketoes torment us very much, and the wolves continually howl night and day round our camp.

1. The White Bear Islands camp on the east bank of the Missouri in Cascade County, Montana. See the captains' entries for June 18, 1805.
2. For this cache, see the captains' entries for June 26, July 9, and July 10, 1805. Lewis describes the damage in his entry for this day.
3. Drouillard.

Monday 14th. There was a pleasant morning.— We staid here also to day; and the musketoes continued to torment us until about noon, when a fine breeze of wind arose and drove them, for a while away. We deposited the most valuable part of our baggage and stores on a large island so that if the Indians came they would not get it.

Tuesday 15th. We had pleasant weather. One of our men[1] started to go down to the other end of the portage, to see if the periogue was safe, which we had left there; and, in the afternoon, the man[2] who had gone after the horses returned unsuccessful; but as he saw some fresh Indian signs he supposes they were stolen and taken back over the dividing ridge.[3] Capt. Lewis therefore concluded to take fewer men and horses with him than he had intended on his excursion up Maria's river. In the evening, the man[4] who had started to go to the other end of the portage, returned without being there. A white bear met him at Willow creek, that so frightened his horse that he threw him off among the feet of the animal; but he fortunately (being too near to shoot) had sufficient presence of mind to hit the bear on the head with his gun; and the stroke so stunned it, that it gave him time to get up a tree close by before it could seize him. The blow, however, broke the gun and rendered it useless; and the bear watched him about three hours and went away; when he came down, caught his horse about two miles distant, and returned to camp. These bears are very numerous in this part of the country and very dangerous, as they will attack a man every oportunity.

1. McNeal, says Lewis.
2. Drouillard.
3. That is, taken back west of the Continental Divide.
4. McNeal.

Wednesday 16th. There was a fine morning. We collected our horses, of which Capt. Lewis took six, and left four to haul the canoes and baggage over the portage; and then started to go up Maria's river with only three hunters.[1] We[2] continued here to repair our waggons or truckles to transport the baggage and canoes on when the men with them should arrive.—[3] The musquitoes are still very troublesome.

When Capt. Lewis left us, he gave orders that we should wait at the mouth of Maria's river to the 1st of Sept., at which time, should he not arrive, we were to proceed on and join Capt. Clarke at the mouth of the Yellow-stone river, and then to return home: but informed us, that should his life and health be preserved, he would meet us at the mouth of Maria's river on the 5th of August.

1. Drouillard and the Field brothers went with Lewis. See Lewis's entries of July 16–28 for his account of this trip.
2. With Gass were Werner, Frazer, Thompson, McNeal, and Goodrich.
3. The party Clark was expected to send down from the Three Forks of the Missouri with the canoes that had been cached on the upper Beaverhead River in August 1805.

Thursday 17th. We had a pleasant day, and high wind; which drives away the musquitoes and relieves us from those tormenting insects.

Friday 18th. There was another plesant day, and I went down with three of the men to the lower end of the portage[1] to examine the periogue and deposit there, and found all safe. We took some tobacco out of the deposit, covered up all again, until the party should arrive with the canoes, and returned to camp.

1. The lower portage camp was on the Missouri, Chouteau County, Montana, below the mouth of Belt Creek; see the captains' entries for June 16, 1805.

Saturday 19th. The weather continues pleasant and most of the men are employed in dressing skins, as we have got all ready for crossing the portage as soon as the canoes arrive. The musquitoes were very troublesome to day. At 3 o'clock in the afternoon, a sergeant and nine men[1] arrived at our camp, with the canoes and some baggage. They informed me that they had a good passage over the mountains to the Missouri;[2] and on their way, saw a boiling-hot spring,[3] which in twenty-five minutes would boil meat put into it, quite well and fit for eating.— This spring is on the head waters of Wisdom river.[4] They had got to the canoe-deposit on the 8th instant[5] and found every thing safe: the whole party then came down to the forks at the mouth of Jefferson river;[6] where Capt. Clarke with ten men and the interpreter left them,[7] and went up Gallatin's river in order to cross over to the Jaune, or Yellow-stone river.[8] They had plenty of provisions all the way. In the evening we hauled the canoes out to dry.

1. Ordway led this detachment with the canoes, sent down from the Three Forks of the Missouri by Clark; see Ordway's journal for July 13–19 for the journey. With him were Collins, Colter, Cruzatte, Howard, Lepage, Potts, Weiser, Whitehouse, and Willard.

2. See Clark's entries for July 3–13, 1806, for his detachment's journey from Travelers' Rest to the Three Forks.

3. Jackson Hot Spring, just east of Jackson in Beaverhead County, Montana. See Clark's and Ordway's entries for July 8, 1806.

4. The name the captains had given the Big Hole River; see their entries for August 4–5, 1805.

5. At Camp Fortunate at the forks of the Beaverhead River, Beaverhead County, Montana, established on August 17, 1805. For the cache there, see Lewis's entry of August 20, 1805.

6. The Three Forks of the Missouri, Broadwater County, Montana.

7. With Clark were Pryor, Shields, Shannon, Bratton, Labiche, Windsor, Hall, Gibson, Charbonneau, Sacagawea, and Jean Baptiste Charbonneau.

8. For Clark's exploration of the Yellowstone, or *Roche Jaune*, River, see his entries of July 13–August 12, 1806.

Sunday 20th.   We had a fine day; but the musquitoes were very bad. We concluded to stay here all day, as the men, who had come with the canoes were fatigued; and, in the evening tried our horses in harness and found they would draw very well.

Monday 21st.   A plesant morning. One of the men went out for the horses; and the rest of us put two canoes on the waggons, and moved them forward by hand some distance, when the man returned without finding the horses. Two more than went out look for them, and at noon came back without finding them. In the afternoon, some more men went out to look for them, who at night returned also without seeing any thing of them; and we lay where the canoes were all night.[1]

1. Neither Gass nor Ordway gives enough information to locate their camps along the Great Falls portage route with any confidence. They were in Cascade County, Montana, south or southeast of the city of Great Falls.

Tuesday 22nd.   We had a fine morning. Eight of us started in various directions to look for the horses, and in a short time two of the men found them; harnessed them in the waggons and moved on about four miles, when one of the axletrees broke; and they returned to the river to mend it. Myself and one of the men did not return till dark, and then came to the place where the canoes were up on the plains, with some of the men. Here a heavy shower of rain came on with thunder and lightning; and we remained at this place all night.

Wednesday 23rd.   There was a plesant morning after the rain; and I went with the man who came with me last night, and joined the party at the river. They had repaired the waggons, and put on two more canoes; one of which was very large and gave us a great deal of trouble, as we could not make axletrees out of the willow that would stand more than six or eight miles. At 5 o'clock we got to Willow creek,[1] and encamped for the night; and made a new axletree. In our way to day, one of the men[2] cut his leg very bad with a knife, which so lamed him that he had to ride in one of the canoes.

1. Box Elder Creek, Cascade County, Montana, some seven miles east of the city of Great Falls.
2. Weiser, says Ordway.

Thursday 24th. This was a cloudy morning. I was very much indisposed last night and am yet very unwell. I therefore staid at this camp, and the party went back for two more canoes. About three o'clock, one of the waggons with a canoe arrived; and the party with it; having let the horses feed a while, and taken dinner, they proceeded on to Portage river.[1] About an hour after they started, a very heavy shower of rain, accompanied with thunder and lightning, came on, and lasted about an hour and a half. After this we had a fine evening, and a little before sunset the other waggon with a canoe arrived; when we encamped for the night. The man who cut his leg is still very lame, and continues at this camp.

1. Belt Creek, the boundary between Cascade and Chouteau counties, Montana.

Friday 25th. This was a fine morning with a very heavy dew. The party set out early for Portage river with the canoe; and in a short time, the men with the other waggon came back; I was by this time so much recovered as to be able to return with the party for another canoe; which is all we will bring over, as the other is heavy, and injured; and we expect that the five small ones with the periogues, will be sufficient to carry ourselves and baggage down the Missouri. About 2 o'clock, the waggons met at Willow creek, when we had another very heavy shower of rain accompanied with thunder and lightning. At 3 o'clock we set out with both the waggons and 2 canoes to Portage river; it rained on us hard all the way, and the road was so muddy that the horses were not able to haul the loads, without the assistance of every man at the waggons. At night we arrived at Portage river,[1] and then had four canoes there safe.

1. Apparently they camped on Belt Creek where the portage route reached its banks, in Cascade County, Montana, a mile or so above its mouth on the Missouri River.

Saturday 26th. The morning was cloudy. Eight of us went back to Willow creek for the other canoe, and the rest of the party[1] were employed in taking down the canoes and baggage to the lower end of the portage, where the periogue had been left.[2] It rained very hard all night, which has made the plains so muddy, that it is with the greatest difficulty we can get along with the canoe; though in the evening, after a hard day's labour, we got her safe to Portage river, and the men run her down to the lower landing place, where we encamped. A few drops of rain fell in the course of the day.

1. Ordway says Colter and Potts ran the canoes down the rapids to the lower portage camp.

2. Where the white pirogue was hidden near the lower portage camp below Belt Creek, Chouteau County, Montana, on June 18, 1805.

Sunday 27th. In a fine clear pleasant morning, myself and one of the men[1] crossed the river with the horses, in order to go by land to the mouth of Maria's river: the rest of the party here are to go by water. We proceeded on through the plains about twenty miles, and in our way saw a great many buffaloe. We then struck Tansy or Rose river,[2] which we kept down about ten miles, and encamped.[3] The land along this river is handsomely covered with Cotton wood timber and there is an abundance of game of different kinds. In our way we killed a buffaloe and a goat.[4] The wolves in packs occasinally hunt these goats, which are too swift to be run down and taken by a single wolf. The wolves having fixed upon their intended prey and taken their stations, a part of the pack commence the chase, and running it in a circle, are at certain intervals relieved by others. In this manner they are able to run a goat down. At the falls where the wolves are plenty, I had an opportunity of seeing one of these hunts.

1. With Gass was Willard, according to Ordway.

2. Teton River, Chouteau County, Montana.

3. Gass's camp on the Teton River was probably within a few miles of Fort Benton, Chouteau County.

4. Gass again uses the party's old name for the pronghorn.

Monday 28th. The morning was fine and pleasant, and at an early hour we proceeded down the river. In our way we killed six goats or antelopes and seven buffaloe; and about one o'clock came to the point at the mouth of Maria's river,[1] where we met with the party who had come down from the falls by water, and who had just arrived; and also unexpectedly with Captain Lewis and the three men who had gone with him. They had joined the party descending the river this forenoon, after riding one hundred and twenty miles since yesterday morning, when they had a skirmish with a party of the Prairie Grossventres, or Bigbellied Indians who inhabit the plains up Maria's river; of which they gave the following account.[2] On the evening of the 26th Captain Lewis and his party met with eight of those Indians, who seemed very friendly and gave them two robes. In return Captain Lewis gave one of them, who was a chief, a medal; and they all continued together during the night; but after break of day the next morning, the Indians snatched up three of our men's guns and ran off with them. One Indian had the guns of two men, who pursued and caught him; and one of them killed him with his knife;[3] and they got back the guns. Another had Captain Lewis's gun, but immediately gave it up. The party then went to catch their horses, and found the Indians driving them off; when Captain Lewis shot one of them, and gave him a mortal wound; who notwithstanding returned the fire, but without hurting the Captain. So our men got all their own horses but one, and a number of those belonging to the Indians, as they ran off in confusion and left every thing they had. Our men then saddled their horses, and made towards the Missouri as fast as possible; after Captain Lewis had satisfied himself with respect to the geography of the country up Maria's river.

We this day took the articles out of the place of deposit, and examined the large red periogue we left here,[4] and found it too rotten to take down the river. We therefore took what nails out of it we could, left our horses on the plains and proceeded down the river. About the time we started a heavy gust of rain and hail, accompanied with thunder and lightning came on and lasted about an hour, after which we had a cloudy wet afternoon, and in the evening we encamped[5] about twenty-five miles below the forks.

1. Where the Marias River meets the Missouri, Chouteau County, Montana, the site of the party's camp of June 3–12, 1805.

2. See Lewis's account of this episode in his journal entries of July 26–27. These Indians were Piegan Blackfeet. Gass follows Lewis in identifying them as *Gros Ventres,* that is, Atsinas, who were allies of the Blackfeet. Non-Indians referred to them as *Gros Ventres,* or Big Bellies,

of the Prairie, as distinguished from the *Gros Ventres* of the Missouri, who were the Hidatsas, a wholly unrelated people.

3. By Lewis's account the Indians seized the guns of all four of the party; the Field brothers pursued, and Reubin stabbed the Piegan.

4. They cached the red pirogue on an island in the then mouth of Marias River, on June 10, 1805.

5. On the south bank of the Missouri in Chouteau County, a little below the mouth of Crow Coulee.

Tuesday 29th. Early in a cloudy morning we commenced our voyage from the mouth of Maria's river; and the current of the Missouri being very swift, we went down rapidly. At noon we saw some Ibex or Bighorns, at the entrance of a range of high rough hills;[1] and we halted and killed two of them. Having dined we proceeded on again, and in our way, during the afternoon, killed seven more of these mountain sheep. There are few other animals in this range of high country. In the evening, we encamped[2] opposite the mouth of Slaughter river, and Captain Lewis had four of those animals skeletonized, to take with him to the seat of Government of the United States. A considerable quantity of rain fell in the course of the day.

1. At the Stone Walls and White Cliffs of the Missouri, Chouteau County, Montana, from Ordway's description.

2. About a mile above and opposite the mouth of Arrow Creek (the party's Slaughter River), Chouteau County, at the site of the party's westbound camp of May 29, 1805.

Wednesday 30th. We embarked early in a cloudy morning with some rain. In our way through this high range of mountains, we killed four more of the large horned animals, two buffaloe, two beaver and a bear.

The water of the river is thick and muddy, on account of the late falls of rain, which wash those clay hills very much. We went down the river upwards of 70 miles to day, and encamped[1] on a prairie island. Heavy rain fell at intervals during the day.

1. Lewis is in conflict with Ordway and Gass on this campsite; the two sergeants place it on Goodrichs Island, while Lewis would have it above a nameless island in Blaine County, Montana, a few miles below Cow Creek.

Thursday 31st. We set out early, though it continued at intervals to rain hard. About 10 o'clock we saw a great gang of elk on a small island, where we halted and in a short time killed fifteen of them. We took the skins and the best parts of the meat, and proceeded. At noon we halted, and in a short time killed fifteen of them. We took the skins and the best parts of the meat, and proceeded. At noon we halted to dine, and had then a very heavy shower of rain. We also killed another of the large horned animals or mountain sheep.— We remained here about an hour, then proceeded on, and will soon be clear of this range of high rough country. In our way this afternoon, we killed two mule and twelve other deer, and two beaver. Though the afternoon was wet and disagreeable, we came 70 miles to day.[1]

1. They camped at some old Indian lodges eight miles below the mouth of Rock Creek, Phillips County, Montana, by Lewis's account.

Friday 1st of Aug. 1806. We embarked early in a wet disagreeable morning, and in a short time saw a large brown or grizly bear swimming in the river, which we killed, and took on board; passed the mouth of Muscle shoal river;[1] and at noon halted to dine at some old Indian lodges.[2] Captain Lewis being afraid, from the dampness of the weather, that the skins he had procured of these big-horned animals would spoil, thought it adviseable to stay here this afternoon, and dry them by a fire in these old lodges; and some of the men went out to hunt. About an hour after we landed here, a large bear came so close to our camp, that one of the men[3] shot and killed it from our fire. In the evening our hunters came in and had killed several deer. The afternoon was cloudy with some rain; and having made a fire and put the skins to dry with two men to attend them, made our arrangements for the night.

1. Musselshell River, on the Petroleum-Garfield county line, Montana.
2. Where they stayed until August 3, in Petroleum or Phillips County, Montana, some two or three miles below the camp of May 19, 1805, and just above what was later called Horse-shoe Point, in an area now inundated by Fort Peck Reservoir. Lewis says they were about fifteen miles below the mouth of the Musselshell River.
3. Lewis and Ordway indicate that several men fired on the bear.

Saturday 2nd.   This was a fine clear morning, and Captain Lewis thought it best to stay here to day also, and dry all our baggage, as it was become damp and wet. Two hunters[1] were sent on in a canoe to hunt; and in the course of the day we got every thing dry and ready to set out the next morning.

1. The Field brothers, as Lewis and Ordway indicate.

Sunday 3rd.   We had a fine morning, and at 6 o'clock got under way and proceeded on. Having gone ten miles we came up with the hunters, who had killed twenty four deer. We went on very rapidly and saw great gangs of elk feeding on the shores, but few buffaloe.[1] At sunset we encamped[2] having gone 73 miles.

1. Lewis agrees with Gass, but Ordway reports seeing buffalo in abundance.
2. In Valley County, Montana, below the mouth of Cattle Creek, and as Lewis notes, about two miles above the camp of May 12, 1805. The site is now inundated by Fort Peck Reservoir.

Monday 4th.   This was another pleasant day and we proceeded on early. One of the small canoes with two hunters[1] did not come up last night. We left another small canoe with some hunters behind[2] and proceeded on. We went very rapidly, and in our way killed a buffaloe, an elk and some deer. At five o'clock we passed the mouth of Milk river,[3] which was very high and the current strong. Having proceeded 88 miles we encamped[4] for the night.

1. Colter and Collins, as Lewis and Ordway both note.
2. Ordway and Willard, who had some mishaps Gass does not narrate; see Ordway's account.
3. Milk River, named by the captains, meets the Missouri in Valley County, Montana.
4. In Valley or McCone County, Montana, about two miles above the camp of May 27, 1805.

Tuesday 5th.   Last night was cloudy and thunder was heard at a distance. About midnight the small canoe[1] we left yesterday came floating down with the current, and would have passed us if our centinel had not hailed it; the hunters in it killed a bear and two deer. This morning was also cloudy, and we halted here till noon in expectation that the other canoe[2] would come down; but there was then no appearance of it; and we began to suspect it had passed in the night. The forenoon had become clear and pleasant, and at noon we got under way. As we went on we killed a very fat buffaloe and some deer; and two hunters[3] who went on a-head in the morning, killed two very large brown bears. At sunset we encamped[4] and at dark a violent gust of rain and wind came on with thunder and lightening, which lasted about an hour; after which we had a fine clear night.

    1. Carrying Ordway and Willard, as Ordway describes.
    2. With Collins and Colter.
    3. The Field brothers.
    4. In McCone County, Montana, some ten miles below Prairie Elk Creek (the party's Little Dry River) and about four miles southwest of Wolf Point.

Wednesday 6th. We embarked early, and had a fine morning, but high wind. At 12 o'clock the wind blew so violent that it became dangerous to go on, and we halted; and some of the men went out and shot a large buck, but not dead and he got into the river; when two of them pursued in a canoe and caught him. Having remained here three hours, we again went on until night and encamped.[1] We have yet seen nothing of the two hunters who had been left behind in the small canoe.

    1. In Richland County, Montana, some ten miles east of Poplar.

Thursday 7th. The morning was cloudy, and we set out early, after a very heavy shower of rain which fell before day light. We proceeded on very well, and about 4 o'clock arrived at the mouth of Yellow Stone river.[1] We found that Captain Clarke had been encamped on the point some time ago,[2] and had left it. We discovered nothing to inform us where he was gone, except a few words written or traced in the sand,[3] which were "*W. C. a few miles far-ther down on the right hand side.*" Captain Lewis having left a few lines for the two men in the canoe,[4] to inform them, if they are still behind, where we were gone, we continued our voyage. At night we encamped[5] after coming above 100 miles; and though dark, killed a fat buffaloe at the place of our encampment.

1. The Yellowstone enters the Missouri in McKenzie County, North Dakota, just east of the Montana state line.

2. On August 3–4; see Clark's journal.

3. Clark says he also left a note on a pole in the point between the rivers. Lewis says he found a note attached to some elk horns in the camp.

4. Colter and Collins; they rejoined on August 12.

5. In Williams County, North Dakota, a few miles south of Trenton.

Friday 8th: We had a fine clear cool morning with some white frost; proceeded on early and in a short time past one of Captain Clarke's camps.[1] At nine o'clock we halted to repair the periogue,[2] and to dress some skins to make ourselves clothing. The musquitoes are more troublesome here than at any place since we left the falls of the Missouri. A party of men went out to hunt and killed some elk and deer; the rest were employed in dressing deer and cabre skins.

1. Determination of Clark's campsites below the mouth of the Yellowstone is difficult. This was presumably the camp of August 4, 1806, in McKenzie or Williams County, North Dakota; see Clark's entry of August 4.

2. In Williams County, several miles southwest of Williston, where they remained until August 10.

Saturday 9th.   This was another fine day; and most of the men were employed as yesterday; and in making small oars for our canoes. Two of them[1] went over the river and killed an elk and a deer.

1. The Field brothers, as Lewis and Ordway note.

Sunday 10th.   We had a fine morning and were employed in repairing the periogue and dressing skins, until 3 o'clock in the afternoon, when we got the periogue completed, loaded our craft, and at four o'clock proceeded on to the mouth of White-earth river, and encamped[1] opposite it on the same bottom, where we encamped on the 21st April 1805. In the afternoon some drops of rain fell; and the musquitoes here were very bad indeed.

1. The party's White Earth River, not the present stream of that name, is Little Muddy River, Williams County, North Dakota. The camp was in McKenzie County, nearly opposite Williston.

Monday 11th. The morning was pleasant; and we set out early; passed Captain Clarke's encampment of the night of the 8th instant, and proceeded on to the burnt bluffs, where we saw a gang of elk feeding. The canoes were then sent to shore with a party of men to endeavour to kill some of them; and we proceeded on with the periogue. In about half a mile further we saw another gang; when we halted [1] and Captain Lewis and one of the men [2] went out after them. In a short time Captain Lewis returned wounded and very much alarmed; and ordered us to our arms, supposing he had been shot at by Indians. [3] Having prepared for an attack, I went out with three men to reconnoitre and examine the bushes, which are very thick at this place, and could see no Indians; but after some time met with the man who went out with Captain Lewis, and found on inquiry that he had shot him by accident through the hips, and without knowing it pursued the game.— Having made this discovery we returned to the periogue; examined and dressed Captain Lewis's wound; and found the ball, which had lodged in his overalls. The canoes having come down, we proceeded on, after dressing two elk that had been killed at this place, and passed an encampment which Captain Clarke had left in the morning. [4] We found a note here informing us, that the Indians had stolen all the horses which he had sent with a serjeant and party, [5] from Yellow Stone river, and that the serjeant with the party came down in skin canoes and met him at this place. We then proceeded on some distance, and encamped. [6]

1. In an area in McKenzie County, North Dakota, opposite the Crow Hills.

2. Cruzatte.

3. See Lewis's account of the incident at this date.

4. Clark had been there since August 9, some ten miles above Tobacco Creek, McKenzie County, North Dakota. See Clark's entry for August 9.

5. Pryor, accompanied by Shannon, Windsor, and Hall, left Clark's party near Billings, Montana, on July 24, 1806, taking an easterly route on horseback toward the Mandan-Hidatsa villages on the Knife River in North Dakota. He was to deliver a message to North West Company trader Hugh Heney, there or on the Assiniboine River in Canada, seeking his services. Pryor's party lost their horses within a day or two, probably to the Crow Indians. They constructed two bullboats and headed down the Yellowstone and the Missouri, overtaking Clark on August 8, in McKenzie County, North Dakota. See Clark's account on that date.

6. In southwestern Mountrail County, North Dakota, a little above the mouth of White Earth River; the site is now inundated by Garrison Reservoir.

Tuesday 12th. The morning was pleasant and we proceeded on. Captain Lewis is in good spirits; but his wound stiff and sore. Having gone about nine miles we met with two men[1] on the river trapping and hunting. Captain Lewis gave them some ammunition and directions with respect to the river above. They informed us that Captain Clarke and party has passed them yesterday at noon. We proceeded on and at 10 o'clock overtook Captain Clarke and his party,[2] all in good health. The two men[3] with the small canoe, who had been some time absent, came down and joined at the place where we met with the two strangers: and now, (thanks to God) we are all together again in good health, except Captain Lewis, and his wound is not serious.

After the Corps were separated among the mountains,[4] as before mentioned, Captain Clarke's party proceeded on to the Canoe deposit, near the head of the main branch of the Missouri (called Jefferson's river) and having descended with the canoes to the mouth of the branch, which they called Gallatin, Captain Clarke with ten men left those, who were to take down the canoes to the falls; travelled three days up Gallatin's river towards the south, when they crossed a ridge and came upon the waters of the Jaune or Yellow-stone river. Having gone about 100 miles down this river by land they made two canoes, and Captain Clarke having sent off a sergeant and three men with the horses to the Mandan villages, went down himself with six other men by water. On the second day after the sergeant and his party had started for the Mandan villages, the Indians stole the whole of the horses, and the party were obliged to descend the river in skin canoes. Captain Clarke's party in their route had found game plenty of different kinds, buffaloe, elk, deer, beaver, otter and some other animals. They also found the Yellow-Stone river a pleasant and navigable stream, with a rich soil along it; but timber scarce.

We here took the men on board, and left the buffaloe canoes. At night we encamped[5] on a sand beach, as the musquitoes are not so bad there as in the woods.

1. Joseph Dickson and Forrest Hancock; see Lewis's entry of this date for their story.
2. The two parties reunited at the place Clark had stopped for lunch in Mountrail County, North Dakota, some six miles south of Sanish and a little below Little Knife River.
3. Colter and Collins.

4. As noted, Clark's account of the exploration of the Yellowstone appears in his journals for July 3 to August 12, 1806.

5. Near the McKenzie-Mountrail county line, North Dakota.

Wednesday 13th. After a stormy night of wind and rain we set out early in a fine morning; about nine o'clock passed the Little Missouri and went on very well during the whole of the day. In the evening those in some of the small canoes, which were ahead, saw Indians,[1] who fled before they could speak to them. At night we encamped[2] opposite an old wintering village of the Grossventres, which had been deserted some time ago.

1. Mandans or Hidatsas (Gass's "Grossventres").

2. Northeast of Riverdale, McLean County, North Dakota, near the mouth of Snake Creek.

Thursday 14th. The morning of this day was pleasant, and we embarked early. In a short time we arrived near to our old friends the Grossventres and Mandans; and fixed our encampment[1] in a central position, so as to be most convenient to the different villages. The inhabitants of all the villages appeared very glad to see us, and sent us presents of corn, beans and squashes.

1. Apparently on the west side of the Missouri River in Mercer County, North Dakota, and considerably below the first (or lower) Mandan village, Mitutanka.

Friday 15th. We had a fine clear pleasant morning, and continued here all day, to ascertain whether any of the chiefs would go down with us or not.— They had to hold councils among themselves, and we had to wait for their answers.[1] The two hunters[2] we left up the river came down, staid with us here, and got one of our party[3] to join in partnership with them, and to return up the rivers Missouri and Jaune to hunt.

1. See Clark's entries of August 14 and 15.

2. Dickson and Hancock; see August 12.

3. Colter. The next four years would give him fame as an explorer in his own right; see Clark's entry for the day.

Saturday 16th. There was a fine cool day; and we yet remained here, waiting an answer from the natives. Some of these Indians are very kind and obliging; furnishing us with corn, beans and squashes; but there are others very troublesome, and steal whenever they have an opportunity. Yesterday and to-day, they stole several knives and spoons; and three powder-horns, and two pouches, filled with ammunition.

In the afternoon the chief, called the Big-White,[1] concluded to go down with us, and we agreed to stay until 12 o'clock to-morrow, that he might have an opportunity to get ready for his voyage and mission. The Commanding Officers gave discharges to the man who agreed to return with the hunters up the river, and the interpreter;[2] who intends settling among these Indians, and to whom they gave the blacksmith's tools; supposing they might be useful to the nation. They also gave a small piece of ordnance[3] to the Grossventers, which they appeared very fond of.

1. Big White, or Sheheke, of Mitutanka village.
2. Charbonneau, who remained here with Sacagawea and little Jean Baptiste. Only Gass mentions that they gave him the blacksmith's tools, an instance of the Jeffersonian policy of gradually "civilizing" the Indians.
3. The small swivel cannon, which they gave to Le Borgne, or One Eye, the Hidatsa chief.

Sunday 17th. There were some flying clouds this morning, and the weather was cold for the season. The two strange hunters, with the man who had received his discharge and was to go up the river with them, went on early. We lashed our small canoes together, two and two, as we expect they will be more steady this way, and carry larger loads. At noon we dropped down to the village of the Big-White: and he, his wife and a child, with Geesem[1] the interpreter for the Big-White, his wife and two children embarked in two of our canoes to go the United States. We proceeded on at two o'clock; the wind was high, and river rough; and in the evening we encamped[2] having descended about 20 miles.

1. Jusseaume; see Clark's entry of October 27, 1804.
2. Near Hensler, Oliver County, North Dakota.

Monday 18th. We set out early in a cloudy morning, and the wind high. At 10 o'clock we killed two deer, when we halted for an hour and cooked some vension. In the evening we encamped,[1] and some of the men went out and killed five or six more deer.

1. South of Bismarck, Burleigh County, North Dakota, below the mouth of Heart River.

Tuesday 19th. This was a cloudy windy morning; and the water so rough, that our small canoes could not safely ride the waves: so we remained here and several of the men went out to hunt. We do not go on so rapidly as we did higher up the river: but having lashed our small canoes together, we go on very safe and can make 50 or 60 miles a day Captain Lewis is getting much better and we are all in good spirits. At 3 o'clock[1] in the afternoon the wind ceased, and we proceeded on, and met with our hunters on the bank, who had killed six elk and eleven deer. We took the meat on board, proceeded on, and encamped[2] on a sand-beach.

1. Four o'clock, Clark says.
2. In Burleigh County, North Dakota, some ten miles below the previous night's camp and near the camp of October 19, 1804, on the opposite side.

Wednesday 20th. We embarked early after a heavy gust of wind and rain, and proceeded on very well. The forenoon was cloudy, without rain; and in the afternoon the weather became clear and pleasant.— We went about seventy miles, and encamped;[1] where we found the musquitoes very troublesome.

1. In Campbell County, South Dakota, probably below the mouth of Spring Creek.

Thursday 21st. We proceeded on early and had a fine morning. At 10 o'clock we arrived at the first village of the Rickarees,[1] and halted. In our way here we met three Frenchmen[2] in a canoe; one of them a young man who formerly belonged to the North west Company of traders, wished to go with us to the United States; which our Commanding Officers consented to and he was taken on board one of our canoes. When we halted and landed at the villages, the natives generally assembled, and Captain Clarke held a council with them; when they declared they would live in peace with all nations; but that their chiefs and warriors would not go to the United States at present, as they had sent one chief already, and he had not returned.[3] There are also a great many of the Chien, or Dog nation[4] encamped here, in large handsome leather lodges; and who have come to trade with the Rickarees for corn and beans, for which they give in exchange buffaloe meat and robes. They are a very silly superstitious people. Captain Clarke gave one of their chiefs a medal, which he gave back with a buffaloe robe, and said he was afraid of white people, and did not like to take any thing from them: but after some persuasion he accepted the meadal,[5] and we left them. Here a Frenchman[6] joined us to go to St. Louis, who was in the service of Commanding Officers; and we dropped down to the village on the island, and encamped[7] for the night.[8]

1. Clark gives this as the second village, but it was the first going downriver. This was the Arikara village, or villages, on the north bank of the Missouri in Corson County, South Dakota, above the mouth of Grand River.

2. One of them may be Rivet, an expedition *engagé* of 1804. Another is thought to be named Grenier, probably one of the two men the party met on October 18, 1804. See Clark's entries of August 21 and 22.

3. This chief died in Washington. See Clark's entries for the day and for October 9 and November 6, 1806.

4. Cheyennes; Gass is still confusing their name with the French *chien*, "dog."

5. See Clark's account of the incident on this date.

6. Evidently the Roie, or Ross, noted by Ordway on this day. Clark refers to him the next day, calling him Rokey. He was probably the former expedition *engagé* Pierre Roi; see Appendix A, vol. 2.

7. The village of Sawa-haini on Ashley Island, above the mouth of Grand River, between Campbell and Corson counties.

8. McKeehan's note: "We think that some further proof is necessary to establish the weakness and superstition of these Indians. Had the chief persevered in his rejection of the medal, we, instead of thinking him silly and superstitious, would have been inclined to the opinion, that he was the wisest Indian on the Missouri."

Friday 22nd. There was a cloudy wet morning, after a night of hard rain, and we stayed at this village to 12 o'clock. The natives used us friendly, and with kindness; gave us corn and beans, with other articles; but one of them would go down with us. At noon we got under way; and having proceeded twelve miles the weather became clear, and we halted to dry our baggage, which we got very wet last night. At four o'clock we again went on, and had a fine passage till night when we encamped.[1]

1. In Walworth County, South Dakota, some six miles southeast of Mobridge. They had passed Grand River, Corson County, during the day. Clark calls the island Grouse Island; it is later Blue Blanket Island, which the party passed on October 7, 1804.

Saturday 23rd.   We set out early in a fine morning, but the wind was high; and we went on very well till near noon, when the wind blew so hard that we had to halt, and were detained about four hours. Three hunters[1] went on ahead by land, and when we had overtaken them they had killed two elk and some deer, and we halted to take in the meat. Here we had a very heavy shower of rain, which detained us another hour. We encamped[2] at night and found the musquitoes very troublesome.

1. Clark says he sent Shields and the Field brothers ahead to hunt.
2. In Potter County, South Dakota, probably below the crossing of U.S. Highway 212. They had passed Moreau River, Dewey County, during the day.

Sunday 24th.   We had a fine morning, and went on very well till noon, when the wind rose, and blew so strong that we were obliged to halt. Having lain by three hours we again proceeded, but did not go far before we were obliged on account of the wind, again to stop, and encamp[1] for the night.

1. Near the upper end of Lookout Bend, Dewey County, South Dakota, on a site now inundated by Oahe Reservoir.

Monday 25th.   The morning was again pleasant, and we proceeded on early, having sent forward two small canoes with five men[1] to hunt. When we had gone twelve miles, we came to the mouth of the Chien river,[2] where we halted staid till noon, for the purpose of taking an observation. Some of the men went out to hunt, and while we remained here, killed three small deer. At half past 12 o'clock we proceeded on again, and in a short time overtook our canoes with the hunters, that had gone on ahead, and killed three deer. In the evening we encamped[3] in a handsome bottom, and a hunter killed another deer.[4]

1. Shields, Collins, Shannon, and the Field brothers, says Clark.
2. The party first passed the mouth of the Cheyenne River on October 1, 1804; it reaches the Missouri on the boundary between Dewey and Stanley counties, South Dakota.

3. In Hughes County, South Dakota, below the entrance of Chantier Creek, Stanley County.

4. Drouillard, Clark says.

Tuesday 26th. We set out early, and had a pleasant morning; passed Teeton river,[1] but saw no signs of the Teeton band of the Sioux nation. In the evening we passed Landselle's fort;[2] but found no persons inhabiting it. At dark we encamped[3] after coming about sixty miles.

1. They reached Bad River, where they had an unpleasant encounter with the Teton Sioux, on September 24, 1804. It enters the Missouri in Stanley County, South Dakota, opposite Pierre.

2. Loisel's Fort aux Cedres, on the later Dorion Island No. 2; see Clark's entry of September 22, 1804.

3. In Lyman County, South Dakota, some four miles above the mouth of Medicine River.

Wednesday 27th. We again had a pleasant day and embarked early; proceeded on till we came to the upper end of the Great-bend,[1] and there stopped to hunt. As our hunters saw no game, we in a short time continued our voyage round the bend; at the lower end of which we killed an elk. As we were passing an island, we saw a gang of buffaloe feeding on it; when we halted and killed three of them, and encamped[2] on the island for the night.[3]

1. The Big Bend, or Grand Detour, of the Missouri River, in Hughes, Buffalo, and Lyman counties, South Dakota, which the party first passed on September 20 and 21, 1804.

2. A nameless island at the lower end of the Big Bend, between Lyman and Buffalo counties; see Clark's entry for this day for a discussion of its identity. It would now be inundated by Big Bend Reservoir.

3. McKeehan's note: "In a former geographical note (p. 62) [*Ed: see Gass's entry of November 29, 1804*] we stated that the place where Mr. Thompson, Astronomer to the North West Company, took his observations in the year 1798 to ascertain the latitude and longitude of the northern bend of the Missouri, was near the longitude of the Mandan villages. If what Mr Thompson called the northern bend is the same with what Mr Gass calls the great bend (of which there appears little doubt) the longitude of the Mandan villages will be between two and three degrees west of the northern, or great bend; or in about longitude 104 degrees west of London, 29 degrees west of Philadelphia, 11 1.2 degrees west of the mouth of the Missouri, and nearly 20 degrees east of the mouth of the Columbia. This will still show the great errors of those maps of Louisiana, which place the Mandan villages 20 degrees west of

the longitude of the confluence of the Missouri and Mississippi; and less than 12 degrees east of that of the mouth of the Columbia."

David Thompson, to whom McKeehan refers, was a trader and surveyor for the North West Company who made the first detailed maps, based on observation, of many areas of western Canada and the Northwest United States. He visited the Mandan and Hidatsa villages in 1797 and took observations which went into his map of 1798, the one mentioned here. Gass's Great Bend is the Big Bend, or Grand Detour, of the Missouri in South Dakota, where the river makes a loop, a feature appearing on maps before Lewis and Clark. McKeehan has confused it with the presently named Great Bend in North Dakota, where the Missouri turns from a generally easterly to a generally southeasterly course. David Thompson was in the neighborhood of the Great Bend, somewhat below, when he visited the Mandan-Hidatsa villages. He never saw the Big Bend.

Thursday 28th.   We had another pleasant day; embarked early, and proceeded on till about 11 o'clock, when we arrived at Pleasant camp,[1] and halted. We left this camp on the 18th September, 1804. The Commanding Officers wishing to procure and taken down with them the skeltons of some mule deer, and cabre; and knowing that there were but few of those animals lower down the river, continued here the remainder of the day, and sent out six or eight hunters;[2] who returned at night without finding any of the wished for animals, but killed some fat buffaloe and common deer.

1. The party's camp of September 16–18, 1804, near Oacoma in Lyman County, South Dakota. Clark called it "Plumb Camp" on September 17, 1804, but now he agrees with Gass and Ordway in calling it "Pleasant Camp."

2. A number of hunters were sent out this day; Clark mentions Pryor, Shields, Gibson, Willard, and Collins specifically as being sent out from this camp to procure pronghorns.

Friday 29th.   The morning was cloudy and some hunters[1] went on ahead early; while we amused ourselves till 10 o'clock gathering plumbs,[2] of which there is great abundance at this place. We then went on, and passed White river[3] on the south side. The Missouri here is very full of sand bars and shoals, and we find difficulty in getting along. About 2 o'clock we halted to kill some buffaloe, but were unsuccessful, and we proceeded, till evening, and encamped.[4]

1. On the previous day Clark mentions giving orders to Shannon, Collins, Labiche, Willard, and Reubin Field to set out in the morning.

2. Probably the wild plum, *Prunus americana* Marsh.

3. White River meets the Missouri in Lyman County, South Dakota.

4. In Lyman County, a little below Round Island and the camp of September 13, 1804.

Saturday 30th. We had a pleasant morning, and went on early, three hunters[1] starting ahead. We killed some buffaloe and elk in our way, and about 2 o'clock, we met a band of the Teetons,[2] fifty or sixty in number, and halted on the opposite side of the river as we did not wish to have any inter-course with them. Here we waited for three hunters,[3] who were behind; and during our stay eight or nine of the Indians swam to a sand-bar about sixty yards from us, and we found that they were the same rascals, who had given us trouble as we went up. We could not converse with them, but one of our men[4] understanding the language of the Ponis,[5] of which they understood some words; we through him let them know that we wanted to have nothing to do with them; and that if they troubled us, we would kill every one of them. They then withdrew, and the whole party left the river and went off to the hills. Our three hunters returned, and we proceeded on, and in the eve-ning encamped[6] on a sand bar in the river.

1. Clark says he accompanied this hunting party.

2. Teton Sioux, of whom they were wary since their tense encounter in September 1804.

3. The Field brothers and Shannon, according to Clark.

4. Probably Cruzatte or Labiche, possibly Jusseaume or Lepage. It is also possible that Jusseaume's wife helped interpret. See the entries of Clark and Ordway.

5. Gass may mean either Ponca or Pawnee, and the latter could refer to the Arikaras, who were of the same Caddoan language family as the Pawnees. Clark is not much help here.

6. Between Gregory and Charles Mix counties, South Dakota, in the vicinity of later Hot Springs Island, now inundated by Fort Randall Reservoir.

Sunday 31st. There was a cloudy morning, after a disagreeable night of wind and hard rain. We set out early; went on very well all day, and in the evening encamped,[1] where we found the Musketoes very troublesome.

1. In Charles Mix County, South Dakota, near the mouth of Chouteau Creek, which marks the county line.

Monday 1st Sept. 1806. This was a fine pleasant day and we set out early, and about 10 o'clock met nine of the Yonktin band of the Sioux nation of

Indians[1] on the south side of the river. We halted and gave them some corn, and then proceeded on with an unfavourable wind. At night we arrived at our encampment of the 31st of August 1804,[2] where we held a treaty with a band of the Sioux nation, and encamped for the night.

1. Yankton Sioux; see Clark's entries of August 28–31, 1804. Gass here passes over some tense moments for the party, described in some detail by Clark and Ordway.

2. The camp of August 28 to September 1, 1804, was at the Calumet Bluff, Cedar County, Nebraska, where they counciled with the Yanktons. Now they camped opposite in Yankton County, South Dakota.

Tuesday 2nd.   We had a fine morning, but high wind; set out early, and went on till noon, when we halted, and some men went out and killed two fine fat buffaloe cows; and brought in the best of the meat. The musketoes are very troublesome. We again started and went on about two miles, when the wind blew so violent that we had to encamp[1] for the night, on a large sand-bar, where the musketoes are not so bad, as where there are woods or bushes.

1. A few miles below James River. It is unclear whether they are on the Nebraska side in Cedar County or the South Dakota side in Yankton County.

Wednesday 3rd.   In a pleasant morning we got early under way, and went very well all day. About 5 o'clock in the afternoon, we met a Mr. Aird,[1] a trader, who was going up the Missouri, and we encamped[2] with him. At sunset a violent gust of wind and rain, with thunder and lightning came on and lasted two hours.

1. James Aird, a native Scotsman now a U.S. citizen for trading purposes; see Clark's entry for this day.

2. The location of this camp is unclear. It would have been some miles upriver from Sioux City, Iowa, on either the Nebraska or the South Dakota side.

Thursday 4th.   There was a cloudy morning. We exchanged some corn with Mr. Aird for tobacco, which our party stood much in need of; and his party, having lost a boat load of provisions in their way up, wanted the corn. We then proceeded on till we came to our old camp near the Maha village,[1] where we halted to dry our baggage, which got very wet last night, and remained all night. The natives are all out in the plains.

1. The Omaha village, which they had visited on August 13, 1804, was just south of Homer, Dakota County, Nebraska. The camp was in either Dakota County or in Woodbury County, Iowa. Gass, like Ordway, fails to mention that some of the party visited Sergeant Floyd's grave at Sioux City, Iowa, covering it after it had been opened by Indians.

Friday 5th   This was a fine morning, and we early embarked, and went on very well, till night, when we encamped[1] on a sand-bar, where the musketoes were very troublesome.

1. In Monona County, Iowa, a few miles south of Onawa.

Saturday 6th.   We set out early, in a fine morning; saw a number of pelicans, and about 8 o'clock a gang of elk, when some hunters went out, but returned without killing any. At 11 o'clock we met a barge belonging to a Mr. Shotto,[1] of St. Louis, loaded with merchandize, for the purpose of trading with the Sioux nation of Indians. We got some spirituous liquors from this party the first we had tasted since the 4th of July 1805, and remained with them about three hours; sent some hunter a head, and proceeded on till about three o'clock in the afternoon, when we halted, and waited for the hunters at the place agreed on to meet them, but they did not come in, and we encamped[2] for the night.

1. René Auguste Chouteau. See Clark's entry for a discussion of the identity of the leader of this party.
2. In either Harrison County, Iowa, or Burt or Washington County, Nebraska.

Sunday 7th.   We had a pleasant morning. The hunters[1] not having come in we left a canoe,[2] with directions to wait till 12 o'clock for them; and proceeded on. About 9 o'clock we met with our hunters, but they had not killed any thing; and at 11 halted to hunt and wait for the canoe. In a short time we killed three elk and brought in the meat; and the canoe having come up we proceeded on, and at sunset encamped.[3] The musketoes are not so troublesome as they were some time ago.

1. The Field brothers, Clark notes.
2. Containing Ordway and four men.
3. In either Harrison County, Iowa, or Washington County, Nebraska, near Blair, Nebraska.

Monday 8th.   We again had a plesant morning; and proceeded on early; at 10 o'clock we passed council bluffs[1] where we held the first council with the Ottos on the 1st, 2nd, and 3rd of August 1804, and in the evening encamped[2] on a small island, having gone on very well during the day.

1. The Council Bluff near Fort Calhoun, Washington County, Nebraska, where they camped from July 30 to August 3, 1804, and counciled with the Otos and Missouris.
2. At the White Catfish camp of July 22–27, 1804, near the Mills-Pottawattamie county line, in Iowa.

Tuesday 9th.   We embarked early and in a short time passed the mouth of the great river Platte;[1] went on very well all day, and at night encamped[2] on a small sand beach opposite the Bald-pated prairie.

1. The Platte meets the Missouri between Cass and Sarpy counties, Nebraska.
2. In either Nemaha County, Nebraska, or Atchison County, Missouri, northeast of Peru, Nebraska, depending on the course of the Missouri River at the time. The bald-pated prairie was first noted on July 16, 1804.

Wednesday 10th.   We had a pleasant morning, embarked early and went on very well. At 4 o'clock P. M. we met a periogue with four men,[1] going to trade with the Loups or Wolf Indians,[2] who live up the river Platte. We remained with these men about an hour, got some whiskey from them, and then continued our voyage. In a short time, we met another periogue and seven men,[3] going to trade with the Mahas,[4] who live on the Missouri. We staid some time with these men, then proceeded and at night encamped[5] on a willow island.

1. Clark gives the leader's name as "Alexander La fass" or "la frost."
2. The Wolf (Loup) or Skiri Pawnees, on the Platte and Loup rivers.
3. Clark gives the leader's name as La Craw, probably Joseph La Croix.
4. The Omahas.
5. About four miles above the mouth of the Big Nemaha River, in either Richardson County, Nebraska, or Holt County, Missouri.

Thursday 11th. We set out early; and had a cloudy morning, and slight showers of rain during the forenoon. At two in the afternoon we stopped to hunt, and soon killed two deer and a turkey: then proceeded on and at sunset encamped[1] on an island.

1. On Nodaway Island in either Andrew or Buchanan County, Missouri. The island was first noted on July 8, 1804.

Friday 12th. The morning was fine and we again embarked early. In half an hour we met two periogues going up to trade; staid with them a short time and went on. About an hour after, we met with a Mr. M'Clelland[1] in a large boat with twelve men, going up to trade with the Mahas. Our commanding officers were acquainted with Mr. M'Clelland, and we halted and remained with him all day,[2] in order to get some satisfactory information from him, after our long absence from the United States. He, and two Frenchmen[3] who were with him had severally instructions from the government to make inquiry after our party; as they were beginning to be uneasy about us.

1. Robert McClellan, who was already known to the captains; see Clark's entry for this day.
2. At St. Michael's Prairie, Buchanan County, Missouri, near St. Joseph, first noted on July 7, 1804.
3. Gravelines and Dorion, Sr., both of whom had met the party previously; see June 12 and October 8, 1804, respectively. Clark describes the missions of these men in this day's entry.

Saturday 13th. We had a pleasant morning after some rain that fell yesterday, and again proceeded on early with unfavourable wind. At 10, we halted to hunt, staid about three hours and killed four deer. We then continued our voyage to sun set and encamped.[1] We had a few musketoes, but they were not so bad as we had found them higher up the river.

1. In either Buchanan County, Missouri, or Doniphan County, Kansas.

Sunday 14th. In a fine morning we proceeded on early and went very well, until 3 o'clock when we met three large batteaux[1] loaded with merchandize, going up to different nations of Indians for the purpose of trade. The people in them were very glad to see us, and gave us some whiskey, pork, and biscuit. We remained with them two hours and again went on. We killed five deer on the bank to day, as we floated down: and saw a fine young horse. At sun set, we encamped[2] on a small island.

    1. Clark indicates they were led by "Mr. Lacroy, Mr. Aiten & Mr. Coutau," the last perhaps Charles Courtin.

    2. Near Leavenworth, Kansas.

Monday 15th. The morning was pleasant and we embarked early. In a short time we killed a fine large elk; at 11 o'clock passed the Kanzon river,[1] and encamped[2] at sun set.

    1. The Kansas River, reaching the Missouri in Wyandotte County, Kansas.

    2. Above the mouth of Little Blue River on the opposite side in Clay County, Missouri.

Tuesday 16th. This was another pleasant day. We proceeded on early, and at 9 o'clock met a large periogue with eight men,[1] going to trade with the Ponis nation of Indians[2] on the river Platte about seventy or eighty miles from its mouth. At 11 we met a batteaux and two canoes going up to the Kanowas nation,[3] who live on a river of the same name. We halted with them a while, then proceeded on, and at sunset encamped[4] on an island.

    1. Led by a member of the Robidoux family of St. Louis, perhaps Joseph Robidoux, the founder of St. Joseph.

    2. Ordway says they were going to trade with the Kansa Indians.

    3. Kansa Indians.

    4. Between Carroll and Lafayette counties, Missouri, a few miles up the Missouri River from Waverly.

Wednesday 17th. We went on early and had a pleasant day, but very warm. One of our party last night caught a large catfish,[1] supposed to weigh 100 pounds. We got a great many papaws[2] on our way to-day: a kind of fruit in great abundance on the Missouri from the river Platte to its mouth; and also down the Mississippi. About 11 o'clock we passed through a bad part of the river, where it was so filled with sawyers that we could hardly find room to pass through safe. About two in the afternoon we met a large keel-boat, commanded by a Captain M'Clanen,[3] loaded with merchandize and bound to the Spanish country by the way of the river Platte. He intended to go by land across the mountain, and get the Spaniards to bring their gold and silver on this side, where he could take his goods and trade with them. He had fifteen hands, an imterpreter and a black. He intends to discharge his men on this side of the mountain, and to get some of the Ponis, who live on the river Platte to accompany him to the Spanish country. Mr. M'Clanen gave all our party as much whiskey as they could drink, and a bag of biscuit. Some of the men were sent on ahead in two small canoes to hunt, and we encamped[4] here for the night.

1. Perhaps a blue catfish, *Ictalurus furcatus.*
2. Pawpaw, *Asimina triloba* (L.) Dun.
3. John McClallen, or McClellan; see Clark's entry for this day.
4. The camp was in the area of Malta Bend, Saline County, Missouri. See Clark's entries for this day and June 15, 1804.

Thursday 18th. We gave Mr. M'Clanen a keg of corn; took our leave of him and proceeded on. In a short time, passed the mouth of the river Grand,[1] and soon after overtook the hunters, who had not killed any thing. We continued our voyage all day without waiting to hunt; gathering some papaws on the shores, and in the evening encamped[2] on an island.

1. Grand River now meets the Missouri between Carroll and Chariton counties, Missouri; the mouth may have been further upriver in 1806.
2. Opposite the mouth of the Lamine River, which joins the Missouri in Cooper County, Missouri, a few miles above Bonneville.

The 19th, was a fine day, and at day light we continued our voyage; passed the mouth of Mine river;[1] saw several turkeys on the shores, but did not delay a moment to hunt: being so anxious to reach St. Louis, where, without any important occurrence, we arrived on the 23rd,[2] and were received with great kindness and marks of friendship by the inhabitants, after an absence of two years, four months and ten days.

1. Lamine River; see September 18.
2. Gass obviously did not bother with his journal in the rush of the last few days of the journey. For the details of their reception in St. Louis, see the last entries in Clark's and Ordway's journals.

Sources Cited

Bailey, L. H. *Manual of Cultivated Plants.* Rev. ed. New York: Macmillan, 1949.

Betts, Robert B. "'The writingest explorers of their time': New Estimates of the Number of Words in the Published Journals of the Lewis and Clark Expedition." *We Proceeded On* 7 (August 1981): 4–9.

Clarke, Charles G. *The Men of the Lewis and Clark Expedition: A Biographical Roster of the Fifty-one Members and a Composite Diary of Their Activities from All Known Sources.* Glendale, Calif.: Arthur H. Clark, 1970.

Coues, Elliott, ed. *History of the Expedition under the Command of Lewis and Clark.* . . . 1893. Reprint. 3 vols. New York: Dover Publications, 1965.

Cutright, Paul Russell. *A History of the Lewis and Clark Journals.* Norman: University of Oklahoma Press, 1976.

———. *Lewis and Clark: Pioneering Naturalists.* Urbana: University of Illinois Press, 1969.

Forrest, Earle R. *Patrick Gass: Lewis and Clark's Last Man.* Independence, Pa.: privately published, 1950.

Gilmore, Melvin R. *Uses of Plants by the Indians of the Missouri River Region.* 1919. Reprint. Lincoln: University of Nebraska Press, 1977.

Hitchcock, C. Leo, Arthur Cronquist, Marion Ownbey, and J. W. Thompson. *Vascular Plants of the Pacific Northwest.* 5 vols. Seattle: University of Washington Press, 1955–69.

Jackson, Donald, ed. *Letters of the Lewis and Clark Expedition with Related Documents, 1783–1854.* 2d ed. 2 vols. Urbana: University of Illinois Press, 1978.

Jacob, John G. *The Life and Times of Patrick Gass.* Wellsburg, Va.: Jacob and Smith, 1859.

McGirr, Newman F. "Patrick Gass and His Journal of the Lewis and Clark Expedition." *West Virginia History* 3 (April 1942): 205–12.

Moulton, Gary E., ed. *Atlas of the Lewis and Clark Expedition.* Lincoln: University of Nebraska Press, 1983.

Ronda, James P. "Frazer's Razor: The Ethnohistory of a Common Object." *We Proceeded On* 7 (August 1981): 12–13.

Smith, James S., and Kathryn Smith. "Sedulous Sergeant, Patrick Gass." *Montana, the Magazine of Western History* 5 (Summer 1955): 20–27.

Wheeler, Olin D. *The Trail of Lewis and Clark, 1804–1806.* 2 vols. New York: G. P. Putnam's Sons, 1904.

Index